EXAM ESSENTIALS PRACTICE TESTS

Cambridge English: Advanced (CAE)

1

Charles Osbourne
with Carol Nuttall
with new material by Tom Bradbury
and Claire Morris

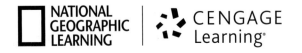

Australia • Brazil • Japan • Korea • Mexico • Singapore • Spain • United Kingdom • United States

NATIONAL GEOGRAPHIC LEARNING | **CENGAGE Learning**

Exam Essentials Practice Tests 1
Cambridge English: Advanced (CAE)
(without key)

Charles Osbourne with some new material by
Tom Bradbury, Claire Morris and Carol Nuttall

Publisher: Gavin McLean

Publishing Consultant: Karen Spiller

Editorial Project Manager: Stephanie Parker

Development Editor: Andrew Reid

Strategic Marketing Manager: Charlotte Ellis

Project Editor: Tom Relf

Manufacturing Buyer: Eyvett Davis

Cover design: Oliver Hutton

Compositor: Cenveo® Publisher Services

National Geographic Liaison: Wesley Della Volla

Audio: Martin Williamson,
   Prolingua Productions

DVD-ROM: Tom, Dick and Debbie Ltd

Contributing writer: Susan Yokes
   (video materials)

ISBN: 978-1-285-74499-5

National Geographic Learning
Cheriton House, North Way, Andover, Hampshire, SP10 5BE
United Kingdom

Cengage Learning is a leading provider of customized learning solutions with office locations around the globe, including Singapore, the United Kingdom, Australia, Mexico, Brazil and Japan. Locate your local office at: **international.cengage.com/region**

Cengage Learning products are represented in Canada by Nelson Education, Ltd.

Visit National Geographic Learning online at **ngl.cengage.com**

Visit our corporate website at **www.cengage.com**

Photos

pp 52 l (Juniors Bildarchiv GmbH/Alamy), 169 t (Eric Fougere/Vip Images/Corbis UK Ltd), 169 c (Dan Wooller/Rex Features), 169 br (Imagebroker/Alamy), 170 t (Monkey Business Images/Shutterstock), 170 c (Radius Images/Alamy), 170 b (Bartosz Hadyniak/Getty Images), 172 t (Adam Blasberg/Getty Images), 172 c (Marco Kesseler/Alamy), 172 b (OJO Images Ltd/Alamy), 173 t (Aurora Photos/Alamy), 173 c (117717/Getty Images), 173 b (Image Source/Getty Images), 175 t (F1online digitale Bildagentur GmbH/Alamy), 175 bl (Chad Ehlers/Alamy), 175 br (NASA Photo/Alamy), 176 t (PhotosIndia.com LLC/Alamy), 176 c (Stockbroker/Alamy), 176 b (Ryan Smith/Somos Images/Corbis UK Ltd), 178 t (Robert Harding Picture Library Ltd/Alamy), 178 c (Leo Mason sports photos/Alamy), 178 b (Imagebroker/Alamy), 179 t (CL Studio/Alamy), 179 c (Krzysztof Slusarczyk/Shutterstock), 179 b (Getty Images), 181 t (Corbis UK Ltd), 181 c (Paul Brown/Alamy), 181 b (David Grossman/Alamy), 182 t (ZSSD/Getty Images), 182 bl (Marmaduke St. John/Alamy), 182 br (Auremar/Shutterstock), 184 t (Svetikd/Getty Images), 184 bl (Picture Partners/Alamy), 184 br (Vicki Beaver/Alamy), 185 t (Prodakszyn/Shutterstock), 185 bl (Jupiter Images/Getty Images), 185 br (Leungchopan/Shutterstock), 187 t (Ocean/Corbis UK Ltd), 187 c (Blend Images/Alamy), 187 b (ZUMA Press, Inc./Alamy), 188 t (Zigy Kaluzny/Getty Images), 188 c (lightpoet/Shutterstock), 188 bl (Scottish Viewpoint/Alamy), 190 t (Pascal Saez/Alamy), 190 c (Michael S. Yamashita/Corbis UK Ltd), 190 b (Photodisc/Getty Images), 191 c (Christopher Pillitz/Getty Images), 191 c (Reuters/Corbis UK Ltd), 191 b (Paul Glendell/Alamy),

Texts

Adapted from 'Peach of an idea: The founders of Innocent Drinks' by Richard Wray, *The Guardian*, 7 August 2004, Copyright Guardian News & Media Ltd 2004. Adapted from 'Language jobs that translate globally' by Kate Hilpern, *The Independent*, 16 October 2012, copyright The Independent. Adapted from 'Satellite Archaeology' by Hannah Bloch, http://ngm.nationalgeographic.com/2013/02/explore/satellite-archaeology. Adapted from 'Mind your languages' by Matthew Brace, *Geographical*, Vol.71, No.11, November 1999, Copyright © Geographical 1999. Adapted from 'Citizen Scientists' by A. R. Williams, http://ngm.nationalgeographic.com/2013/03/explore/citizen-scientists. Adapted from 'Read it and weep! Research shows modern day books contain 14% less emotion than books published at the beginning of the 1900s... but are far more paranoid' by Nick McDermott, Daily Mail online, 20 March 2013, reproduced with permission from Solo Syndication. Adapted from 'Back to basics' by Ashley Seager, *The Guardian*, 13 July 2004, Copyright Guardian News & Media Ltd 2004. Adapted from 'Close encounters of the wild kind' by Christian Amodeo, *Geographical*, Vol.76, No.2, February 2004, Copyright © Geographical 2004. Adapted from 'Missing Out: In Praise Of The Unlived Life, By Adam Phillips' by Christina Patterson, 16 June 2012, http://www.independent.co.uk/arts-entertainment/books/reviews/missing-out-in-praise-of-the-unlived-life-by-adam-phillips-7851441.html#, copyright The Independent. Adapted from 'Wired for Culture' by Tom Chivers, *The Telegraph*, 6 March 2012, © Telegraph Media Group Limited 2012. Adapted from 'Teach Us To Sit Still by Tim Parks' review by John Preston, *The Telegraph*, 11 July 2010, © Telegraph Media Group Limited 2010. Adapted from 'The Antidote by Oliver Burkeman' by B. J. Epstein, http://www.walesartsreview.org/the-antidote-by-oliver-burkeman/, with permission from Wales Art Review. Adapted from 'Field science: When your degree takes you to the jungle' by Tamara Williams, 27 February 2013, http://www.independent.co.uk/student/student-life/field-science-when-your-degree-takes-you-to-the-jungle-8512656.html?origin=internalSearch#, copyright The Independent. Adapted from 'Bred to Soar' by Jeffrey P. Cohn, published in *Américas Magazine* (Volume 56, #5, 2004) © 2004 Organization of American States. Reprinted from *Américas Magazine*, the official publication of the Organization of American States (OAS). Adapted from 'Scientists and their emotions: the highs and the lows' by Ewan Birney, *The Observer*, 10 February 2013, Copyright Guardian News & Media Ltd. 2013. Adapted from 'Why the humble mushroom is being hailed as a superfood' by Angela Epstein, *The Mail on Sunday*, 19 October 2008, reproduced with permission from Solo Syndication. Adapted from 'How sound and smell can create perfect harmony' by Cassie Barton, *The Guardian*, 22 October 2012, Copyright Guardian News & Media Ltd 2012. Adapted from 'Neolithic discovery: why Orkney is the centre of ancient Britain' by Robin McKie, *The Observer*, 7 October 2012, Copyright Guardian News & Media Ltd 2012. Adapted from 'David Hockney, Philip Pullman, Kirsty Wark: my favourite masterpiece' by Jonathan Jones, *The Guardian*, 13 October 2011, Copyright Guardian News & Media Ltd 2011.

Although every effort has been made to contact copyright holders before publication, this has not always been possible. If notified, the publisher will undertake to rectify any errors or omissions at the earliest opportunity. Note that the sample answer sheets in the Practice tests are not the updated official answer sheets provided by Cambridge as these were not available at the time of publication.

Printed in China by RR Donnelley
Print Year: 2015   Print Number: 03

Contents

CAMBRIDGE ENGLISH: ADVANCED

Paper 1: READING AND USE OF ENGLISH (1 hour 30 minutes)

Part	Task type and focus	Number of questions	Task format
1	**Multiple-choice cloze** Task focus: vocabulary	8	A multiple-choice cloze text with eight gaps, followed by eight four-option questions.
2	**Open cloze** Task focus: grammar and some vocabulary	8	A modified cloze text with eight gaps which you fill with the appropriate word.
3	**Word formation** Task focus: vocabulary	8	A text with eight gaps. You are asked to complete the text by making an appropriate word from the word prompt you are given for each gap.
4	**Key word transformations** Task focus: grammar and vocabulary	6	This task consists of six discrete key word transformations. You are asked to complete a sentence which means the same as the given sentence using the key word.
5	**Multiple choice** Task focus: reading for detailed understanding of a text, gist, opinion, attitude, tone, purpose, main idea, meaning from context, implication, text organisation features	6	You answer six four-option multiple-choice questions on a text.
6	**Short texts** Task focus: reading to understand meaning across different texts.	4	You read four short texts by different writers on a similar topic, and with a similar purpose. Reading across the texts, you identify similarities and differences in the themes and opinions of the writers.
7	**Missing paragraphs** Task focus: close reading of a text, identifying references and meanings across discourse.	6	You read a text from which six paragraphs have been removed. There is one extra paragraph. You decide which paragraphs complete each gap in the text.
8	**Multiple matching** Task focus: reading for specific information in a text, detail, opinion, attitude	10	You match ten questions to different texts or different sections of a text.

Paper 2: WRITING (1 hour 30 minutes)

Part	Task type and focus	Number of questions	Task format
1	**Question 1** Essay	Part 1 is compulsory. 220–260 words	You write an essay based on a given title and accompanying ideas, including one of your own.
2	**Questions 2–4** may include an email/a letter, a report, a review or a proposal	You have a choice from three tasks. 220–260 words	You carry out a writing task, using the appropriate style and format.

Paper 3: LISTENING (40 minutes approximately)

Part	Task type and focus	Number of questions	Task format
1	**Multiple choice** Task focus: understanding gist, detail, function, purpose, feeling, attitude, opinion, genre, agreement, etc.	6	A series of short unrelated extracts, from monologues or exchanges between interacting speakers. There is one three-option question for each extract.
2	**Sentence completion** Task focus: detail, specific information, stated opinion	8	A monologue. The task consists of eight gapped sentences.
3	**Multiple choice** Task focus: understanding attitude and opinion, main idea, specific information and gist	6	A listening text involving interacting speakers. You have six four-option multiple-choice questions, and need to decide what the correct answer is.
4	**Multiple matching** Task focus: understanding mood and attitude, main ideas, specific information and context	10	Five short monologues, all on a similar theme. You listen once and match each speaker to information from two separate lists.

Paper 4: SPEAKING (15 minutes approximately)

Part	Task type and focus	Input	Task format
1 **Interview** (2 mins)	The interlocutor asks each candidate to say a little about themselves.	Verbal questions	You must be able to • give personal information. • talk about present circumstances / past experiences. • talk about future plans.
2 **Individual long turn** (4 mins)	Each candidate talks about a pair of photographs for 1 minute, followed by a 30-second response from the second candidate.	Visual stimuli, with verbal and written instructions	You must be able to • give information. • express your opinions. • relate photos to yourself and your own experience.
3 **Two-way collaborative task** (4 mins)	The interlocutor asks candidates to carry out a task based on written prompts.	A written question with written stimuli and verbal instructions	You must be able to • exchange information and opinions. • express and justify opinions. • agree, disagree or partly agree. • suggest and speculate.
4 **Discussion** (5 mins)	The interlocutor asks candidates general opinion questions related to the topic covered in Part 3.	Verbal prompts	You must be able to • exchange information and opinions. • express and justify opinions. • agree, disagree or partly agree.

Exam Essentials Practice Tests is a series of materials published by National Geographic Learning for students preparing for the major EFL/ESL examinations: Cambridge English: First (FCE); Cambridge English: Advanced (CAE); and International English Language Testing System (IELTS). The series is characterised by the close attention each component pays to developing a detailed knowledge of the skills and strategies needed for success in each paper or part of the exams.

Cambridge English: Advanced (CAE) Practice Tests helps learners become aware of the Cambridge English: Advanced (CAE) exam requirements, offers details about the format and language in the exam, and helps learners develop exam skills necessary for success. The book also provides extensive practice in all parts of the exam, using the actual test format.

Taking the Exam

Cambridge English: Advanced is one of a series of five Cambridge English exams corresponding to different levels of the Common European Framework of Reference for Languages (CEFR):

• Cambridge English: Key (KET) CEFR Level A2

• Cambridge English: Preliminary (PET) CEFR Level B1

• Cambridge English: First (FCE) CEFR Level B2

• Cambridge English: Advanced (CAE) CEFR Level C1

• Cambridge English: Proficiency (CPE) CEFR Level C2

Cambridge English: Advanced is widely recognised by universities and similar educational institutions, and in commerce and industry, as proof that the holder of this qualification can take a course of study in English at university level, and also carry out managerial and professional work effectively. It can also be used as proof of English skills when applying for employment in English-speaking environments.

The exam can be taken on many dates during a year, and can be taken on paper or on a computer. It consists of four Papers.

Paper 1 Reading and Use of English (1 hour 30 minutes)

• Part 1 is a multiple-choice cloze task. You read a text with eight gaps. This is followed by eight four-option multiple-choice questions. You need to complete each gap with the correct option. Part 1 tests your knowledge of vocabulary, including idioms, fixed phrases, phrasal verbs, collocations and shades of meaning.

• Part 2 is an open cloze task. You read a text with eight gaps. You need to complete each gap with an appropriate word. Part 2 tests your knowledge of the structure of the language – grammar and some vocabulary.

• Part 3 is a word formation task. You read a short text with eight gaps. You need to complete each gap with an appropriate word formed from a prompt word in capitals that appears to the right of the text on the same line as the gap. Part 3 tests your knowledge of how words are formed from other words.

• Part 4 consists of six sentences, each of which is followed by a word and a gapped sentence. You need to complete the gapped sentence so that its meaning is the same as the first sentence using three to six words, including the word given. Part 4 tests your knowledge of vocabulary and grammar.

• Part 5 consists of a long text with six four-option multiple-choice questions. Part 5 tests your ability to read for detail, gist, opinion, attitude, purpose, implication and text organisation features such as reference and comparison.

• Part 6 consists of four short texts written by four different people about the same subject, together with four questions. The questions test your ability to understand the opinions and attitudes expressed in the texts and to identify when writers agree and disagree with each other.

• Part 7 consists of a long text from which six paragraphs have been removed and placed in jumbled order after the text. You have to decide from where in the text the paragraphs have been removed. Part 7 tests your understanding of how a text is structured.

• Part 8 consists of a long text with several sections or several short texts. There are 10 questions which require you to decide which section of the long text or which short text each one refers to. Part 8 tests your ability to read for specific information, detail, opinion and attitude.

Paper 2 Writing (1 hour 30 minutes)

- Part 1 is compulsory. You are required to write an essay in 220–260 words. Before you write your answer, you must read the instructions as well as an input text or texts. Part 1 focuses on your ability to evaluate, express opinions, hypothesise, etc. Persuasion is always an important element in your writing in Part 1.

- There are three questions to choose from in Part 2. For questions 2–4, you are required to write an email/letter, a proposal, a report or a review in 220–260 words. Part 2 focuses on your ability to give opinions, persuade, justify, give advice, compare, etc.

- Both parts of the Writing Paper test your ability to write a text according to instructions in an appropriate style and register for a given purpose and target reader. Effective text organisation, accuracy and a good range of vocabulary are also important.

Paper 3 Listening (approximately 40 minutes)

- Part 1 consists of three short monologues or texts involving interacting speakers. You are required to answer two three-option multiple-choice questions for each extract. Part 1 tests your ability to understand feeling, attitude, opinion, purpose, function, agreement, course of action, general gist, detail, etc.

- Part 2 consists of a long monologue. You are required to complete eight gapped sentences with information you hear on the recording. Each gap is completed by one, two or three words or a number. Part 2 tests your ability to understand specific information and stated opinion.

- Part 3 consists of a text involving interacting speakers. You are required to answer six four-option multiple-choice questions. Part 3 tests your ability to understand attitude and opinion.

- Part 4 consists of five short monologues on a related theme. There are two tasks in this part. Both tasks require you choose from a list of options the opinion that each speaker expresses. Part 4 tests your ability to understand gist, attitude and main point and to interpret context.

Paper 4 Speaking (approximately 15 minutes)

The Speaking Paper generally involves two candidates and two examiners.

- In Part 1 you have a brief conversation with the examiner. Part 1 tests your ability to give personal information and use social and interactional language.

- In Part 2 the examiner gives you and the other candidate visual and written prompts. Each candidate is required to use the prompts he/she is given to talk for a minute. He/She is also required to answer a question based on the other candidate's prompts in 30 seconds. Part 2 tests your ability to organise a larger unit of discourse to compare, describe, express opinions and speculate.

- In Part 3 the examiner gives you and the other candidate visual and written prompts. You are required to use the prompts to have a conversation with the other candidate. Part 3 tests your ability to sustain an interaction, exchange ideas, express and justify opinions, agree and/or disagree, suggest, evaluate, reach a decision through negotiation, etc.

- In Part 4 the examiner asks you questions based on the topics you talked about in Part 3. You are required to have a three-way discussion with the examiner and the other candidate. Part 4 tests your ability to exchange information, express and justify opinions, agree and/or disagree.

Preparing for the exam

In preparing for the four Papers, the following points should be taken into account.

Reading and Use of English

To prepare for the **Use of English** (Parts 1, 2, 3 and 4), you need to develop your awareness and use of both grammatical structures and vocabulary. You need to know how structures such as verb forms, modal and auxiliary verbs, pronouns, prepositions, conjunctions, modifiers and determiners are used correctly in a variety of different types of text. You also need a good knowledge of vocabulary, so learn whole phrases rather than single words in isolation, how words and phrases are used in combination with other words, how words can have different meanings and uses, and how different words can be formed from a root. It helps to read widely and to pay attention to grammar and vocabulary as you read. Make use of dictionaries and grammar books (except when doing the tests), and develop an efficient system for recording the new vocabulary and grammar you encounter.

To prepare for the **Reading** (Parts 5, 6, 7 and 8), you should read from a range of material: newspapers, magazines, journals, novels, leaflets, brochures, etc. When you read, pay attention to text organisation features, train yourself to recognise the author's purpose in writing and his or her tone, and learn to read between the lines for what is implied rather than stated explicitly. It is important to practise different reading strategies that can be used for different parts of the Reading Paper, for example skimming for the main idea and gist, scanning to locate specific information or reading closely to determine the writer's precise meaning.

Writing

You need to be familiar with all the text types you may be required to write in the exam. You should also be aware of the criteria that will be used in marking your texts.

- Has the candidate achieved the purpose stated in the instructions?
- Does the text have a positive general effect on the target reader?
- Does the text cover all the content points?
- Is the text organised effectively and are ideas linked appropriately?
- Has language been used accurately?
- Does the text have a good range of vocabulary and grammatical features?
- Is the register appropriate for the task?
- Is the layout appropriate?

Listening

You should practise listening to a wide variety of spoken English: announcements, speeches, lectures, talks, radio broadcasts, anecdotes, radio interviews, discussions, etc. You should also practise listening for different purposes: to understand gist, identify context or attitude or find specific information.

Speaking

You should practise speaking English as much as possible. It is important to master conversational skills such as turn taking and the appropriate way to participate in a discussion, giving full but natural answers to questions and requesting clarification.

Further information can be obtained from the Cambridge English website: www.cambridgeenglish.org

Practice Tests: contents

Cambridge English: Advanced (CAE) in the *Exam Essentials Practice Tests* series prepares candidates for the Cambridge English: Advanced examination by providing **eight full practice tests,** which accurately reflect the latest exam specifications.

There are **three guided tests** at the beginning, which feature **essential tips** to practise exam strategy. These tips offer guidance and general strategies for approaching each task. Other tips offer advice relevant to specific questions in the guided tests. These guided tests will help students prepare for each paper, while the following five **tests (without guidance)** will offer students thorough practice at a realistic exam level.

The **DVD-ROM** accompanying the book includes the audio materials for all the Listening Papers. These accurately reflect the exam in both style and content. Moreover, the audio materials for Tests 1 and 2 have been recorded with the repetitions and full pauses, exactly as in the exam itself.

A **writing bank** includes **sample answers** for the kinds of tasks that occur in Paper 2 (Writing), writing tips in the form of notes and **useful phrases** for the different task types. Varied **visual materials** for Paper 4 (Speaking) have also been included, while a **language bank** supplies useful phrases and expressions for use in the Speaking Paper.

There is also a **glossary** for each test, explaining vocabulary that is likely to be unfamiliar to students.

Clear and straightforward design simplifies use of the book. **Exam overview** tables ensure that key information is readily accessible, while a specially designed menu makes it easy to navigate through the different parts and papers of each practice test.

You will find **sample exam answer sheets** on pages 166–168 which you can photocopy and use to note down your answers. These will help you practise using the answer sheets you will be given in the real exam.

For more practice, there is also an additional book of tests for this exam: *Exam Essentials Practice Tests 2 Cambridge English: Advanced (CAE)*.

Practice Tests: principles

In writing this book, three guiding principles have been observed.

Firstly, that it should be useful for teachers, students sitting the Cambridge English: Advanced exam for the first time or re-sitting the exam, whether they are working alone or in a class. Students approaching the exam for the first time would be best advised to work through the book linearly, developing their skills and confidence; those re-sitting the exam can consult the Exam overview tables to concentrate on particular areas for targeted revision. The **without key** edition can be used by students working in a class, while the **with key** edition includes a detailed **answer key and all the audio scripts,** ensuring that students working alone can benefit from support while attempting these tests.

The second principle is that the questions should accurately reflect the range of questions found in the Cambridge English: Advanced exam. Thus students obtain guidance concerning the general content and the best way of approaching the tasks from the questions themselves. Seeing the questions in this light – as instructions to the candidate from the examiner rather than intimidating challenges – also helps students feel less daunted by the whole experience of sitting a major exam like this.

The third principle is that the texts used in the practice tests should be not only representative of those used in the exam, but also varied and interesting. Everyone finds it easier to learn if the subject matter is relevant to his or her lifestyle and interests. In choosing, editing and creating the texts here, we have done our utmost to ensure that the experience of working with this book is as stimulating and rewarding as possible.

This edition of *Exam Essentials* for students of Cambridge English: Advanced (CAE) includes a brand new DVD-ROM which focuses on the Speaking test component of the Cambridge English: Advanced examination. The DVD-ROM includes two videos:

• a complete Cambridge English: Advanced Speaking test.
• a short clip giving valuable advice about the Cambridge English: Advanced Speaking test.

To maximise learning from the complete Cambridge English: Advanced Speaking test, the following PDFs are also available on the DVD-ROM:

• a worksheet for individual or class use.
• an answer key for the worksheet.
• the complete script of the Speaking test.

A complete Speaking test

A full Cambridge English: Advanced Speaking test interview is approximately 15 minutes in length. Please note that the interview shown on this DVD-ROM is a slightly extended version of the Speaking test. This allows for a wide range of language and types of response to be included. This interview also features high-level candidates whose performance would achieve a good pass in the exam. The video therefore provides a good model to follow. Don't worry if you feel you may not perform to this high standard in every area of the test. You will need to demonstrate a good level, but you will not need to use every structure or item of vocabulary perfectly in order to pass the test.

The video clearly details:

• the role of the examiners.
• the timings of the test.
• the four parts of the test and what is involved in each one.

The role of the examiners

There are two examiners in the test room. Examiner 1 (the interlocutor) asks the candidates questions and handles the tasks. He or she has to keep to very strict timings and has a script to follow. Unscripted conversation or questions are therefore not possible. This is to ensure that each candidate receives equal treatment. Examiner 2 (the assessor) does not usually speak in the test, except to greet the candidates. However, Examiner 2 will make notes. Both examiners give marks to the candidates.

The timings of the test

Part 1: Interview – 2 minutes (3 minutes for groups of three)

Part 2: Individual long turn – 4 minutes (6 minutes for groups of three)

Part 3: Collaborative task – 4 minutes (6 minutes for groups of three)

Part 4: Discussion – 5 minutes (8 minutes for groups of three)

The four parts of the test

Part 1: Interview – this includes greeting the candidates, introducing the examiners and general questions about yourself.

Part 2: Individual long turn – this involves talking about two out of three pictures and briefly answering a question about your partner's pictures after he/she has spoken.

Part 3: Collaborative task – this is where both candidates talk about prompts on a diagram, and reach a decision through negotiation.

Part 4: Discussion – the interlocutor leads a discussion by asking candidates questions. Candidates exchange information and opinions related to the topic in Part 3.

How each part of the test should be answered

The video offers tips for improving candidates' performance in each of the four parts. In Part 1, candidates need to give personal information, talk about their present circumstances, talk about past experiences and future plans as well as express opinions. In Part 2, candidates need to express their opinions through comparing, hypothesising and speculating on the pictures given. In Part 3, candidates need to work together to exchange ideas and opinions, agree or disagree, suggest, speculate, evaluate and reach a decision through negotiation. In Part 4, candidates express and justify their opinions and agree and disagree.

Tips and advice

Following the Speaking test, there is a short clip to supplement the speaking tips given in the book. In this section, which is about five minutes long, an examiner gives some tips and advice about how to do well in the Cambridge English: Advanced Speaking test.

The worksheet

This printable worksheet accompanies the complete Cambridge English: Advanced Speaking test. Although primarily designed for self-study, the worksheet can also be used in the classroom. It provides in-depth information about the Speaking test and focuses on the language each candidate uses in the video.

The worksheet is divided into four sections which relate to each part of the Speaking test. It includes activities which:

• draw students' attention to key features of the candidate's response.
• relate these features to the marking criteria used by the examiners.
• give the student practice in developing their own answers for similar questions.

A separate answer key and a full video script are also provided.

For questions **1–8**, read the text below and decide which answer (**A, B, C** or **D**) best fits each gap. There is an example at the beginning (**0**).

Mark your answers **on the separate answer sheet**.

Example:

| 0 | A | event | B | aspect | C | field | D | division |

0	A	B	C	D
	⎵	**▬**	⎵	⎵

Essential tips

▶ Read through the whole text to get a general idea of what it is about.

▶ The correct option must have the correct meaning. It can also be part of a phrase, collocation, idiom, phrasal verb or expression.

▶ The correct option must fit in the sentence structurally. All the four options will be the right part of speech (noun, adjective, verb, adverb, etc.), but only one will be correct in the context of the sentence. For instance, the correct option may be the only word that is followed by a preposition that comes after the gap. So, check the words on either side of the gap carefully to see what collocates with them.

Question 2: One of the options does not collocate with *time*. Of the other three options, only one has the correct meaning of 'best'.

Question 3: Only one of the options forms a fixed expression with *what is* and has the meaning of 'in addition' or 'moreover'.

Question 4: All four options can form phrasal verbs with *out*, but only one collocates with *activities* to mean 'perform activities'.

Question 6: Only one option collocates with *convinced*.

Nature's clocks

Our biological clocks govern almost every (**0**) .... of our lives. Our sensitivity to stimuli (**1**) .... over the course of the day, and our ability to perform certain functions is subject to fluctuations. The middle of the day, for example, is the (**2**) .... time for tasks such as making decisions. Anything that demands physical co-ordination, on the other hand, is best attempted in the early evening. What is (**3**) ...., there is a dramatic drop in performance if these activities are (**4**) .... out at other times. The risk of accident in a factory, for example, is 20% higher during the night (**5**) ....

Primitive humans lived in tune with the daily cycle of light and dark. Today, we are (**6**) .... convinced that we can impose schedules on our lives at will. Sooner or later, however, we pay a (**7**) .... for ignoring our natural rhythms. A good example is jet lag, caused when we confuse our body's biological clocks by (**8**) .... several time zones. Jet lag often lasts for several days and can badly affect our decision-making ability.

1	A	modifies	B	ranges	C	varies	D	wavers
2	A	peak	B	summit	C	maximum	D	optimum
3	A	more	B	else	C	different	D	besides
4	A	made	B	gone	C	carried	D	set
5	A	labour	B	work	C	duty	D	shift
6	A	powerfully	B	firmly	C	steadily	D	highly
7	A	price	B	fine	C	fee	D	cost
8	A	landing	B	penetrating	C	crossing	D	travelling

For questions **9–16**, read the text below and think of the word which best fits each gap. Use only **one** word in each gap. There is an example at the beginning (**0**).

Write your answers **IN CAPITAL LETTERS on the separate answer sheet**.

Example: 0 | I | N |

Antarctica in danger

The last 20 years have seen a dramatic increase (**0**) .... the numbers of visitors to Antarctica. These (**9**) .... only include scientists who are researching (**10**) .... crucial issues as climate change and its impact on the polar regions, but also more and more tourists. Some tourists simply want to see the last unspoiled continent. Some, on the (**11**) .... hand, seek more active pursuits like adventure sports. However, environmentalists are concerned that the growing tourist industry may (**12**) .... endangering the Antarctic environment and sowing the seeds of its destruction.

(**13**) .... of the problems facing the area is pollution resulting from tourism. Careless visitors throw rubbish into the sea, without realising (**14**) .... harmful this can be to wildlife. Just (**15**) .... damaging, perhaps more so, is oil spilt from ships insufficiently reinforced to withstand collisions (**16**) .... icebergs. Oil from even a small spill can remain an environmental hazard for many years, and there are increasing numbers of icebergs breaking off the continental ice sheet due to global warming.

Essential tips

- ▶ Read through the whole text to get a general idea of what it is about.

- ▶ Decide what word(s) in the sentence are grammatically related to the gapped word. This will help you decide what part of speech is needed (auxiliary verb, pronoun, article, preposition, etc.).

- ▶ Read the whole sentence to see if the word you need is part of a longer phrase, such as *either ... or ...* .

- ▶ It may be that two (or even three) words could fit in the gap, so do not assume the word you are thinking of is wrong if you can also think of one or two alternatives.

Question 9: Read the whole sentence carefully. Notice *but also* in the last part of the sentence. Think of the structure *... only ... but also*.

Question 10: Look carefully at the words either side of the gap. Climate change is an example of a crucial issue. Can you think of a word to go with *as* to indicate an example?

Question 11: The gapped word is part of a phrase: *on the ... hand*. Read the previous sentence before deciding on the word for the gap.

Question 12: Which verb usually comes before a continuous (*-ing*) verb form? Which verb form comes after *may* and other modal verbs?

PAPER 1 Reading and ▸ Part 1
Use of English Part 2
Part 3
PAPER 2 Writing Part 4
Part 5
PAPER 3 Listening Part 6
Part 7
PAPER 4 Speaking Part 8

For questions **17–24**, read the text below. Use the word given in capitals at the end of some of the lines to form a word that fits in the gap **in the same line**. There is an example at the beginning (**0**).

Write your answers **IN CAPITAL LETTERS on the separate answer sheet.**

Example: | 0 | A | C | T | I | V | I | T | Y | | | | | | | | | | |

Essential tips

▸ Read through the whole text to get a general idea of what it is about.

▸ Decide what type of word is needed in each gap (e.g. verb, noun, adjective or adverb).

▸ Look at the word in capital letters. You may need to change its form to fit the gap.

▸ Think about what prefixes and suffixes you could add.

▸ Some words will need more than one change.

▸ Check the spelling carefully and consider whether the word should be singular or plural.

Question 17: Think carefully about the type of word you need here. You will need to add both a prefix and a suffix.

Question 19: The gapped word forms part of the expression *in ... with*, which means 'matching something'.

Question 22: You need to make a verb from a noun here. Make sure you use the correct verb form. There are two ways of spelling this word, and both can be correct.

Elephant training

If you are travelling in Thailand, you can now take part in
an (**0**) .... of an unusual kind. For a sum of money which   **ACTIVE**
is (**17**) .... modest, you can spend a few days at   **CREDIBLE**
an elephant-conservation centre training to be a
mahout (elephant driver).

Primarily set up in an endeavour to preserve the (**18**) ....   **MAJESTY**
Thai elephant, the centre welcomes tourism as a means
of funding itself. Nevertheless, its programme remains
strictly in (**19**) .... with the traditions of *Kachasart*, the ancient   **KEEP**
method of studying elephants, and the *mahouts* build up very
close relationships with their elephants. Training is believed
to be (**20**) .... to the elephants, providing them with physical   **BENEFIT**
and mental (**21**) .... Their well-being is considered of   **STIMULATE**
utmost importance.

The elephants are captive, of course, and the centre
has been (**22**) .... for not allowing them to go free.   **CRITIC**
The reality, however, is that (**23**) .... deforestation has   **EXTEND**
left wild elephants struggling to survive in habitats that
are shrinking almost on a (**24**) .... basis, and the centre   **DAY**
offers them a sanctuary – for the time being at least.

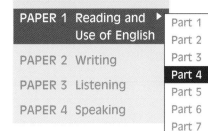
PAPER 1 Reading and ▸
       Use of English

PAPER 2 Writing

PAPER 3 Listening

PAPER 4 Speaking

Part 1
Part 2
Part 3
Part 4
Part 5
Part 6
Part 7
Part 8

For questions **25–30**, complete the second sentence so that it has a similar meaning to the first sentence, using the word given. **Do not change the word given.** You must use between **three** and **six** words, including the word given. Here is an example (**0**).

Example:

0 Jane regretted speaking so rudely to the old lady.

MORE

Jane .... politely to the old lady.

Example: | **0** | WISHED SHE HAD SPOKEN MORE |

Write **only** the missing words **IN CAPITAL LETTERS on the separate answer sheet**.

25 Pop in for a chat whenever you are in town.

HAPPEN

If .... in town, pop in for a chat.

26 Paula had just reached the gate when it began to rain.

THAN

No sooner .... it began to rain.

27 'Mark wrote that poem, not Ian,' said Helen.

IT

According to Helen, ... that poem, not Ian.

28 Even if it is expensive, they want to stay in the hotel by the beach.

MAY

Expensive ...., they want to stay in the hotel by the beach.

29 Unless you tell the truth, the school trip will be cancelled.

MEAN

Your failure .... the cancellation of the school trip.

30 Noriko has never been here before, so it is possible that she has got lost.

HAVE

Noriko .... it is the first time she has ever been here.

Essential tips

▸ For each question, read both sentences carefully. The second sentence must convey the same information as the first sentence, but in different words.

▸ The key word in capital letters must be used without changing its form in any way.

▸ You may need to change the order in which you give the information, and the form of some words from the first sentence.

▸ Some questions may require you to change from a negative sentence to a positive one, or from a passive structure to an active one (or the other way round – be prepared for this!).

▸ You must use between three and six words in your answer. If you write too few words or too many, you will lose marks.

Question 26: Think about the word order here. Certain negative structures at the start of a sentence are followed by inversion (e.g. *Never **before had** Caroline seen such a beautiful garden*).

Question 27: How can you use *it* to emphasise that Mark, not Ian, wrote the poem?

Question 30: How can you express the idea of possibility? You need a structure with a modal verb (more than one modal verb is possible). You will also need a suitable linking word.

PAPER 1 Reading and ▸
        Use of English
PAPER 2 Writing
PAPER 3 Listening
PAPER 4 Speaking

Part 1
Part 2
Part 3
Part 4
Part 5
Part 6
Part 7
Part 8

You are going to read a magazine article. For questions **31–36**, choose the answer (**A, B, C** or **D**) which you think fits best according to the text.

Mark your answers **on the separate answer sheet**.

The beauties of the stone age

Jane Howard reviews some ancient works of art.

I have just come home after viewing some astonishing works of art that were recently discovered in Church Hole cave in Nottinghamshire. They are not drawings, as one would expect, but etchings – shapes cut into the rock – and they depict a huge range of wild animals. The artists who created them lived around 13,000 years ago, and the images are remarkable on a variety of counts. First of all, their sheer number is staggering: there are 90 in all. Moreover, 58 of them are on the ceiling. This is extremely rare in cave art, according to a leading expert, Dr Wilbur Samson of Central Midlands University. 'Wall pictures are the norm,' he says. 'But more importantly, the Church Hole etchings are an incredible artistic achievement. They can hold their own in comparison with the best found in continental Europe.' I am not a student of the subject, so I have to take his word for it. However, you do not have to be an expert to appreciate their beauty.

In fact, it is the wider significance of the etchings that is likely to attract most attention in academic circles, since they radically alter our view of life in Britain during this epoch. It had previously been thought that ice-age hunters in this country were isolated from people in more central areas of Europe, but the Church Hole images prove that ancient Britons were part of a way of living, thinking and seeing the world that had spread right across the continent. And they were at least as sophisticated as their counterparts on the mainland.

News of such exciting discoveries spreads rapidly, and thanks to the internet and mobile phones, a great many people probably knew about this discovery within hours of the initial expedition returning. As a result, some etchings may already have been adversely affected, albeit inadvertently, by eager visitors. In a regrettably late response, the site has been cordoned off with a high, rather intimidating fence, and warning notices have been posted.

An initial survey of the site last year failed to reveal the presence of the etchings. The reason lies in the expectations of the researchers. They had been looking for the usual type of cave drawing or painting, which shows up best under direct light. Consequently, they used powerful torches, shining them straight onto the rock face. However, the Church Hole images are modifications of the rock itself, and show up best when seen from a certain angle in the natural light of early morning. Having been fortunate to see them at this hour, I can only say that I was deeply – and unexpectedly – moved. While most cave art often seems to have been created in a shadowy past very remote from us, these somehow convey the impression that they were made yesterday.

Dr Samson feels that the lighting factor provides important information about the likely function of these works of art. 'I think the artists knew very well that the etchings would hardly be visible except early in the morning. We can therefore deduce that the chamber was used for rituals involving animal worship, and that they were conducted just after dawn, as a preliminary to the day's hunting.'

However, such ideas are controversial in the world of archaeology and human origins. Dr Olivia Caruthers of the Reardon Institute remains unconvinced that the function of the etchings at Church Hole can be determined with any certainty. 'When we know so little about the social life of early humans, it would be foolish to insist on any rigid interpretation. We should, in my view, begin by tentatively assuming that their creators were motivated in part by aesthetic considerations – while of course being prepared to modify this verdict at a later date, if and when new evidence emerges.'

To which I can only add that I felt deeply privileged to have been able to view Church Hole. It is a site of tremendous importance culturally and is part of the heritage, not only of this country, but the world as a whole.

▸ This part of the exam tests your detailed understanding of a text, including the views and attitudes expressed.

▸ Read through the text quickly to get a general idea of what it is about. Do not worry if there are words or phrases you don't understand.

▸ The questions follow the order of the text. Read each question or question stem carefully and underline the key words.

▸ Look in the text for the answer to the question. One of the options will express the same idea, but don't expect that it will do so in the words of the text.

Question 31: An option can only be correct if all the information contained in it is accurate. Look at option A: are the images in Church Hole 'unique examples of ceiling art'? The text says they are 'extremely rare in cave art'. Is this the same? Look at option B: are the images in Church Hole 'particularly beautiful'? And are they 'paintings'?

Question 33: Look at option A. What does the writer say about the discovery of the images being made public? Look at option B. If something is 'vulnerable to damage', what might happen to it? Look at option C. The text says 'many people probably knew about the discovery within hours of the initial expedition returning'. Is this the same as saying 'many people visited the cave within hours'? Look at option D. Were the measures definitely ineffective?

Question 35: Sometimes you will find words from the options in the text. Be careful: the meaning in the text is not necessarily the same as that in the answer options. Here, option D says the hunters 'kept animals in the cave', but the text says the cave was used for 'rituals involving animal worship', which is not the same thing.

31 According to the text, the images in Church Hole cave are
- A unique examples of ceiling art.
- B particularly beautiful cave paintings.
- C superior in quality to other cave art in Britain.
- D aesthetically exceptional in their own right.

32 What is the cultural significance of these images?
- A They indicate that people from central Europe had settled in Britain.
- B They prove that ancient Britons hunted over large areas.
- C They reveal the existence of a single ice-age culture in Europe.
- D They suggest that people in Europe were more advanced than Britons.

33 According to the text,
- A the discovery of the images should not have been made public.
- B the images in the cave are vulnerable to damage.
- C many people visited the cave within hours of its discovery.
- D the measures taken to protect the images have proved ineffective.

34 Why were the images not discovered during the initial survey?
- A They were not viewed from the right direction.
- B People were not expecting to find any images.
- C The search took place at the wrong time of day.
- D The torches used were too bright.

35 What conclusion does Dr Samson draw from the lighting factor?
- A Rituals were common in animal worship.
- B The artists never intended to make the images visible.
- C The images were intended to be seen at a certain time of day.
- D Ice-age hunters kept animals in the cave.

36 According to Dr Caruthers,
- A we cannot make inferences from cave art.
- B the images in Church Hole do not serve any particular purpose.
- C experts know absolutely nothing about life 13,000 years ago.
- D the reasons such images were created are open to question.

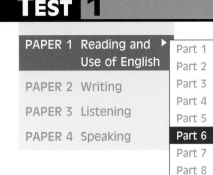
PAPER 1 Reading and ▶   Part 1
         Use of English   Part 2

PAPER 2 Writing   Part 3
                              Part 4
PAPER 3 Listening   Part 5

PAPER 4 Speaking   **Part 6**
                              Part 7
                              Part 8

You are going to read four contributions to a debate about the value of sending people into space. For questions **37–40**, choose from the contributions **A–D**. The contributions may be chosen more than once.

Mark your answers **on the separate answer sheet**.

Manned space missions

Is it a good idea to send people into space? Four scientists give their views.

A

What are we looking for out in space? That's the question that needs asking. The only thing we bring back is knowledge, and robots outperform astronauts in that respect. They are cheaper to put into space, they can stay there longer and they can collect and retain far more information. The early manned space flights generated genuine interest around the world, but who really cares nowadays, apart from a minority in whose interest it is that vast sums should continue to be invested? Who really believes it will ever be feasible to ship back large quantities of valuable materials from the moon, Mars or another planet, let alone migrate to these places in the event of a catastrophe? What is the priority? To try to create a station on Mars which could accommodate a handful of people, or to do something here to try to resolve global warming?

B

Space exploration, whether manned or not, is hugely expensive, and this is probably a key reason why it seems to have lost its appeal for many people. The fact is, however, that our galaxy is littered with giant meteors like the one that struck the Earth 16 million years ago, wiped out the dinosaurs and precipitated an ice age. Other cosmic dangers exist, as do threats on Earth itself, and one day the human species may only survive by settling in a new home. If we are to form colonies on the moon or other places in space, we have no alternative but to go there ourselves and do it, and that requires preparation. Robots tend to be good at certain tasks like collecting data, but their ability to think critically and creatively and to engage in problem-solving is limited. Some experiments that can only be conducted in space require physical and intellectual dexterity and these are skills that only humans possess.

C

People with a vested interest will say that for humans to travel beyond the Earth is important for the prestige and glamour of space exploration, and for the way it draws young minds into science and technology. However, for the cost of putting a few people into space for a few days, science education in schools could be transformed by creating smaller classes, new laboratories and equipment. Now, wouldn't that be exciting! So much of the investment in manned missions goes into keeping astronauts alive and safe, and the really useful science takes second place. The idea that humans will ever be able to (or want to) settle on the moon or anywhere else in space is unthinkable, so investment for that purpose is ludicrous, but the technological stimulus gained from the development of robotics and computer programmes that can deal with things in real time without people around has immense value on Earth, as well as in space.

D

Manned space flight is not primarily about science. The truth is that developments in science and computer design mean that satellites, robots and other technology are probably better than astronauts at collecting information from space which we can use on Earth. But people do not get excited when they see robots launched into space. Computers attached to a rocket don't stimulate the imagination or the enthusiasm for space exploration. And we do need to explore space, whatever the financial implications. In the long term, we need to find out whether we can survive outside the Earth's orbit. It's a question of our species' survival. Astrophysicists have worked out that at some point in the future – we do not know when – the sun will engulf the Earth, and for the species to continue, when that happens, we need to be elsewhere.

Which writer

has a different opinion from the others about the
inspirational significance of manned space missions?

`37` `[  ]`

has a similar view to writer B about the importance
of establishing whether humans can live on other planets?

`38` `[  ]`

expresses a different view from the others regarding
the relative efficiency of manned missions for carrying
out research?

`39` `[  ]`

shares writer A's opinion about the cost effectiveness
of sending people into space?

`40` `[  ]`

Essential tips

▶ This part of the exam tests your ability to understand
opinions and attitudes expressed in different texts and to
identify whether different writers agree or disagree with
each other. There are always four short texts by different
writers, and the four texts are all on the same subject.

▶ Read the main title and the four texts quickly to get a
general idea of what they are about. Don't worry if there
are words or phrases you don't understand.

▶ Look carefully at the four questions, highlighting the key
words in each.

▶ Read the first text and highlight the sections of the text
that refer to each of the questions. Write the question
numbers next to the relevant parts of the text. Then do
the same for each text.

▶ Then look across the four texts and compare the sections
that refer to Question 37. Read them carefully and
decide which ones express similar views and which have
different views.

Question 37: The key words in this question are *different
opinion from the others* and *inspirational significance*. All
the questions are about 'manned space missions' so there
is no need to highlight that. You need to find three views
that are similar and one that is different. The relevant part
of Text A is: *The early manned space flights generated
genuine interest around the world, but who really cares
nowadays ...?* The relevant part in text B is: *it seems to have
lost its appeal for many people*. Are they similar or different
opinions? Now, go through the same process with texts
C and D.

Question 40: The key words here are: *shares writer A's
opinion* and *cost effectiveness*. All the texts are about
sending people into space so there is no point highlighting
that. The relevant part of text A is: *They are cheaper to put
into space, they can stay there longer and they can collect
and retain far more information*. If you look at the previous
sentence, it is clear that *they* refers to 'robots'. So, writer A
believes that robots are more cost-effective than humans in
space. Now, look through the other three texts and highlight
references to cost. Which one expresses a similar view to
that of writer A?

PAPER 1 Reading and ▸ Part 1
Use of English Part 2

PAPER 2 Writing Part 3
Part 4
PAPER 3 Listening Part 5

PAPER 4 Speaking Part 6
Part 7
Part 8

You are going to read a newspaper about a company that makes fruit drinks. Six paragraphs have been removed from the article. Choose from the paragraphs **A–G** the one which fits each gap (**41–46**). There is one extra paragraph which you do not need to use.

Mark your answers **on the separate answer sheet**.

Peach of an idea

At the end of the 1990s, three friends in their mid-20s, Adam Balon, Richard Reed and Jon Wright were thinking of starting a business. They took £500 worth of fruit to a music festival in west London, made a huge batch of smoothies – fruit drinks blended with milk and yoghurt – and asked their customers for a verdict.

41

Looking back, they now admit that they were amazingly naïve, thinking it would just take off once they had the recipes and packaging figured out. In fact, the three budding entrepreneurs had nine months living on credit cards and overdrafts before they sold their first smoothie.

42

Only five years later, though, Innocent had become Britain's leading brand of smoothie, selling about 40% of the 50 million downed annually by British drinkers. Eight years after that, Innocent employed 250 staff, were selling over 200 million smoothies per week around the world, and a majority stake in the company had been bought up by the international giant, Coca Cola. What was the recipe for this startling success?

43

Innocent's refusal to compromise on this point presented them with some problems when they first started talking to potential suppliers, Adam says. This was when they discovered the truth about the majority of so-called natural fruit drinks.

44

'Naïvety', adds Richard, who is always ready with a soundbite, 'can be a great asset in business because you challenge the status quo.' Although Innocent's drinks are fiendishly healthy, the company has always been very careful not to preach. 'Everyone knows what they're supposed to do,' says Richard. 'But people just don't, especially when they live in a city. We just thought, "Wouldn't it be great to make it easy to get hold of this natural fresh goodness?" Then at least you've got one healthy habit in a world of bad ones.'

45

'In essence,' explains Jon, 'we simply froze some of our smoothies and threw in a bit of egg to make it all stick together.' To help testers make up their minds about which combinations worked, they dusted off the old "yes" and "no" bins and put them out again. And once again their methods proved fruitful.

46

'We didn't rule it out completely,' says Richard. 'But the three of us have always gone away once every three months to talk about what we want out of the business and we've always been in the same place. So as long as we're excited and challenged and proud of the business, we're going to want to be a part of it.'

A Most are made from concentrated juice with water – and perhaps sweeteners, colours and preservatives – added. 'We didn't even know about that when we started,' Adam explains. 'It was when we started talking to people and they said, "OK, we'll use orange concentrate," and we said, "What's *concentrate*?" and they explained it and we said, "No, we want orange juice."'

B Probably something to do with pure, unadulterated ingredients with a dash of quirky advertising. As one campaign put it, their drinks are not made *from* fruit, they *are* fruit.

C 'We decided to keep it simple,' says Richard. We had a bin that said "yes" and a bin that said "no", and at the end of the weekend the "yes" bin was full of empty bottles. We quit our jobs the next day.'

D Their early years of success coincided with increasing consumer concerns about healthy eating, and Innocent soon became worth a lot of money to potential buyers. Was there ever a temptation in those early years to sell up and go and live on a desert island?

E They also seem to have managed to stay friends, and the fact that each member of the team brings a different and complementary set of skills to Innocent seems to have helped them avoid any big bust-ups over strategy.

F So, at another festival in 2004, the Innocent team tried extending their range of products into desserts. 'For us there was this problem of Sunday evenings, sitting down to watch a film with a big tub of ice cream – it's nice to munch through it, but very bad for you,' Richard adds.

G They found that the finances were the basic stumbling block. But they eventually had a lucky break when Maurice Pinto, a wealthy American businessman, decided to invest in them. In total, it took 15 months from the initial idea to taking the product to market.

Essential tips

▶ This part of the exam tests your understanding of how a text is organised and how paragraphs relate to each other. For example, a paragraph might give details about an idea mentioned previously, or it may present another side of an argument.

▶ Read through the text quickly to get a general idea of what it is about. Don't worry if there are words you don't understand.

▶ Look for links between the main text and the gapped paragraphs. The gapped paragraph may have links either to the paragraph before it or to the paragraph after it, or even to both.

▶ Look for theme and language links. For example:

• references to people, places and times;

• words or phrases that refer back or forward to another word, phrase or idea in the text. For example, if the first line of a paragraph says something like *This becomes clear when we look at ...* then *this* refers back to something expressed in the previous paragraph.

• linking devices such as *firstly, secondly, furthermore, on the other hand, however*. These will help you to find connections between paragraphs.

▶ When you have found a paragraph that may fill a gap, read the paragraph that comes before it and the one that comes after it to see that they fit together.

▶ Re-read the completed text and make sure it makes sense.

Question 41: The last sentence in the previous paragraph describes how Balon, Reed and Wright 'asked their customers for a verdict'. Which gapped paragraph describes how customers gave their opinion?

Question 43: The previous paragraph ends with the question *What was the recipe for this startling success?* Look for a gapped paragraph which seems to answer this question.

Question 44: The previous paragraph ends with the sentence. *This was when they discovered the truth about the majority of so-called 'natural fruit drinks'.* Look for a gapped paragraph which describes this 'truth'.

You are going to read a magazine article in which four people talk about careers involving foreign languages. For questions **47–56**, choose from the people (**A–D**).

Mark your answers **on the separate answer sheet**.

Which person

mentions being discouraged from studying languages?	**47**
expresses sympathy for those who find language learning difficult?	**48**
points out a common misconception about what it takes to learn a language?	**49**
enjoys the respect shown due to their language skills?	**50**
emphasises the impact learning a foreign language can have on mother-tongue use?	**51**
describes suffering embarrassment through ignorance of a language?	**52**
admits to having been unaware of their abilities?	**53**
mentions the excitement experienced when working with languages?	**54**
points out what language skills can indicate about someone's personality?	**55**
claims that a lack of career focus is common among language students?	**56**

Essential tips

▶ In this part of the exam, you are required to read several short texts to find specific information, which may include an opinion or the expression of an attitude.

▶ Read the instructions, the title and the questions.

▶ Skim through the texts quickly to get a general idea of what they are about. Don't worry if there are words you don't understand.

▶ Read each question again and make sure you understand what it is asking. Underline the key words in the questions (the words that show you what you should look for in the text).

▶ Scan the texts for ideas or words that relate to the question. Read the relevant parts of the texts carefully.

▶ Remember that the part of the text that gives the answer for each question will almost certainly not use the same words; instead, it will express the idea in a different way.

▶ All the texts are about the same topic, so similar points may be made in two or three texts. When you match a question with a text, make sure it reflects exactly what is in that text.

Question 47: The word *discouraged* is used in the question. Look for other words in the texts that express the same idea. Then check that the part of the text you find also expresses the idea of studying languages.

Question 48: Think of other words or phrases that express the same idea as *find language learning difficult*. Then scan the texts for references to this. Make sure the one you choose contains the idea that the writer expresses sympathy.

Question 49: If the statement is expressed in difficult language, you need to examine it carefully. What is meant by 'a common misconception'? '*Mis-*' refers to something wrong and *conception* means an idea, so 'a wrong idea'. Then think carefully about the meaning of 'what it takes to learn a language'. There may be more than one 'wrong idea' in the texts, and there may be more than one reference to learning languages.

Careers with foreign languages

A Jack Reynolds – interpreter in the UK

Most of my friends studied subjects like business or engineering, and I suspect they thought learning foreign languages was pointless, especially if your first language is English. That changed when I became the interpreter for a couple of Brazilian footballers who'd joined Manchester United. When my friends realised who I was spending time with, my coolness rating definitely shot up, which has been nice. I've always been interested in languages. I did French and Spanish at school and then added Portuguese at university. To be honest, I've never seen myself as a brilliant linguist – I was never the best in my class – but I've worked at it, and when I went to Brazil after university I decided to forget any shyness I might have, and immerse myself in the local culture. When I came back to the UK, I was good enough to qualify as an interpreter. Apart from the sports work, I interpret at conferences. That gets my adrenaline going more than being with the footballers, actually.

B Ana Ramirez – educational consultant

I did a degree in English and Russian at university in Spain. I enjoyed it but I'm ashamed to admit that I had no idea what I was going to do with it when I finished. I was by no means the only one from my course in that position, and there's a similar thing in other countries, from what I've seen. After a few false starts, I ended up working for a Europe-wide organisation which administers various educational projects. I travel around Europe and Russia a lot, so I get to practise my languages. Part of our brief is to promote language learning and I genuinely believe in it. Interestingly, one thing it's given me, apart from a job and the opportunity to meet people around the world, is a greater awareness of my strengths and weaknesses in Spanish. Unfortunately, I hear lots of people saying 'I'd like to have another language, but it's beyond my abilities.' The truth is, though, that anyone can learn a language. We all learn our mother tongue, after all. You just need the right conditions and attitude. I absolutely believe that.

C Helen Murdoch – IT project manager

I'm naturally curious and hate not understanding people, and that's what's always attracted me to languages. It works the other way round, too. When we're recruiting for a challenging IT project, I always think the candidates who are multilingual tend to be more adaptable and open-minded, which certainly helps us. I went to university in the 1980s, and in those days, languages were seen as no more than a 'nice-to-have'. When I told my father I'd decided to study French, he said, 'Are you sure? Wouldn't something more substantial be better?' So, I combined it with a management degree. With the increasingly competitive marketplace, I think that view's changed. My work has taken me to different countries, and helped me improve my French and pick up Arabic and Turkish, an opportunity not available to everyone sadly. I've seen at first-hand the difference that knowing a language can make. I once committed a major blunder in an office in Japan. Had I spoken Japanese, I would have known not to do it, and would have avoided a couple of very awkward days afterwards.

D Timo Heikkinen – student

I'm in my final year at university. I'm studying Chinese but I also speak English, Swedish, Russian, German and French, and Greek because my mum's half-Greek, and Finnish as I'm from Finland. I recently won a prize for achievement in learning languages. To be honest, I hadn't considered myself unusual because I've picked up languages from going to different countries with my parents who work for international companies. I realise now, however, that I do have a flair for languages; I've been told I even write well in Finnish and Greek. I'm not sure what I'll be doing next year. I've had a few offers but I'm not very decisive. Quite a lot of people I know are really good at their subjects – maths, physics or whatever – but languages defeat them and that seriously narrows their options. I'm glad I'm not in their shoes.

PAPER 1 Reading and
             Use of English

PAPER 2 Writing

PAPER 3 Listening

PAPER 4 Speaking

Essential tips

▸ In Paper 2, you must answer two questions. The question in Part 1 is compulsory. In Part 2, there are three questions, and you have to answer one of them.

▸ In Part 1, you will be asked to write an essay for a particular purpose and target reader.

▸ Part 1 tests your ability to respond to the input material in an appropriate style, evaluating information, expressing opinions, etc. All tasks require you to be persuasive. Read the instructions carefully and underline the key words that tell you what you are being asked to do.

▸ The input information in Part 1 may be from a variety of different texts: notes, letters, reports, advertisements, diagrams, etc. Make sure you read it carefully and understand what information it conveys before you start writing.

▸ Think about the appropriate register for your writing: formal, semi-formal, neutral or informal.

▸ Don't try to write out your answer in a rough draft before you produce a final draft; you will not have enough time. Instead, plan what you will say in each section/paragraph of your writing.

▸ Divide your writing into three sections: introduction, main body and conclusion. Think about what you will say in each part. Plan approximately how many words should be in each section of your writing.

▸ Write your essay. Use your own words as far as possible; don't copy the information from the input texts.

▸ When you have finished, check your spelling and punctuation. Make sure the examiner can read your writing.

▸ See the **Writing bank** on pages 193–205 for examples of different types of writing.

PAPER 1 Reading and
Use of English

PAPER 2 Writing ▶ **Part 1**
Part 2

PAPER 3 Listening

PAPER 4 Speaking

You **must** answer this question. Write your answer in **220–260** words in an appropriate style on the separate answer sheet.

---

1 Your class has attended a lecture on what governments could do to minimise the use of fossil fuels. You have made the notes below.

> **Methods of minimising the use of fossil fuels**
>
> - recycling
> - increaing taxes on petrol
> - increasing use of nuclear energy

> **Some opinions expressed in the discussion:**
>
> 'Is the technology for recycling adequately developed?'
>
> 'Increased taxation will not be a sufficient deterrent.'
>
> 'Nuclear energy is too risky.'

Write an **essay** for your tutor discussing **two** of the methods in your notes. You should **explain which method you think is more important** for governments to consider, and provide reasons to support your opinion.

You may, if you wish, make use of the opinions expressed in the discussion, but you should use your own words as far as possible.

Essential tips

▶ When you write an essay, think about the appropriate register and tone for the question you are answering. Who is going to read your essay?

▶ In your essay, you must describe the general idea What information should you give? Is it necessary to mention who 'you' are in this essay?

▶ What is the reason for writing the essay? What effect do you want it to have on the reader? What do you hope to achieve by writing it? Do you want to convince the reader about anything? Think about the language you will need to achieve this goal.

▶ The notes and opinions provide you with information, and you can develop your own arguments around them.

PAPER 1 Reading and
             Use of English
PAPER 2 Writing ▶ Part 1
                            Part 2
PAPER 3 Listening
PAPER 4 Speaking

Write an answer to **one** of the questions **2–4** in this part. Write your answer in **220–260** words in an appropriate style on the separate answer sheet. Put the question number in the box at the top of the page.

2 You would like to start a radio station at the college where you are a student. You have decided to send a proposal to the principal, asking for permission and practical assistance. Your proposal should include the following:

- why you think the radio station would be beneficial
- what sort of programmes you would begin with
- what sort of support, practical and financial, you would need.

Write your **proposal**.

3 You have seen the following blog in an online magazine for young people.

> I live in a small village and long to move into the city. I am 18 years old and have just left school. What are the good things about city life? What about the disadvantages? Would I be mad to leave my village, or would I be opening up great new opportunities?
>
> Paul

Write your **email** to Paul giving your views.

4 A British television channel is interested in making a documentary about public transport in different parts of the world. You have been asked to write a report for the channel, addressing the following questions.

- What means of public transport in your region are the most popular?
- What is being done to improve these facilities and encourage the use of public transport?
- What more could be done?

Write your **report**.

Essential tips

- In Part 2, you must choose one task. However, you should be familiar with all the possible types of text you might need to write.

- Read each question carefully. Before you choose a question, ask yourself if you know enough vocabulary on the subject and can employ it in the required register and text type.

- In Part 2 questions, you have more freedom to use your imagination and come up with information that is not in the input material.

  If you are writing a report or proposal, consider whether to use headings and bullet points or numbered lists.

Question 2
- What style would be appropriate for this proposal? Bear in mind that the proposal is written by a college student to the principal of the college.

- Consider your three sections: introduction, main body and conclusion. The introduction could state simply what you want, and the conclusion could repeat this request, perhaps with some extra force or promise of success. The words 'Introduction' and 'Conclusion' could also be headings. What will the main body contain? What will the heading(s) be?

- Don't worry about precise figures, for example, how much money would be needed to start the radio station. You are not expected to know this.

Question 3 : You are writing to a young person, so use a lively, informal style, bringing in anecdotes and advice related to your experience.

Question 4
- In order to answer this question, you must be familiar with the format of a report. You need to write clear paragraphs and use headings. You may also want to use other features such as bullet points or numbered lists.

- Remember that a report must have a clear introduction and conclusion as well. In your introduction, state what the report is about and who it is for. In your conclusion, summarise the information contained in your report. See the Writing bank on page 200.

- You need to include information about the public transport in your region. At the same time, your task is to produce a good piece of writing, so as long as the points you make sound reasonable, they do not all have to be factually correct. For instance, if you want to say that most people in your region travel to work by car, you could invent a survey that shows 25% of workers say they travel to work by car. It doesn't matter if this survey was never actually carried out.

- The question asks you to give your opinion about how the situation may change in the future. Therefore, you can use the first person to say what you think.

PAPER 1 Reading and
Use of English

PAPER 2 Writing

PAPER 3 Listening ▸ | Part 1
Part 2
PAPER 4 Speaking | Part 3
Part 4

Essential tips

▸ Before you listen to each extract, you will be given time (15 seconds) to read the questions. Make good use of this time, and try to predict what you are going to hear.

▸ Listen carefully before choosing the answer. The options may contain words you hear on the recording, but the meaning of the sentence may be different!

▸ Some questions ask you about the speaker's feelings or attitude to something. Listen to the speaker's tone of voice and the way he/she speaks. It may be necessary to listen to the whole extract before making your choice.

Question 1: More than one option may seem possible here. Why did Nigel join the project?

Question 2: Listen carefully to Jenny's tone of voice.

Questions 3 and 4: Some of the vocabulary is specialised, but you can understand the meaning from the rest of the text.

🎧 **Track 1**

You will hear three different extracts. For questions **1–6**, choose the answer (**A**, **B** or **C**) which fits best according to what you hear. There are two questions for each extract.

Extract One

You hear two friends talking about an experience one of them had as a volunteer.

1 Nigel joined the Blue Ventures project because
   A a friend of his encouraged him to do volunteer work.
   B he had always dreamed of going to Madagascar.
   C he thought the experience would be useful to him.

2 Which word best describes Jenny's reaction to Nigel's account?
   A enthusiasm
   B disinterest
   C envy

Extract Two

You hear two students at law school talking about possible future jobs.

3 When Rich finishes his course, he
   A would like to work in commerce.
   B will join a top firm of solicitors.
   C intends to do postgraduate study.

4 Jenny will work in the area of
   A criminal law.
   B property law.
   C human rights law.

Extract Three

You hear two friends talking about a football match they have just watched.

5 Maggie thinks that England
   A deserved to lose.
   B were not confident enough.
   C were unfortunate.

6 According to Steve,
   A Gerrard was unfairly treated.
   B England played badly.
   C Russia didn't play well.

PAPER 1 Reading and
Use of English

PAPER 2 Writing

PAPER 3 Listening

PAPER 4 Speaking

Part 1
Part 2
Part 3
Part 4

Track 2

You will hear a writer talking about a book she has written on the subject of aspirin.
For questions **7–14**, complete the sentences with a word or a short phrase.

THE STORY OF ASPIRIN

Doctors in (**7**) .... treated their patients with a
medicine derived from the bark of the willow.

Edward Stone believed that (**8**) .... was similar to
quinine.

The active ingredient of aspirin was isolated in (**9**) ....

Unfortunately, salicylic acid can affect the (**10**) ....
quite badly.

The first commercially available aspirins were made by Bayer, a
(**11**) ....

However, there was little (**12**) .... into the way aspirin
works for nearly 70 years.

Some scientists think that people over (**13**) .... should
take aspirin to prevent certain diseases.

It appears that (**14**) .... grown without artificial
chemicals also contain the active ingredients of aspirin.

Essential tips

▶ Read the instructions and
find out the subject of the
recording.

▶ Read the questions carefully
and think about the sort of
information you might need to
complete the gaps.

▶ Each gap is completed by
one, two or three words, or a
number.

▶ Decide what grammatical form
the gapped word or words
should have.

▶ You will hear the words you
need on the recording, but not
in the same sentences as the
questions. You need to listen
for the ideas expressed on the
recording.

▶ You will hear the recording
twice, so you will have a
chance to fill in any gaps you
miss the first time.

Question 7: What sort of word
could come after *in*: a time, a
place, or an expression with the
preposition *in*? Listen for any of
these.

Question 10: The recording
is about a medicine, and this
sentence mentions an acid
that can affect something or
somebody quite badly. Who or
what could this be?

Question 12: The sentence is
about something that happened
or lasted for nearly 70 years, so
you should listen for information
about this period. Also consider
what could fit with the phrase
'into the way aspirin works'.

Question 14: The gapped word
must describe something like
a plant, which can be grown
without artificial chemicals,
so listen for a word with this
meaning.

PAPER 1 Reading and
　　　　 Use of English

PAPER 2 Writing

PAPER 3 Listening ▶

PAPER 4 Speaking

Part 1
Part 2
Part 3
Part 4

Essential tips

This part of the exam is usually a multiple-choice task, but it could also be a sentence-completion task. If it is a sentence-completion task, look back at the tips for Parts 1 and 2. If it is a multiple-choice task, read the following tips.

▶ Read the instructions and find out the subject of the recording.

▶ Read the questions or question stems carefully and underline the key words.

▶ The questions follow the order of the recording, but the final question may be about the recording as a whole.

Question 15: Option A suggests most people, especially the critics, liked the ballet; option B implies some people liked it and some didn't; option C implies most people didn't like it; and option D implies that people who love animals liked the ballet. Which of these ideas does the recording convey?

Question 18: Think about different ways to express that something 'is of greatest interest to audiences'. You should also be prepared for the information to be given in a different order. For example, the speaker may describe something that happened and then say afterwards that it interested audiences.

Question 19: The question tells you that Stan will talk about something that went wrong when he saw the ballet. Which option best describes what happened?

🎧 Track 3

You will hear part of an interview with Stan Levin, a dance critic, about a modern ballet production involving animals. For questions **15–20**, choose the answer (**A**, **B**, **C** or **D**) which fits best according to what you hear.

15 We gather that the ballet being discussed here
　　A　has received general critical acclaim.
　　B　has caused considerable controversy.
　　C　has not been well received on the whole.
　　D　has become popular with animals-lovers.

16 It appears that the function of the dogs in the ballet is to
　　A　reflect what happens to the human characters.
　　B　act as a contrast to the human characters.
　　C　show how wild animals behave in a civilised society.
　　D　symbolise homeless people.

17 How does Stan feel about the increasing use of technology in dance?
　　A　He thinks this trend has gone too far.
　　B　He prefers more traditional approaches to dance.
　　C　He does not approve of it in principle.
　　D　He believes it is creating a new art form.

18 What aspect of the ballet is of greatest interest to audiences?
　　A　the way the dogs behave during dance sequences
　　B　the way the dogs perform their tricks
　　C　the sight of the dogs in a pack
　　D　the way the dogs copy the actions of one character

19 What caused the lapse in mood during the performance Stan saw?
　　A　the inability of the dogs to concentrate
　　B　the audience's unwillingness to accept the dogs
　　C　the behaviour of a member of the audience
　　D　the inability of dogs and humans to work as a team

20 What aspect of the performance made the most powerful impression on Stan?
　　A　the implicit potential for violence
　　B　the aggression shown by the dogs
　　C　the bond between the dogs and the tramp
　　D　the primitive appearance of the dogs

PAPER 1 Reading and
              Use of English

PAPER 2 Writing

PAPER 3 Listening ▶   Part 1
                           Part 2

PAPER 4 Speaking   Part 3

                            Part 4

Essential tips

▶ Read the instructions and find out who will be talking and what they will be talking about.

▶ You have two tasks to think about at the same time, each relating to one type of statement made by the speakers. So the first time you hear each speaker, be prepared for a piece of information that corresponds to an option in the first task; the second time, listen for a piece of information that corresponds to an option in the second task.

▶ The answer options do not repeat what the speakers say; they express the ideas in different words. Read each option carefully, and be prepared to hear the information expressed in a different form.

▶ Each task has three options you do not need.

Questions 21–25
Option A: If something has a 'social function', what does it have? How might you express the idea that learning English has a social function?

Option B: What sort of jobs are 'sedentary' and what could be a problem for people working in these jobs?

Option F: What are some examples of 'high-level sporting events', and how are the competitors regarded in the community?

Option H: If this option is correct for one of the speakers, it must mean that the person had 'an injury'. What kinds of things can happen when people have an injury?

Questions 26–30
Option G: What ways are there to express that something is a 'commitment'? If you commit yourself to do something, what do you do or say?

Option H: How else could a speaker talk about 'genetic make-up'?

🎧 **Track 4**

You will hear five short extracts in which people talk about fitness and health.

While you listen, you must complete both tasks.

TASK ONE

For questions **21–25**, choose from list **A–H**, what each person says is his or her reason for attending a gym regularly.

A   The gym has a social function for me.

                                 Speaker 1 | 21 |

B   I have a sedentary job.

                                 Speaker 2 | 22 |

C   My company pays for me to attend a gym.

                                 Speaker 3 | 23 |

D   I'm studying sport science at college.

                                 Speaker 4 | 24 |

E   Being fit gives me a sense of achievement.

                                 Speaker 5 | 25 |

F   I compete in high-level sporting events.

G   I come here with members of my cycling club.

H   I started exercising regularly after an injury.

TASK TWO

For questions **26–30**, choose from list **A–H** what opinion each speaker expresses about fitness and health, generally.

A   It is alarming that so many people have an unhealthy lifestyle.

                                 Speaker 1 | 26 |

B   Being good at sport commands respect.

                                 Speaker 2 | 27 |

C   I find it hard to commit myself to exercising.

                                 Speaker 3 | 28 |

D   Diet is as important as exercise.

                                 Speaker 4 | 29 |

E   Exercise machines are extremely boring.

                                 Speaker 5 | 30 |

F   Achieving health requires self-sacrifice.

G   Exercise is necessary to keep weight under control.

H   Genetic make-up has a lot to do with fitness.

Essential tips

Part 1

▶ In this part of the exam, you must show that you can use English appropriately to interact with another person using general social language. You will be expected to answer questions about yourself: your family, home, interests, education and future plans.

▶ Make sure you answer the questions you have been asked and don't talk about something different.

▶ Don't try to prepare for this part of the exam by learning a prepared speech – the examiner may ask you something different.

Part 2

▶ In this part of the exam, you have to talk on a subject for about a minute. This is a long time when you have to talk in an exam. Make sure you practise talking for this length of time.

▶ The examiner could ask you to compare things, contrast them, identify them or speculate about them. He/She will give you three pictures and ask you to talk about them.

▶ In this part of the test, you are asked to compare and contrast the pictures, and to speculate about why someone is doing something, or what advantages something might have. Make sure you answer the two questions that you are asked.

▶ While the other candidate is talking, listen carefully. The examiner will ask you an extra question related to what the other candidate has been talking about.

Part 1 (2 minutes)

The examiner will ask you a few questions about yourself and about a general topic. For example, the examiner may ask you:

• Where are you from?
• What do you do here?
• What did you like most about the area where you grew up?

Part 2 (4 minutes)

You will each be asked to talk on your own for about a minute. You will each be given three different pictures to talk about. After your partner has finished speaking, you will be asked a brief question connected with your partner's photographs.

Costumes (compare, contrast and speculate)

Turn to pictures 1–3 on page 169 which show people in costumes.

(*Candidate A*), it's your turn first. Here are your pictures. They show **people in different costumes**.

I'd like you to compare **two** of the pictures and say **why these people are dressed in this way and how the people might be feeling**.

(*Candidate B*), **which of these costumes do you think is most comfortable? Why?**

Working environments (compare, contrast and speculate)

Turn to pictures 1–3 on page **170** which show different working environments.

Now, (*Candidate B*), here are your pictures. **They show different working environments**.

I'd like you to compare **two** of these workplaces, and say **what the advantages and disadvantages of working there might be**.

(*Candidate A*), **which of these environments would you prefer to work in? Why?**

Part 3 (4 minutes)

Look at page 171 which shows some things related to modern life.

Modern times (discuss, evaluate and select)

Here are some aspects of modern life and a question for you to discuss.

First, you have some time to look at the task.

(*Pause 15 seconds*)

Now talk to each other about **the advantages and disadvantages of each aspect of modern life**.

Now you have about a minute to decide **which two aspects best illustrate that modern life has both advantages and disadvantages**.

Part 4 (5 minutes)

The examiner will encourage you to develop the topic of your discussion in Part 3 by asking questions such as:

• Which aspects of life in the past, which no longer exist, do you think were positive? Could they be revived? (Why? / Why not?)

• Should developments in technology be restricted in any way? (Why? / Why not?)

• What sort of difficulties do young people face today, but that previous generations did not have to confront, or not to the same extent?

• Why do older people sometimes become nostalgic about the past?

PAPER 1	Reading and	▶	Part 1
	Use of English		Part 2
PAPER 2	Writing		Part 3
			Part 4
PAPER 3	Listening		Part 5
PAPER 4	Speaking		Part 6
			Part 7
			Part 8

For questions **1–8**, read the text below and decide which answer (**A, B, C** or **D**) best fits each gap. There is an example at the beginning (**0**).

Mark your answers **on the separate answer sheet**.

Example:

| **0** | **A** situation | **B** business | **C** function | **D** case |

| 0 | A | **B** | C | D |

Essential tips

▶ Read the title and the whole text quickly for general meaning.

▶ Remember – the gapped word may be part of an idiom, expression or phrasal verb. It may collocate with another word, or be part of a fixed phrase.

▶ If you do not know which option to choose, read out the sentence with each of the options in turn. Choose the option that sounds best in context.

▶ Check the clauses and phrases on each side of the gap to see whether the presence of a word here dictates the choice of a word for the gap.

Question 1: The words at the start of the sentence (*There's no getting away from it*) indicate the meaning of the word needed for the gap.

Question 3: Look at the whole sentence. In their research, scientists want satellite images to be as clear and accurate as possible. Which word expresses this idea?

Question 5: The options tell you that this is a phrasal verb with *make*. Which one means 'see' or 'detect'?

Question 7: This is a fixed phrase used to describe a way of learning something: you try something new and you learn something if it goes wrong.

Satellite archaeology

Archaeology is a messy (**0**) .... There's no getting away from it; digging holes in the ground is an (**1**) .... part of archaeological work. But there is a new way to search without a shovel. Satellite images are now used to (**2**) .... buried objects in landscapes with astonishing (**3**) .... In the same way that medical (**4**) .... let doctors examine parts of the body they couldn't otherwise see, satellite images help scientists find and map long-lost rivers, roads and cities, and make (**5**) .... archaeological features in places which are very difficult to survey from the ground. 'There's much we miss on the ground,' emphasises archaeologist Sarah Parcak, a (**6**) .... in using satellite imagery.

Through 'thousands of hours' of trial and (**7**) ...., Parcak has developed techniques using satellite imagery which allow her to detect (**8**) .... changes in the surface of the land caused by objects like bricks buried underground. In 2011, her team discovered evidence of hundreds of dwellings at the 3,000-year-old city of Tanis near the River Nile delta in Egypt. This might have taken a century using traditional methods.

1	**A** inflexible	**B** inevitable	**C** inclusive	**D** infallible
2	**A** disclose	**B** conceive	**C** define	**D** identify
3	**A** attention	**B** measurement	**C** precision	**D** adjustment
4	**A** scans	**B** looks	**C** regards	**D** sights
5	**A** through	**B** out	**C** for	**D** up
6	**A** creator	**B** principal	**C** chief	**D** pioneer
7	**A** failure	**B** mistake	**C** error	**D** fault
8	**A** subtle	**B** thin	**C** mild	**D** soft

Essential tips

▶ Remember: the gapped words will probably not be complex or specialised words. Most of them will be structural items like articles, pronouns or prepositions. A few may form a part of common expressions, etc.

▶ Look at the whole sentence, or even bigger sections of the text, to see if the word you need is part of a longer or parallel structure. For example, you might need the word *other* in the expression *on the other hand*, which will be clear if you find *on one hand* in the previous sentence.

Question 12: The structure *as ... as* is often used with adjectives to compare two things that are the same. Can you think of an expression with *as ... as* that has the more abstract meaning of 'to the extent that'?

Question 14: This gap follows the word *insight*, which means 'understanding'. The preposition *of* usually follows *understanding*, but *insight* takes a different preposition.

Question 16: Read the whole sentence. The first part of the sentence must mean something like 'it seems that the Pirahã ...'.

For questions **9–16**, read the text below and think of the word which best fits each gap. Use only **one** word in each gap. There is an example at the beginning (**0**).

Write your answers **IN CAPITAL LETTERS on the separate answer sheet**.

Example: 0 O R D E R

Finding the right word

Do people need words in (**0**) …….. to think? A study of a tribe living in the Amazon basin could provide the answer to this age-old question. The Pirahã tribe (**9**) …….. be small – there are only about 200 members all told – (**10**) …….. they exhibit a fascinating cultural peculiarity. These people have no words for numbers, (**11**) …….. from *one*, *two* and *many*. What is more, their words for *one* and *two* are very similar. As (**12**) …….. as anyone can tell, this tribe has never had (**13**) …….. sort of vocabulary for numbers, but they appear to survive quite well without it.

Could these people perhaps supply an insight (**14**) …….. the way our minds work? When asked to count some objects, they could not get beyond two or three before starting to make mistakes. This applies even to adults who appear intelligent in (**15**) …….. other way.

So it looks (**16**) …….. though the Pirahã are not very good at counting simply because they lack a vocabulary for numbers. This would suggest that human beings cannot think if they have no words to do so.

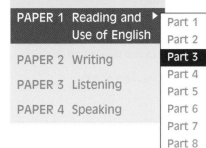

PAPER 1 Reading and ▶ Part 1
Use of English   Part 2
                    Part 3
PAPER 2 Writing   Part 4
                    Part 5
PAPER 3 Listening   Part 6
                    Part 7
PAPER 4 Speaking   Part 8

For questions **17–24**, read the text below. Use the word given in capitals at the end of some of the lines to form a word that fits in the gap **in the same line**. There is an example at the beginning (**0**).

Write your answers **IN CAPITAL LETTERS on the separate answer sheet**.

Example: | 0 | I | N | T | R | I | G | U | I | N | G | | | | | | | | | | |

Essential tips

Question 19: What part of speech do you need? A verb, noun, or an adjective or adverb? You need to read the whole paragraph in order to be sure of the meaning of this sentence. Does the missing word have a positive or negative meaning? Sometimes it is necessary to make two changes to a word, a prefix and a suffix.

Question 21: *Variable* means 'changeable'. However, the word you need here means 'always'. What part of speech do you need, and what changes do you need to make to *variable* in order to form the missing word?

Question 22: The adjective *new* indicates a noun is needed for the gap. Should it be singular or plural?

Question 23: What word could we use here to mean 'add new information to something'?

The jigsaw history puzzle

Of all the games in the world, the jigsaw puzzle must be among the most widely known. Yet its early history presents an (**0**) .... puzzle of its own.   **INTRIGUE**

Officially, the jigsaw puzzle (**17**) .... in England, and   **ORIGIN**
its (**18**) .... was John Spilsbury, a London engraver and   **INVENT**
map maker. It is also an apparently (**19**) .... fact that in   **DISPUTE**
1767 Spilsbury created a puzzle, (**20**) .... known as a   **INITIAL**
'dissected map', by mounting one of his maps on a
piece of hardwood and cutting around the borders of
the countries. His puzzles came to be used in schools
to help children learn geography.

However, as is almost (**21**) .... the case with inventions,   **VARIABLE**
some doubts have been raised about whether Spilsbury's
puzzle was the first. This was an age of exploration, and
new (**22**) .... demanded that maps be constantly   **DISCOVER**
(**23**) .... There is some evidence that two Dutch map   **DATE**
makers have produced map puzzles ten years before
Spilsbury. The evidence is (**24**) ...., however, and   **CONCLUDE**
advertising for their dissected maps only appears in 1779.

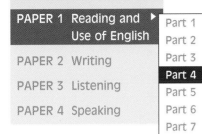
PAPER 1	Reading and ▶	Part 1
	Use of English	Part 2
PAPER 2	Writing	Part 3
		Part 4
PAPER 3	Listening	Part 5
PAPER 4	Speaking	Part 6
		Part 7
		Part 8

Essential tips

Question 26: You need a phrasal verb here which means 'think of something'. Be careful. Do you need a two-part or three-part phrasal verb?

Question 27: You need to make two changes to the second sentence. First, you need a causative structure because someone else is decorating the room, not us. Secondly, think about the word you have been given. It is part of an expression that means 'decorated'.

Question 30: Think about the word order here. Certain negative structures at the start of a sentence are followed by inversion.

For questions **25–30**, complete the second sentence so that it has a similar meaning to the first sentence, using the word given. **Do not change the word given.** You must use between **three** and **six** words, including the word given. Here is an example (**0**).

Example:

0 Jane regretted speaking so rudely to the old lady.

MORE

Jane .... politely to the old lady.

Example: | 0 | WISHED SHE HAD SPOKEN MORE

Write **only** the missing words **IN CAPITAL LETTERS on the separate answer sheet**.

---

25 'Do your homework first, and then you can go to the cinema,' said Jamie's mother.

LONG

Jamie's mother agreed to let him go to the cinema .... his homework first.

26 Harry thought of throwing a surprise party for Katie's birthday.

CAME

Harry .... of throwing a surprise party for Katie's birthday.

27 They are decorating our living room, so the house is a mess.

DONE

We are ...., so the house is a mess!

28 I really hate it when people speak to me like that!

BEING

I really object .... like that!

29 I was just about to call him when he rang me instead.

POINT

I was .... when he rang me instead.

30 The manager gave her secretary strict instructions that no one should be allowed to disturb her.

CIRCUMSTANCES

'Under .... to be disturbed!' the manager told her secretary.

PAPER 1 Reading and ▸   Part 1
        Use of English   Part 2
PAPER 2 Writing   Part 3
                             Part 4
PAPER 3 Listening   Part 5
PAPER 4 Speaking   Part 6
                             Part 7
                             Part 8

You are going to read a magazine article. For questions **31–36**, choose the answer (**A**, **B**, **C** or **D**) which you think fits best according to the text.

Mark your answers **on the separate answer sheet**.

The Cinderella story

The basic story is very old indeed and familiar to most of us. The heroine, Cinderella, is treated cruelly by her stepmother and mocked by her two ugly stepsisters. Even though her father loves her, she can't tell him how unhappy she is because her stepmother has bewitched him. One day, Cinderella's stepmother and stepsisters are invited to a ball at the royal palace. Cinderella is told she cannot go and is understandably very unhappy. However, her fairy godmother comes to the rescue and, waving her magic wand, produces some beautiful clothes for Cinderella, as well as a carriage to convey her to the ball. There, she dances with the handsome prince, who falls in love with her, not only because she is beautiful but also because she is good and gracious. Cinderella has been warned that the magic will wear off at midnight, so when the clock strikes 12, she hurries away, leaving behind a glass slipper. Next day, the prince, smitten by her charms, comes looking for the girl whose foot fits the glass slipper. He finds Cinderella and they marry amid general rejoicing.

Just a sweet, pretty tale? Not in the view of Ellen Macintosh, who has written extensively about fairy tales. 'This story features the stock, two-dimensional characters of most fairy tales, and little character development is attempted,' she says. Indeed, although her comment does make one wonder why simplicity of this sort should be out of place in a story for children. Be that as it may, Ellen's main problem is with what the story implies. 'Instead of standing up to her cruel stepmother and absurd stepsisters, Cinderella just waits for a fairy godmother to appear and solve her problems. But wouldn't you want a daughter of yours to show more spirit?'

The story is enduring, whatever its shortcomings, and it doesn't take much in the way of analytical skills to see its influence on a number of recent Hollywood productions, all aimed at girls aged five to 15. In these versions for the silver screen, the Cinderella character no longer has to clean the house and has no siblings to make her life a misery, though she persists in not showing much backbone. The character of the rich and handsome stranger, however, is retained, and in some cases really is a prince. The role of the fairy godmother is often played by coincidence or sheer luck. We live in an enlightened age when even very young children might reject the notion of fairies. The wicked stepmother may be transformed into a villain of some sort. In the majority of film versions, the heroine has a profession and is even permitted to continue working after marrying her prince – this is the 21st century, after all.

Doesn't the success of these films indicate that the story has relevance to children even today? 'Yes,' admits Ellen, who sees its message as being rooted in a fundamental childhood desire for love and attention. 'Most children experience a sense of inner loneliness as they are growing up and empathise with the protagonist who faces some sort of test or challenge. This can be seen in the original story of Cinderella, where the fairy godmother tells the heroine that she must learn to be gracious and confident if she is to go to the ball. She has to grow spiritually, and by maturing, she becomes attractive to the prince, thus ensuring that the ending of the story will be happy. 'In the later versions, this element is missing,' says Ellen, 'and the theme of the story is simply that a girl's role in life is to be more beautiful than other little girls so that she can carry off the prize: the handsome prince. Is this really what we want girls to grow up believing?'

▶ Remember – in this part of the exam, you need to understand the details of a text, as well as the writer's opinion, attitude and purpose.

▶ You can approach this part in two slightly different ways. However, you should begin by reading the instructions and the title of the text. Then you can either skim the text first before you read the questions, or read the questions first before you skim the text.

▶ There will be six questions or question stems. Read each question carefully and, without looking at the options, scan the text for the answer or for a suitable and accurate way to complete the question stem.

▶ Think about the meaning of what you read, and only then see if you can match the relevant section of the text with one of the options.

▶ The correct option is unlikely to use the same words as the text to express an idea.

Question 31: You are being asked about the writer's view, not Ellen MacIntosh's. Look for a section of the text where the writer describes Ellen's ideas and then gives her opinion of these ideas.

Question 33: This question is about films based on the Cinderella story. Look in the text for the word *film* or any other word which means the same thing, for example, *movie*. When you find the relevant section of the text, read it carefully. Then, see which option corresponds precisely to what the text says.

Question 36: Even though you may be nervous and in a hurry, you must think carefully about the meaning of the questions. Which word in the question stem shows you are being asked to find a *difference* between the original story and the modern version?

31 What does the writer imply about fairy tales in the second paragraph?
   A Fully developed characters would improve them.
   B The stories lines are very straightforward.
   C It is unrealistic to expect character development.
   D It is a mistake to consider them sweet and pretty.

32 What is Ellen's primary objection to the Cinderella story?
   A The heroine is treated cruelly.
   B The heroine is not assertive enough.
   C The ugly stepsisters are figures of ridicule.
   D The stepmother is not a convincing character.

33 Modern film adaptations of the story tend to present a Cinderella
   A whose character remains basically unchanged.
   B who is luckier than she is in the original story.
   C whose circumstances are unusual.
   D that many children might find unconvincing.

34 Modern variants on the story generally
   A portray Cinderella as a successful professional.
   B imply that Cinderella will become a real princess.
   C reflect children's beliefs.
   D make concessions to modern women's lives.

35 In Ellen's view, what makes the Cinderella story so appealing?
   A Children can identify with the heroine.
   B Little girls enjoy being challenged.
   C It has an element of magic.
   D Cinderella is more beautiful than other girls.

36 Unlike the original tale, modern versions of the Cinderella story
   A suggest that girls do not need strength of character.
   B do not require the heroine to develop.
   C underestimate the power of love.
   D are aimed solely at young children.

You are going to read four reviews of a book about the connection between music and the brain. For questions **37–40**, choose from the reviews **A–D**. The reviews may be chosen more than once.

Mark your answers **on the separate answer sheet**.

This is your brain on music: the science of a human obsession by Daniel Levitin

Four reviewers comment on Daniel Levitin's book about the neuroscience of music.

A

Scientific analysis of difficult concepts regarding how music works and the psychological processes involved in our interactions with it is something few of us are comfortable with, but in trying to keep things simple for a non-specialist audience, as far as technical terms are concerned, Levitin too often ends up dumbing down. A number of small errors obvious to a knowledgeable musician – like the tonic pitch of a scale being referred to as the *root*, when only chords have roots – fuel this sense of irritation. It's a fascinating subject, however, made more so by Levitin's decision to explain it against the background of his own intriguing narrative. A successful rock musician for many years, he switched careers and became a professor of psychology and music. This background shows in his sensitive choice of familiar tunes and songs that he uses to illustrate concepts and theories.

B

We can all enjoy music, yet the theory of it can seem excessively complex, and you'd think the study of its effect on the brain even more so. The success of this book, by a musician and record producer turned neuroscientist, is both that it goes out of its way to make the general reader feel at ease, and that it celebrates our extraordinary capacity for analysing and understanding music. Consider the job the brain has to do in separating and processing even, say, the sound of a cat's purr over a refrigerator's hum, merely by analysing the way that various air molecules cause the eardrum to vibrate. Then go and listen to your favourite piece of orchestral music or even pop music. Levitin's anecdotes about famous musicians he has met and played with are worth passing over, but the rest of this excellent introduction will leave your brain buzzing.

C

Setting jargon aside in favour of everyday terminology, Levitin gives readers enough background to understand what to listen for in music and to connect what they hear to his science. Having been a musician and producer in the music industry before turning to science, Levitin knows about communication, and wisely weaves in stories about music making and working with musicians to make the science easier to relate to. The bulk of the music Levitin talks about, however, is pop. Classical music, or modern music in that tradition, is sometimes referred to in patronising terms, but for the researcher interested in the achievements of the brain, one might think that classical music's larger structures and more complex achievements would provoke greater interest. It is also disappointing to come across flawed accounts of certain aspects of musical acoustics and music theory. But overall, this book is an admirable contribution to popular science.

D

It is to Levitin's credit that this book contains clear, well-informed explanations of a range of musical phenomena and their underlying psychological processes. It should be stimulating and accessible to the non-specialist. His attempt to make the science easier to grasp by regular reference to his own career in music – as a musician, producer and neuroscientist – is well intentioned, but there are times when we could do with fewer funny stories and more attention to detail. This is more than just a stylistic point. There are misleading descriptions of significant research work, for example. The choice of music to illustrate his arguments is refreshingly free of high-art bias but it draws so strongly on Levitin's own musical preferences that some readers who do not share his musical tastes may feel lost. Despite my misgivings, however, Levitin's efforts to show a lay audience how music is at the centre of human experience and evolution are to be applauded.

Which reviewer

has a similar view to reviewer C regarding Levitin's selection of musical examples? [37]

takes a different view to the others about the accuracy of the book's content? [38]

shares reviewer D's opinion about the extent to which Levitin includes information about himself? [39]

has a different opinion from the others regarding the suitability of the writing style for the target readers? [40]

Essential tips

- ▶ Remember – in this part of the exam, you have to decide whether four different writers have similar or different opinions and attitudes about a particular subject.

- ▶ Read the title and the texts quickly for general understanding.

- ▶ Highlight the key words in each question.

- ▶ Read the first text and highlight the sections that are relevant to each question. Remember to write the question numbers in the relevant places. Do the same for each text.

- ▶ Then look across the four texts and compare the sections that refer to each question in turn. Read the opinions carefully and decide which ones are similar and which are different.

Question 37: The key words in this question are *similar views to reviewer* C and *selection of musical examples*. The section of text C referring to 'musical examples' is: *The bulk of the music Levitin talks about, however, is pop. Classical music, or modern music in that tradition, is sometimes referred to in patronising terms, but ... one might think that its larger structures and more complex achievements would provoke greater interest and even richer evidence.* This implies that the reviewer thinks the selection is too limited. Reviewer A refers to a *sensitive choice of familiar tunes and songs which he uses to illustrate concepts and theories*, which is very different from the criticism suggested in C. Look for what reviewers B and D say about the musical selection and decide which is similar to reviewer C's opinion.

Question 38: The key words here are: *different view to the others* and *accuracy of ... content*. Reviewer A refers to *a number of small errors obvious to a knowledgeable musician*. Reviewer B refers to a subject which is *excessively complex* but makes no reference to any errors. So, A and B have different views on the issue of accuracy. Look carefully at texts C and D, and decide whether they share reviewer A or reviewer B's view on this.

PAPER 1 Reading and ▶ Part 1
Use of English   Part 2

PAPER 2 Writing   Part 3
                    Part 4
PAPER 3 Listening   Part 5

PAPER 4 Speaking   Part 6
                    Part 7
                    Part 8

You are going to read a magazine article. Six paragraphs have been removed from the article. Choose from the paragraphs **A–G** the one which fits each gap (**41–46**). There is one extra paragraph which you do not need to use.

Mark your answers **on the separate answer sheet**.

Mind your languages

Thousands of the world's languages are dying, taking to the grave not just words but records of civilisations and cultures that we may never fully know or understand. Linguists have calculated that of the 6,000 languages currently spoken worldwide most will disappear over the next 100 years. As many as 1,000 languages have died in the past 400 years. Conversely, the handful of major international languages are forging ahead.

41

But the vast majority of the world never had need of phrases in *Heiltsuk*, a Native Indian language from British Columbia in Canada, which is now dead. Nor will most people be interested in learning any of the 800 languages spoken on the island of Papua New Guinea, many of which are threatened. Frederik Kortlandt, from Leiden University in Holland, is one of several linguists around the world who are determined to document as many of the world's remaining endangered languages as possible.

42

Periodically, linguists and other interested parties meet to discuss their work. One such conference held in Nepal focused on the issue of how to save some Himalayan languages spoken by just a handful of people. A great number of languages in the greater Himalayan region are endangered or have already reached the point of no return.

43

The trouble is, such materials often do not exist. Kortlandt knows a language is disappearing when the younger generation does not use it any more. When a language is spoken by fewer than 40 people, he calculates that it will die out. Occasionally, however,

researchers get lucky. *Kamassian*, a language from the Upper Yenisey region of Russia, was supposed to have died out, until two old women who still spoke it turned up at a conference in Tallinn, Estonia in the early 1970s.

44

'Would you ask this to a biologist looking for disappearing species?' Kortlandt asks. 'Why should languages, the mouthpiece of threatened cultures, be less interesting than unknown species? Language is the defining characteristic of the human species. These people say things to each other which are very different from the things we say, and think very different thoughts, which are often incomprehensible to us.'

45

Take, for example, the vast potential for modern medicine that lies within tropical rainforests. For centuries, forest tribes have known about the healing properties of certain plants, but it is only recently that the outside world has discovered that the rainforests hold potential cures for some of the world's major diseases. All this knowledge could be lost if the tribes and their languages die out without being documented.

46

We will only be able to find them and benefit from their properties through one or more of the 300 languages and dialects spoken on the islands. If the languages die, so too will the medicinal knowledge of naturally occurring tonics, rubs and potions. Science could be left wondering what we might have found.

A This is one of the things worrying linguists working in Fiji in the South Pacific. There are hundreds of known remedies in Fiji's forests. The guava leaf relieves diarrhoea, the udi tree eases sore throats, and hibiscus leaf tea is used by expectant mothers. There are possibly several more yet to be discovered.

B 'I accept this,' says Kortlandt, 'but at the very least, we can record as much as we can of these endangered languages before they die out altogether. Such an undertaking naturally requires support from international organisations.' But what progress is being in this respect?

C Kortlandt elaborates further: 'If you want to understand the human species, you have to take the full range of human thought into consideration. The disappearance of a language means the disappearance of a culture. It is not only words that disappear, but also knowledge about many things.'

D To non-linguists while particular stories like this can be fascinating, it must seem odd to get worked up about the broader issue. Why waste so much time saving languages spoken by so few? Why look back instead of forward?

E For example, Chinese is now spoken by 1,000 million people and English by 350 million. Spanish is spoken by 250 million people and growing fast.

F 'There are about 200 languages spoken in this area, but only a few have been properly described,' says Kortlandt. The problem is it can take years to document a language. 'We are generally happy when we have a group of texts we can read and understand with the help of a reliable grammar and dictionary.'

G This often means trekking to some of the most inaccessible parts of the Earth and can require consummate diplomacy in dealing with remote tribes, some of which may be meeting outsiders for the first time and may be wary of strangers asking for so much information about their language.

Essential tips

▶ Remember – in this part of the exam you need to understand the structure and organisation of a text (how its paragraphs work together). First look at the instructions and the title of the text. Then skim the gapped text for the general meaning and notice how it develops ideas, opinions or events.

▶ You may need to consider more than one gap at a time in order to work out which paragraph goes where. Do not rely simply on recognising repeated names, dates, etc.

Question 41: In the paragraph after the gap, the word *But* shows that a contrast is being described. It is likely that the contrast is between the extinct or threatened languages referred to and the *major international languages* mentioned in the paragraph before the gap.

Question 43: The paragraph before the gap refers to *the greater Himalayan region.* Is there a gapped paragraph which, using different words, refers to a region?

Also, the paragraph after the gap begins with a reference back to 'such materials'. Can you find anything about 'materials' in any of the gapped paragraphs?

Question 44: The paragraph after the gap begins with Kortlandt referring to something that has been asked. Can you find a gapped paragraph with a question in it? Check carefully that it fits the gap.

PAPER 1 Reading and ▶
Use of English

PAPER 2 Writing

PAPER 3 Listening

PAPER 4 Speaking

Part 1
Part 2
Part 3
Part 4
Part 5
Part 6
Part 7
Part 8

You are going to read an article in which four people talk about careers involving foreign languages. For questions **47–56**, choose from the people (**A–D**).

Mark your answers **on the separate answer sheet**.

In which section of the article are the following mentioned?

an enhanced appreciation of other people's work	**47**
thoughts about the future	**48**
the financial necessity for engaging in other ventures as well	**49**
encouragement from a family member	**50**
advice from a specialist	**51**
the value of assessing one's abilities objectively	**52**
identifying potential customers	**53**
an impulsive decision	**54**
a feeling of apprehension about making a major change	**55**
academic qualifications which were never used	**56**

Essential tips

▶ You should begin by reading the instructions and the title of the text. Then you can either skim the text first before you read the questions, or read the questions first before you skim the text. Experiment and see which way works better for you.

▶ Don't waste time reading the text in detail. You only need to match specific information in the text with the questions.

Question 49: Some questions use language which you will need to think about carefully. Here, for example, the question is about the need to do other jobs to make money, but this simple idea is expressed formally. The reverse may also occur: the question may express an idea in simple language but the text will use more formal language.

Question 54: An *impulsive decision* is one taken suddenly without any planning. Which person does this fit best?

Question 55: *Apprehension* means feeling anxious or nervous. The person who experienced this feeling is unlikely to have used exactly these words, but, using other words, they will have described their nervousness before a change.

Turning a hobby into a career

It may seem idealistic or risky to exchange one's regular job for the uncertainty of earning your living from a hobby – but more and more people are attempting to do just that.

A I had piano lessons when I was young, and I did have some talent. But it became obvious I'd never be good enough for a career on the stage. In a way, I was lucky. If I hadn't realised that early on, I probably would have carried on dreaming that my big break would come. As it is, I became a music teacher instead, and in my free time I started to dabble in the technical side of music production. Then an aunt died, leaving me some cash, and I set up my own recording studio! Of course, there is a downside to turning a hobby into a career. I love my job so much that I used to work seven days a week, but after a while, I realised you need to switch off occasionally. My job has definitely added depth to the way I listen to music; now I can really understand why someone's using a certain technique or piece of equipment.

B I studied medicine, but when I finished medical school, I had a sort of crisis. I knew I couldn't go on with it! I'd have been an awful doctor. But I was keen on amateur dramatics and I enjoyed putting on plays at the local youth centre. So I started wondering if I could make a living from teaching drama. A friend suggested I should offer acting lessons for children. It was tricky and at first, I couldn't work out how to find people who would pay for their children to attend the kind of courses I wanted to run. Then someone at an organisation called Business Link, which helps people set up their own businesses, suggested advertising on the internet! I was contacted by a surprising number of interested people and five years down the line, I'm still doing all right. The classes themselves aren't terribly lucrative, but I supplement my income by giving talks to amateur dramatics societies and writing articles for magazines.

C When I left college, I started working in a bank, but my heart was never really in it. The problem was partly the environment: I don't like working in an office. I'm more of an outdoor person – and I'd always been crazy about surfing. One summer while I was on holiday, I got chatting to the owner of a surf shop. It turned out he was good friends with a cousin of mine. He said he wanted to sell up and I jumped at the chance to buy the business from him! Looking back, I can see how lucky I was. It's incredibly difficult to set up a shop like that from scratch. Besides, being an avid surfer myself, I assumed a lot of other people must share that interest – which isn't the case! It took me a while to realise how naive I was. Now that I've learnt the ropes, I'm considering either expanding – more shops, managers and so on – or diversifying, perhaps producing my own surf boards! The second option is more likely because it interests me a lot.

D I wanted to study graphic design when I left school, but I didn't have good enough grades. So I got a job in a garage instead and for the next 10 years, I worked as a car mechanic. But while I was working, I did some evening courses in industrial design. I even built a car of my own from spare parts. Then I got the idea of building a bike – a four-wheel delivery bike – and the next thing I knew, my wife was urging me to set up my own company! I had to take a very deep breath before I finally took the plunge. I'd done my best to prepare for it, taking a course in Business Management in my spare time, and I knew I'd be working longer hours for less money, at least at first. The big difficulty was the uncertainty of not knowing how much would be coming in each month. And things were pretty tough for the first few years – looking back, I can see that I underestimated the amount of paperwork I'd have to do – but I've never regretted it.

Essential tips

▸ In Paper 2, you must answer two questions, so it is essential to use your time effectively. This does not mean you should start writing at once and write as much as you can! You must take the time to prepare before you begin writing.

▸ Make sure you understand the instructions. Read the question several times, underlining the key words that describe your task.

▸ Think about the register of your writing: should it be formal or informal? What layout is appropriate?

▸ Writing Part 2 tasks will include an email or a letter, a proposal, a report, or a review. Your answer for Part 2 must be between 220 and 260 words.

▸ The input for Part 2 questions is much shorter than that for Part 1. You must use the information given, but also use your imagination intelligently to come up with more information. You will need to spend time preparing your answer, as for Part 1.

▸ In Part 2, you must answer one question, so think carefully about the task that you feel most comfortable with. Are you confident you know which register to use and if a particular format or layout is necessary? Do you have a good range of vocabulary relevant to this task? Can you express clear views on the subject (if the question requires you to do so)?

▸ You don't need to write a rough draft – there isn't time for that. Make a plan or an outline instead.

▸ Your writing should normally have three sections: an introduction, the main body and a conclusion. Note down approximately how many words should be in each section.

▸ Note down a few words or phrases to remind yourself what you must say in each section.

▸ Take a few minutes to look at your plan and make sure the information flows well. If it doesn't, you can still change your mind and put something in the conclusion instead of the main body, for instance.

▸ See the Writing bank on page 193–205 for examples of different types of writing and sample answers.

PAPER 1 Reading and
Use of English

PAPER 2 Writing ▶ **Part 1**
Part 2

PAPER 3 Listening

PAPER 4 Speaking

Essential tips

▸ You could consider the issue
from two or more viewpoints,
e.g. economic (green), or
political (popularity with the
townspeople). You could
argue for a compromise or
come down strongly in favour
of one position . Assemble
the points you want to make
and state them clearly and
concisely. Your essay should
be thought-provoking and
persuasive.

You **must** answer this question. Write your answer in **220–260** words in an
appropriate style on the separate answer sheet.

1 Your class has attended a lecture on what governments could do to minimise the
use of cars in the city centre. You have made the notes below.

Methods of reducing use of cars in town:

- restrict parking
- cheaper public transport
- congestion charges

**Some opinions expressed in the
seminar:**

'People would park illegally.'

'Travelling by public transport is slow
and not suitable for everyone.'

'It would be expensive to administer
congestion charges.'

Write an **essay** for your tutor discussing **two** of the methods in your notes. You
should **explain which method you think is better** for the local government to
consider, and provide reasons to support your opinion.

You may, if you wish, make use of the opinions expressed in the discussion, but
you should use your own words as far as possible.

PAPER 1 Reading and
Use of English

PAPER 2 Writing ▶ Part 1
                        Part 2

PAPER 3 Listening

PAPER 4 Speaking

Write an answer to **one** of the questions **2–4** in this part. Write your answer in **220–260** words in an appropriate style on the separate answer sheet. Put the question number in the box at the top of the page.

2   Read this extract from a letter you received from an international youth organisation.

> We are conducting a survey on the importance of regional culture to young people around the world. Please write a report on this survey, describing how young people in your region feel about the history and culture of that region, and how you think this may change in the future.

Write your **report**.

3   You recently returned from a holiday abroad. On the flight out, the aircraft was delayed and you missed your onward connection. Your luggage was taken to the wrong destination and not returned to you for two days. Write a letter to the airline describing how your holiday was affected. Say how you feel about their service, and ask for compensation.

Write your **letter**.

4   A website that specialises in film reviews has asked you to write a review of the film version of a book you have read, comparing the film to the book. You should comment on the portrayal of the characters, the development of the main themes, and whether you think the film is as good as the book or not. Give reasons for your opinions.

Write your **review**.

Essential tips

Question 2

▶ What style would be appropriate for this report? Bear in mind that the report is written for an international organisation.

▶ When writing a report, you need to give your paragraphs headings. Use the details of the question to help you organise your answer into paragraphs with suitable headings. This will help you focus on what information you need to include.

▶ Try to use examples from your own experience, if possible.

Question 3

▶ You are writing to a company, so use a formal, appropriate style. Remember to answer each point in the instructions.

Question 4

▶ Begin by giving a general description of what you are reviewing. Remember that the reader may not have experienced this book or film. Then, give your opinions on the film or book. Remember to phrase these as opinions, not as facts.

PAPER 1 Reading and
Use of English

PAPER 2 Writing

PAPER 3 Listening ▶

PAPER 4 Speaking

Part 1
Part 2
Part 3
Part 4

Essential tips

Question 2: Read the options carefully during the pause before you hear the recording. Then listen to the speaker talking about doing Tai Chi. What does she say takes years of practice?

Question 3: Read the question stem carefully. What information do you have to focus on?

Question 6: All the options may appear possible, but listen carefully to what the speaker actually realised.

Track 5

You will hear three different extracts. For questions **1–6**, choose the answer (**A, B** or **C**) which fits best according to what you hear. There are two questions for each extract.

Extract One

You hear part of an interview with a Tai Chi instructor.

1   According to Ruth, Tai Chi
    A   needs to be performed indoors.
    B   is a series of exercises.
    C   represents a way of life.

2   One of the most difficult things about learning Tai Chi is
    A   that you have to do it out of doors.
    B   achieving harmony between your movements.
    C   remembering the complex dance sequences.

Extract Two

You hear two people discussing taking a year off before going to university.

3   Before going to work in China, the man had not expected the job to be
    A   rewarding.
    B   easy.
    C   boring.

4   The woman's experience made her realise that
    A   marketing was a difficult career for women.
    B   working in a hotel was very challenging.
    C   she had made the wrong choice of career.

Extract Three

You hear part of an interview with an illusionist.

5   Daniel's interest in magic arose from his
    A   ambition to become an entertainer.
    B   desire to impress someone.
    C   trips to the cinema as a boy.

6   According to Daniel, one similarity between magic and film-making is
    A   the debt they owe to technology.
    B   the disbelief they arouse in the audience.
    C   the power they have over the audience.

PAPER 1 Reading and
          Use of English

PAPER 2 Writing

PAPER 3 Listening ▶

PAPER 4 Speaking

Part 1
Part 2
Part 3
Part 4

Essential tips

▶ As with all listening tasks, make the best use of the time you are given before you hear the recording. Read the instructions carefully, look at the title and the questions, and imagine what the recording might say.

▶ Remember: you will hear the words you need but not in the same context as the question. Note, however, that you can answer a question with a synonym, or paraphrase an idea, as long as the synonym or paraphrase completes the question appropriately.

▶ Bear in mind the question after the one you are trying to answer, so if you miss the information you need, you can move on to the next question.

Question 7: The word or words you need must describe the person's occupation or role. This sort of information might be given at the beginning of the talk, so make sure you are listening carefully from the very start of the recording!

Question 10: From the context you can guess that the speaker will mention a profession. You might try to imagine which professions a farmer and his wife might aspire to for their son.

Question 11: The speaker will say that he studied something, but remember that another way to say that you did something is to imagine what would have happened if you had not done it.

Question 14: There are many phrases with *in* which might fit here, such as *in luxury*, but that is unlikely. Probably the word you need will be the name of a place. The text may use a different structure, so you might not hear the preposition *in*.

Track 6

You will hear a writer talking about a biography she has written. For questions **7–14**, complete the sentences with a word or a short phrase.

AN INTERESTING CHARACTER

The speaker has written a book about (**7**) ....
                                                              called Robert Tewbridge.

Tewbridge's father was a (**8**) .... in Scotland.

Tewbridge's parents wanted him to become (**9**) ....

Tewbridge earned his living by writing (**10**) ....
                                                              for various publications.

The speaker learnt a great deal about Tewbridge's character
                        from studying his (**11**) ....

It appears that Tewbridge and his (**12**) ....
                                                              were close friends.

Tewbridge spent many years studying (**13**) ....

He lived in (**14**) .... for the last 30 years of his life.

PAPER 1 Reading and
          Use of English

PAPER 2 Writing

PAPER 3 Listening ▶

PAPER 4 Speaking

Part 1
Part 2
Part 3
Part 4

Track 7

You will hear part of an interview with Betsy Boom, owner of a chain of fashion shops. For questions **15–20**, choose the answer (**A**, **B**, **C** or **D**) which fits best according to what you hear.

15 What aspect of shopping does Betsy enjoy most?
    A experimenting with different styles
    B finding a bargain
    C comparing items in different shops
    D being given advice

16 What does she dislike about expensive clothes shops?
    A There isn't a wide selection of goods.
    B The assistants are unfriendly.
    C Customers are ignored.
    D Customers are expected to spend a lot of money.

17 When people first went into one of Betsy's shops, they often felt
    A flattered.
    B amused.
    C awkward.
    D dizzy.

18 The members of staff in Betsy's shop
    A were offended at the demands Betsy made.
    B found it hard to adjust to the new surroundings.
    C disliked dealing with shy and difficult customers.
    D came to enjoy the atmosphere after a while.

19 What is the most rewarding aspect of the business for Betsy?
    A seeing customers overcome their inhibitions
    B proving to others that her idea was a good one
    C watching the staff relax in their new roles
    D being able to provide fashionable clothes at low prices

20 What does Betsy feel is the danger she faces now?
    A becoming complacent
    B growing arrogant
    C being afraid to try something new
    D suffering financially if fashions change

Essential tips

▶ Prepare for what you will hear on the recording: read the instructions and think about the subject. Consider who the speakers will be.

▶ Remember: you will not hear the exact words of the question in the recording, so concentrate on the ideas expressed.

▶ The questions follow the order of the recording, but the final question may be about the recording as a whole.

Question 16: The question refers to Betsy's feelings about expensive shops. If you hear one of the words in the options, check that Betsy is using it to talk about expensive clothes shops.

Question 17: To prepare for this question, think how you would explain the feelings in the options. In the recording you will hear one of these feelings expressed in different words.

Question 19: How might Betsy express *most rewarding* in other words? Now think about the meaning of the options. What does *overcome their inhibitions* in option A mean, for example?

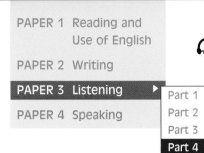
PAPER 1 Reading and
            Use of English

PAPER 2 Writing

PAPER 3 Listening ▶   Part 1

PAPER 4 Speaking   Part 2

                      Part 3

                      Part 4

Essential tips

▶ Read the instructions carefully. Look at the options for Task One, and consider what each person's job entails before you attempt this task.

▶ Aim to complete Task One the first time you listen, and Task Two the second time. Then check that you feel happy with your choices for Task One. On listening the second time, you may notice something you missed the first time.

Question 22: Listen carefully to what the speaker says. She mentions helping 'university students'. Who might she be?

Question 24: The speaker says that 'Here at Head Office, we show our employees exactly how much energy can be saved by adopting particular practices.' Who would be likely to talk about the company and its staff in this way?

Question 26: Listen to everything the speaker says before making your choice. What point does he make about workers' awareness?

Question 29: The speaker talks about how the company goes further than simply imposing new regulations at work. What do they do?

Track 8

You will hear five short extracts in which people talk about environmental initiatives.

While you listen, you must complete both tasks.

TASK ONE

For questions **21–25**, choose from list **A–H**, the person who is speaking.

A   a public health officer

B   a sales representative

C   the company manager

D   a careers advice officer

E   a marketing executive

F   a marketing executive

G   an environmental activist

H   an office cleaner

Speaker 1	21
Speaker 2	22
Speaker 3	23
Speaker 4	24
Speaker 5	25

TASK TWO

For questions **26–30**, choose from list **A–H** what view each speaker is expressing.

A   Consumers should put more pressure on companies to adopt environmental schemes.

B   Few companies prioritise conservation.

C   We should be more optimistic about what companies are doing about the environment.

D   Few office workers realise how much they could do to conserve energy.

E   Companies need to explain environmental initiatives to their employees.

F   Young people don't buy from companies without sound environmental policies.

G   The provision of incentives will encourage staff to adopt company schemes.

H   Young job seekers demand a work environment that reflects their values.

Speaker 1	26
Speaker 2	27
Speaker 3	28
Speaker 4	29
Speaker 5	30

Essential tips

Part 3

▶ In this part of the exam, you and the other candidate have to work together to perform a task, such as exchanging ideas or reaching a decision.

▶ Listen carefully to the examiner's instructions.

▶ You have to talk for two minutes, so it is important that you really discuss the issue. You must ask your partner about his/her views and not only give your own.

▶ There is no right or wrong answer. The only important thing is to exchange ideas and express your opinions. However, don't try too hard to persuade your partner. It is acceptable if you each come to different conclusions.

Part 4

▶ In this part of the exam, you will be asked to discuss topics related to the task in Part 3. The focus is on expressing your opinions and agreeing/disagreeing.

▶ Make sure you don't just give one-word responses to the examiner's questions. Include expressions like 'In my opinion', 'It seems to me' or 'I'm not sure that I agree'.

▶ You should listen carefully to your partner because the examiner will ask you if you agree, or have another opinion.

Part 1 (2 minutes)

The examiner will ask you a few questions about yourself and about a general topic. For example, the examiner may ask you:

• What kind of outdoor activities do you enjoy?
• Which sports are popular in your region?
• Which sports do you enjoy watching and playing, and which do you find boring?

Part 2 (4 minutes)

You will each be asked to talk on your own for about a minute. You will each be given three different pictures to talk about. After your partner has finished speaking, you will be asked a brief question connected with your partner's photographs.

> ### Anticipation (compare, contrast and speculate)

Turn to pictures 1–3 on page 172 which show people waiting for something. (*Candidate A*), it's your turn first. Here are your pictures. They show **people anticipating something**.

I'd like you to compare and contrast **two** of the pictures and say **what these people could be anticipating that makes them look this way. How do you think they are feeling?**

(*Candidate B*), **which person do you think is the most nervous? Why?**

> ### Being alone (compare, contrast and speculate)

Turn to pictures 1–3 on page **173** which show people spending time alone.

Now, (*Candidate B*), here are your pictures. **They show people alone**.

I'd like you to compare and contrast **two** of these pictures, and say **why the people are alone, and how you think they are feeling.**

(*Candidate A*), **in which picture do you think the person is least able to cope with being alone? Why?**

Part 3 (4 minutes)

Look at page 174 which shows some situations where people need motivation.

> ### Motivation (discuss, evaluate and select)

Here are some situations where people need motivation and a question for you to discuss.

First, you have some time to look at the task.

(*Pause 15 seconds*)

Now talk to each other about **why people need motivation in these situations.**

Now you have about a minute to decide **which situation needs the most motivation.**

Part 4 (5 minutes)

The examiner will encourage you to develop the topic of your discussion in Part 3 by asking questions such as:

• When do you think it is important for people to be motivated? Are there any times when being motivated is undesirable?
• It is often said that motivation is important in education. Do you agree? (Why? / Why not?)
• What factors motivate people to achieve something?
• How can people motivate themselves?

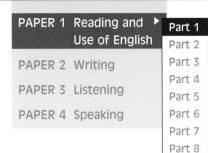

PAPER 1	Reading and Use of English	▶	Part 1
			Part 2
PAPER 2	Writing		Part 3
			Part 4
PAPER 3	Listening		Part 5
			Part 6
PAPER 4	Speaking		Part 7
			Part 8

For questions **1–8**, read the text below and decide which answer (**A**, **B**, **C** or **D**) best fits each gap. There is an example at the beginning (**0**).

Mark your answers **on the separate answer sheet**.

Example:

| 0 | **A** bothered | **B** feared | **C** cared | **D** wondered |

| 0 | A | B | C | D |

Essential tips

Question 3: The word *sighting* after the gap refers to someone having seen one of these insects. For others to know about the sighting, it must have been written down. Which word best fits the idea of it being written down?

Question 7: The word after the gap, *up*, tells you that this is a phrasal verb. The idea here is recruiting or getting people to help.

Question 8: This is an example of collocation. Which verb is normally used with *a part* to mean 'helped' or 'participated'?

Citizen scientists

Experts (**0**) .... that the nine-spotted ladybug, or ladybird as it is known in some countries, was becoming extinct. Then, in 2011, Peter Priolo, a volunteer ladybug hunter, (**1**) .... one sitting on a sunflower in New York. The ladybug population had once been so (**2**) .... in the state of New York that it was the 'official state insect', but the last (**3**) .... sighting of one had been almost 30 years before. Priolo was thrilled. So was the Lost Ladybug Project, which studies different species of North American ladybugs with the assistance of ordinary people, a (**4**) .... known as 'crowdsourcing'. One reason for the ladybug's (**5**) .... may be that other imported insects have (**6**) .... its habitat and are eating its food.

'In future, crowdsourcing may help us stop this happening,' says the project's director, John Losey from Cornell University.

(**7**) .... up ordinary citizens isn't new to science. Amateur astronomers, weather watchers, and other hobbyists going back to the 1700s have all (**8**) .... a part in the development of science. What's different today is the internet, which has helped recruit hundreds of thousands of volunteers over the past decade or so.

1	**A** regarded	**B** glanced	**C** observed	**D** considered
2	**A** widespread	**B** thorough	**C** overall	**D** comprehensive
3	**A** accounted	**B** recorded	**C** marked	**D** entered
4	**A** ritual	**B** habit	**C** manner	**D** practice
5	**A** recession	**B** drop	**C** decline	**D** letdown
6	**A** interfered	**B** invaded	**C** interrupted	**D** involved
7	**A** Signing	**B** Drawing	**C** Bringing	**D** Meeting
8	**A** put	**B** done	**C** added	**D** played

PAPER 1	Reading and ▸	Part 1
	Use of English	**Part 2**
PAPER 2	Writing	Part 3
		Part 4
PAPER 3	Listening	Part 5
PAPER 4	Speaking	Part 6
		Part 7
		Part 8

Essential tips

Question 9: If you look at the whole sentence, you will see that professional builders and members of the public are being grouped together. Can you think of a structure to join the two elements?

Question 13: Can you think of a phrase that means 'generally'?

Question 15: This is a fixed phrase. Both *on* and *lookout* are part of this phrase, which means 'looking for'. Which word is needed to complete it?

For questions **9–16**, read the text below and think of the word which best fits each gap. Use only **one** word in each gap. There is an example at the beginning (**0**).

Write your answers **IN CAPITAL LETTERS on the separate answer sheet.**

Example: | 0 | W | H | O | | | | | | | | | | | | | | | | | | |

Second-hand but better than new

Many people (**0**) …….. are building their own homes or renovating existing buildings these days prefer to buy certain things like doors and fireplaces second-hand. A lot of businesses will supply second-hand materials, (**9**) …….. only to professional builders, but also to ordinary members of the public. People wishing to indulge (**10**) …….. a spot of DIY will be able to find reclamation material, (**11**) …….. second-hand building supplies are known, if they are prepared to look for it, in most parts of the country.

Searching for second-hand goods can be time-consuming, of course, so (**12**) …….. bother? Well, on the (**13**) ……..**,** it makes good financial sense. A second-hand oak door in good condition will be considerably cheaper than a new one, even (**14**) …….. it is only a few years old. Many people, however, are on (**15**) …….. lookout for very old items, ones which can be hundreds of years old. (**16**) …….. articles as these will be expensive, of course, but many are ready to pay high prices for genuine antiques.

For questions **17–24**, read the text below. Use the word given in capitals at the end of some of the lines to form a word that fits in the gap **in the same line**. There is an example at the beginning (**0**).

Write your answers **IN CAPITAL LETTERS on the separate answer sheet.**

Example: | 0 | P | O | P | U | L | A | R | I | T | Y | | | | | | | |

Essential tips

Question 17: The gapped word comes before an adjective. What part of speech do you need?

Question 19: The gapped word is an adjective. Does it have a positive or negative meaning?

Question 21: The gapped word follows an article, so it must be a noun. How do you make a noun from *grow*?

Product placement

The rise in the (**0**) …….. of product placement has been one of the most interesting trends in advertising in the last couple of decades. Branded products are promoted indirectly by using them in films, and the success of this is making it (**17**) …….. desirable. Demand for product placement stemmed, at least (**18**) ….….., from regulations banning the advertising of certain products deemed (**19**) …….. for TV commercials. Films are not subject to the same sort of (**20**) …….. as television.

Other factors have contributed to the (**21**) …….. of product placement, One is these is the (**22**) …….. of consumers, exposed to an advertisement over a period of time, to become more (**23**) …….. in their response to it. They become tired of 'the same old thing' and advertisers are being forced to recognise a (**24**) …….. in their customers which did not exist in the past. People these days are more likely to be influenced by watching film star role models using a product. This is true of consumers in general, but it is particularly applicable to younger people.

POPULAR

INCREASE
ORIGIN

SUIT
CENSOR

GROW
TEND

CRITIC

SOPHISTICATED

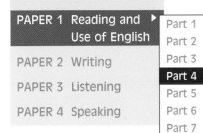

Essential tips

Question 26: Two structural changes are needed here. First, *The wishes of the residents* is now the subject of the sentence so a passive structure is needed. Secondly, a phrase including *into* is required which means the same as 'consider'. Can you think of one?

Question 27: You need a phrase with *placed*. What word can be used with *place* to mean that something is someone's fault?

Question 28: You need a phrasal verb which means 'regret saying something'.

For questions **25–30**, complete the second sentence so that it has a similar meaning to the first sentence, using the word given. **Do not change the word given.** You must use between **three** and **six** words, including the word given. Here is an example (**0**).

Example:

0 Jane regretted speaking so rudely to the old lady.

  MORE

  Jane .... politely to the old lady.

Example: | **0** | WISHED SHE HAD SPOKEN MORE |

Write **only** the missing words **IN CAPITAL LETTERS on the separate answer sheet**.

---

25 Although he studies hard, Christoph never does well in his exams.

  MATTER

  Christoph never does well in his exams, ... he studies.

26 The town council rarely seem to consider the wishes of the residents.

  INTO

  The wishes of the residents rarely .... by the town council.

27 John's mum said it was his own fault the party was ruined.

  PLACED

  John's mum .... for the party being ruined.

28 I'm sorry I said that your new hat looked like a lampshade.

  BACK

  I .... about your new hat looking like a lampshade.

29 There were a lot of people at the resort, but Mandy still had a great time.

  FACT

  Mandy had a great time at the resort .... crowded.

30 'You left my MP3 player on the bus, Joe!' shouted Olivier.

  ACCUSED

  Olivier .... MP3 player on the bus.

You are going to read a review of a book. For questions **31–36**, choose the answer (**A**, **B**, **C** or **D**) which you think fits best according to the text.

Mark your answers **on the separate answer sheet**.

Book review: Jesse Prinz's *Beyond Human Nature*

Jesse Prinz's book *Beyond Human Nature: How Culture and Experience Shape the Human Mind* is a valuable exploration of the age-old 'nature or nuture' debate – whether individual human beings are the product of the genetic features they are born with or of what they experience as they grow up. The book is also firmly part of what we might call the 'neuro-backlash'. In the last decade or so, a host of accessible books have appeared which are fun and provocative, and supplied startling messages about psychology and neuroscience that promised to empower us by decoding the inner workings of human life. But it was really only a matter of time before the re-evaluation of this popular science writing took off.

The controversy over the work of the American journalist Jonah Lehrer only accelerated the widespread reaction. The discovery that, in writing his celebrated books and magazine pieces on neuroscience, Lehrer had been a bit too careless with his facts, quotes, arguments, and conclusions gave way to cries that the simplification of science, in particular of neuroscience, often by science journalists, was once again to blame. The truth is, though, this trend was due to run out of steam. Even some of the best of these books — and there are certainly many worthwhile ones — have begun to seem formulaic.

With any luck, we will now get more books like Jesse Prinz's. While too many of the popular neuroscience authors write as though they are angling for more high-profile speaking work, Prinz is clearly only interested in trying to leave his mark on the nature-versus-nurture debate. Obviously, as Prinz says, we are shaped by both nature and nurture. But while Steven Pinker's influential book, *The Blank Slate,* provides a compelling defence for 'team nature', Prinz identifies himself as an unashamed 'nurturist'.

As such, he is committed to demonstrating that our interactions with our environment — our upbringing, early experiences, culture — have a lot more to do with the way we think, learn language, acquire knowledge, and make moral judgments than anything we are born with. This position has real implications for such big issues as the influence of genetics on intelligence and the effect of biology on gender inequality. And while it might not seem an exciting approach in the manner we have come to expect from recent popular cognitive science books, in the academic world today, it is a minority view—and in terms of certain established theories, very controversial.

Take the debate about language. For years, the field of linguistics has been heavily influenced by Noam Chomsky's notion of a *universal grammar*. Kids might learn a particular language from experience, Chomsky and his followers say, but they are drawing on a set of pre-programmed grammatical rules that we are all born with. It's why, even at a very young age, we are able to create an impressive array of unique, grammatically correct sentences. It's also a prime example of a 'nature' rather than 'nurture' argument.

Prinz takes us through the research that has been done, meticulously examining the logic behind the conclusions of Chomsky and his supporters, and suggests a different explanation. He defends a lesser-known theory that 'children might learn language statistically,' by unconsciously remembering the patterns in the sentences they hear and 'using these to generalise to new cases.' Instead of going for the hard sell, Prinz admits that all he hopes to do is raise the possibility that this alternative theory might be true. This lends his work an air of maturity.

This book should be seen as a notable example of science writing done right. Before discussing the role of genes in the manifestation of different traits, for instance, Prinz spends several pages explaining what genes are, how they work, and how we should think about them. We also get a useful walk through intellectual history as he shows how the nature/nurture pendulum has swung back and forth over thousands of years, and how Prinz's particular approach to these issues descends directly from the 18th-century philosopher David Hume. Although the author seems to want to win the argument, he's generous when it comes to providing evidence for the opposing side – making sure that readers will finish the book with a more thorough understanding of some major debates in science.

Essential tips

- Remember – in this part of the exam you need to understand the writer's opinion, attitude and purpose in a text. You also need to understand details of a text – not just what it says but also how it is organised and how different parts of the text relate to each other.

- Either skim read the text first before you read the questions, or read the questions first before you skim the text.

- Then read the questions carefully. There should be something in each question to help you locate which part of the text it is about. For example, Question 31 here refers to the first paragraph; Question 32 here mentions 'Johan Lehrer's work' and it should be easy to find Johan Lehrer in the second paragraph.

Question 31: This is an example of a question focusing on understanding the organisation of the text. The inverted commas around *neuro-backlash* and the options indicate that these phrases are in the text. It may help you to underline or highlight them in the text. If you do not know what this word means, look in the text for clues to help you. For example, the word *neuroscience* comes halfway through the third sentence. Secondly, what can the word *back* mean? Think about the meaning of *go back* or *give back*. Is this sense of *back* suggested in any of the options? The read the first paragraph carefully and think about how it is organised.

Question 33: This question focuses on understanding a different kind of detail – the attitude expressed by the writer

31 What does the 'neuro-backlash' in the first paragraph refer to?
   A   a host of accessible books
   B   the inner workings of human life
   C   a new vocabulary of buzz words
   D   the re-evaluation of this popular science writing

32 According to the reviewer, the discovery of problems in Jonah Lehrer's work
   A   stemmed from a wider access to information about science.
   B   triggered a new way of thinking about neuro-science.
   C   confirmed a shift in many people's opinions.
   D   led to exaggerated criticism of him.

33 In which of these phrases from the third paragraph does the writer express disapproval?
   A   'angling for high-profile speaking work'
   B   'trying to leave his mark'
   C   'provides a compelling defence'
   D   'identifies himself as an unashamed 'nurturist'

34 The reviewer refers to 'Chomsky's notion of a universal grammar' as an example of
   A   a big issue
   B   an exciting approach
   C   a minority view
   D   an established theory

35 What view of Prinz's work does the reviewer express in the sixth paragraph?
   A   He shows appropriate caution in putting forward his own ideas.
   B   He spends too much time challenging other people's work.
   C   His explanation of difficult concepts is very clear.
   D   His analysis goes into too much detail at times.

36 What point does the reviewer make in the final paragraph?
   A   The book reveals new information about the issues it covers.
   B   Certain theories have always gone in and out of fashion.
   C   The views Prinz puts forward are rather old-fashioned.
   D   Science writers should consider their readers more.

in his choice of certain words. Questions like this may well include vocabulary you do not know (e.g. *angling, leave his mark, compelling, unashamed*). To find out the attitude expressed in a word, you should read the text around each phrase (you should do this even if you think you know the word). For example, you may not know

unashamed nurturist in option D, but there is an explanation of the word *nurture* earlier in the text, so you should be able to work out what a *nurturist* is. Then, consider what the writer says about Prinz elsewhere in the text and whether he is likely to describe him with a word that expresses *disapproval*.

PAPER 1	Reading and Use of English	▶	Part 1
			Part 2
PAPER 2	Writing		Part 3
			Part 4
PAPER 3	Listening		Part 5
			Part 6
PAPER 4	Speaking		Part 7
			Part 8

You are going to read four contributions to a debate about whether economic growth is always a good thing. For questions **37–40**, choose from the contributions **A–D**. The contributions may be chosen more than once.

Mark your answers **on the separate answer sheet**.

Economic growth and prosperity

Will more economic growth deliver prosperity and well-being? Or, with natural resources running out and the threat of climate change, should developed countries abandon the idea of endless growth? Four economists give their views.

A

In the advanced economies of the world, there is mounting evidence that ever-increasing consumption adds little to human well-being. In fact, increasing stress levels, obesity and other social ills suggest it positively impedes it. More urgently, it is now clear that the ecosystems which sustain our economies are collapsing under the impact of this consumption. Economists argue that the environmental impact of an economy, relative to its income, falls as it gets richer – wealthier nations tend to have stricter environmental regulations, for example. There is no alternative but to opt out of further growth. However, the bottom line is that economic growth inevitably leads to increases in greenhouse gas emissions, which accelerates climate change. The implications are complex but include a need to fundamentally rethink the uses to which we put our technological expertise and much tighter regulation of advertising, which incites wholly superfluous consumption.

B

It has become received wisdom that prosperity and economic growth do not go together. More 'stuff', we are told, damages the environment and makes us miserable. Hence, we should limit growth, raise taxes to redistribute affluence, invest in welfare rather than wealth creation, and control or even eliminate commercial advertising, a key trigger of consumption. Frankly, it is tragic that growth has such a bad name. In the space of about two centuries, substantial increases in economic output have brought enormous benefits: longer, healthier lives, shorter working hours, miraculous inventions, the ability to reshape the environment for our own benefit and, surely, greater general well-being. The world is not perfect, of course, and climate change is an issue. But to tackle it, we need more resources and technology, rather than less. We should invest in high-tech energy production, sea walls to resist flooding and other engineering-based solutions, rather than cheap moralising.

C

Economic progress has brought huge benefits for humanity, but in some countries, we appear to have reached the stage where the costs of growth have started to outweigh the benefits. The more we have, the less satisfied we are, and we are running up against natural limits on a finite planet as resources are depleted, biodiversity falls sharply and climate change threatens to destroy us. Should we now give up on economic progress and focus instead on well-being and protecting the planet? While the idea has a certain utopian appeal, the reality for the majority is unimaginable. Even wholesale reform of aspects of modern economies like advertising, the cheerleader for consumerism, is unlikely to be accepted. There is a middle way: to pursue, determinedly, existing environmental policies and to apply our technological expertise to overcome our difficulties, with massive projects to harness solar, wind and wave power, for example.

D

The world is heading for catastrophic climate change, and life in some of the world's most technologically advanced nations, while abounding in consumer products, has evidently not been enhanced in terms of personal relationships, meaningful work and other key values for well-being – indeed, it's quite the opposite. So, should the growth model be dropped? In *The Moral Consequences of Economic Growth*, Benjamin Friedman convincingly argues that rising standards of material prosperity foster opportunity, tolerance, fairness and democracy, and to give up on growth is unlikely to lead to the sort of open, friendly society we want. The way forward, then, is to tackle excessive consumerism and its associated ills by various reforms, such as greater control of advertising, and to strengthen measures to keep global warming and resource depletion within reasonable limits, while the world economy carries on growing.

Which writer

has a different view to the others about continuing to
aim for economic growth?

37 ☐

expresses a different opinion from the others on the link
between continued economic growth and happiness?

38 ☐

takes a similar view to writer B's opinion about economic
growth and the use of technology?

39 ☐

shares writer A's opinion about what the consequences
of economic growth imply for advertising?

40 ☐

Essential tips

▶ Remember that you need to decide whether four
different writers have similar or different views on the
same subject.

▶ Go through each text carefully in turn, highlighting the
sections relating to each question. Write the question
numbers next to the parts you highlight.

▶ Starting with Question 37, compare the views expressed
in all four texts.

Question 37: The key words in this question are *different
view from the others* and *about continuing to aim for
economic growth*. Writer A says: *There is no alternative but
to opt out of further growth.* Writer B says *it is tragic that
growth has such a bad name* and calls for *more resources
and better technology rather than less*, so B appears to be
in favour of continued economic growth. Look carefully at
texts C and D, and decide whether they share A or B's view.

Question 39: The key words here are: *similar view to writer
B's* and *economic growth and the use of technology*. Writer
B says: *we need more resources and technology rather
than less. We should invest in high–tech energy production,
sea walls to resist flooding and other engineering-based
solutions.*

Writer A says we need *to fundamentally rethink the uses to
which we put our technological expertise,* and talks about
superfluous consumption so writer A's view on this issue
seems different from B's. What about writers C and D?

PAPER 1 Reading and ▶ Part 1
Use of English   Part 2

PAPER 2 Writing   Part 3
                       Part 4
PAPER 3 Listening   Part 5

PAPER 4 Speaking   Part 6
                       Part 7
                       Part 8

You are going to read a magazine article. Six paragraphs have been removed from the article. Choose from the paragraphs **A–G** the one which fits each gap (**41–46**). There is one extra paragraph which you do not need to use.

Mark your answers **on the separate answer sheet**.

The lost civilisations of Peru

An expedition in the mountainous regions of southern Peru has found some important remains from the Inca civilisation. Their discovery came when the expedition stumbled across a small, flat area cut into a forested mountainside. At first, it looked like nothing in particular, but then the explorers realised it could have been a platform where Inca priests stood and watched the path of the sun.

| 41 |

Qoriwayrachina, as the site they discovered is known, is of outstanding importance. In fact, it became clear that this was one of the most significant historical finds in South America since the unearthing of Machu Picchu, the fabulous lost city of the Incas, in the 20th century.

| 42 |

For example, recent archaeological work near the Peruvian capital has revealed another ancient city, dating back to well before the Incas. This has reinforced the feelings of many archaeologists that there are many more hidden remains buried for hundreds (or even thousands) of years, still waiting to be found.

| 43 |

But it is the mountains of the Vilcabamba range that perhaps hold the most promise. Vilcabamba, which means 'sacred valley', was the hub of the vast Inca civilisation. In the 16th century, when the Spanish conquest led to the demise of this ancient way of life, this area was the last part of the Inca empire to fall. Hundreds of years later, it slowly began to yield its secrets to archaeologists, Macchu Picchu perhaps being the most notable of a series of impressive finds. By no means everything there has been unearthed, however.

| 44 |

Knowing that there is more to be found is important, because although many valuable Inca sites have been discovered and researched, we still know surprisingly little about the Inca way of life. What's more, studying remains will be of great value, as many are in danger of being ruined forever, either by thieves on the hunt for ancient treasure, or by modern developments such as the building of roads or new towns.

| 45 |

It is not all action-man excitement, however. The best explorers spend time reading the accounts of the Spanish conquerors, studying maps and talking to local people who know their own area and are often willing to reveal the whereabouts of previously unidentified remains. Raising funds to pay for the work is also part of the challenge.

| 46 |

Peter Frost, one of the group which discovered Qoriwayrachina, knows this. As a tour guide, photographer, and travel writer working in the region for 30 years (though not an archaeologist), he has become an expert on the Incas. Since his initial work at Qoriwayrachina, he has led two lengthy expeditions to the area, and has uncovered the ruins of 200 structures and storehouses, an intricately engineered aqueduct, colourful pottery and several tombs, all valuable evidence for the study of the region's past.

A Far from it. Archaeologists know from having found traces of homes and infrastructure, that there are several potentially major sites still waiting for proper investigation.

B The importance of this kind of preparation is underlined by Hugh Thompson in his recent book about exploring for Inca ruins, *The White Rock*. According to him, anyone can go into the jungle and look for ancient remains. However, they may cause a great deal of damage in the process and indeed, the history of Peruvian exploration is littered with failures.

C According to these experts, what we now know as Peru has hosted advanced civilisations for as long as almost anywhere else in the world. The likelihood, therefore, of making further discoveries almost anywhere in the country, is high.

D These worries mean it is fortunate that the urge to discover ruins swallowed by the jungle is still as strong as ever. Many archaeologists feel a keen sense of adventure, seeing themselves in an Indiana Jones fantasy, hunting for lost

civilisations. The thought of finding a lost city, hidden by the jungle for hundreds of years, and containing unimaginable treasures from a mysterious people is, for some, difficult to resist.

E The previous year, 1989, saw a number of expeditions to the region in search of the mythical lost city, but the end result was similarly disappointing. Undeterred, the courageous explorer refuses to abandon his attempts to raise money for one last try.

F But that staggering discovery took place over 100 years ago, and so many explorers, archaeologists and tourists have been in the region since then that one might assume all its secrets have been surrendered. But the mountains of Peru are still full of hidden ruins, as are other parts of the country.

G So, a decision was made to battle on through the thick jungle. Their reward was to uncover significant evidence of the civilisation that once lived there: tombs, a water system, and traces of many other buildings.

Essential tips

Question 42: The last sentence of the previous paragraph mentions a discovery made in a particular period. Which gapped paragraph has a time reference which might relate to this?

Question 44: The last sentence of the previous paragraph contains a negative structure which emphasises that not all the ancient remains have been discovered (*By no means everything has been unearthed, however.*) Which gapped paragraph starts by agreeing with this idea?

Question 46: The previous paragraph describes things explorers do before they go on expeditions. Which gapped paragraph refers to this?

You are going to read an article in which four people talk about careers involving foreign languages. For questions **47–56**, choose from the people (**A–D**).

Mark your answers **on the separate answer sheet**.

Which student

gained an awareness of how frustrating scientific work can be? 47

gained in confidence as a result of the work experience? 48

particularly valued the opportunity to discuss ideas with professional scientists? 49

experienced difficulties in understanding scientific ideas? 50

was impressed by the way their volunteer work resembled a real job? 51

realised the importance of choosing an area of personal interest for voluntary work? 52

discovered something of immediate practical benefit in their research? 53

believes it is wise to volunteer in areas of science that are well-publicised? 54

made the most of a personal misfortune? 55

made a discovery that contradicted expectations? 56

Essential tips

Question 47: When people say that work is 'frustrating', they mean that they are not making the progress they had hoped for. Which student describes a situation like this?

Question 51: All four students volunteered in order to gain experience of work, but which of the four specifically mentions the similarities with 'a real job'?

Question 53: All four students carried out research that would probably be of benefit in some way. But which research led to a discovery with 'immediate' and 'practical' consequences?

Volunteering in science laboratories

A Eric Martens

A talented athlete, Eric Martens trained so hard in his final year at school that he sustained knee injuries, which kept him off the track for months. Rather than becoming discouraged, however, Eric turned to science and landed a voluntary stint in a sports research unit in his summer holidays. 'There are people there who are particularly interested in how human joints develop and function,' says Eric. 'It was brilliant being able to ask them about their work – and challenge it sometimes.' Eric assisted on a number of projects, and eventually was allowed to conduct an experiment himself. Barefoot jogging has become fashionable among some amateur runners. Eric observed a number of experienced joggers running barefoot on treadmills and found that that they still ran as if they were wearing shoes, landing heel-first rather than on the balls of their feet. The impact sustained could easily lead to injury. The implications for runners were obvious and the findings were soon made known more widely. 'It was a great experience,' says Eric. 'I'm definitely thinking of going into research when I finish university.'

B Angela Michaelis

In her final year at school, Angela Michaelis had become fascinated by human behaviour. So, she emailed various people involved in brain research and was eventually offered a placement with a well-known psychologist called Carmen Gago. With Dr Gago's help, Angela wound up investigating trust and turned to a group of people for whom trust is crucial – skydiving instructors. Angela assumed that learners would base the degree of trust they placed in an instructor on levels of experience and perhaps appearance. What novices reported, though, was that it mainly related to the way the instructors talked. 'Dr Gago was impressed,' says Angela. 'And I was pleased because the whole thing was a real challenge. We made several false starts. One skydiving group agreed to take part and then pulled out. Then we had trouble recording the interviews and organising the data. At one stage I wasn't sure it would ever happen. I suppose it's good to know that research can be like this, and I'm glad I was working on something I was curious about. If I hadn't been, I wouldn't have got nearly so much out of it.'

C Katie Oldham

Katie Oldham is also very interested in the human brain. She spent two months helping a neuroscientist, Frank Hebble, explore how the brain reacts to sudden changes in the environment, such as sounds or touches. She mapped how brain activity shifts when these changes occur, using a technique that measures electrical pulses in the brain. Such maps may help doctors who study children with certain medical conditions. 'It was intimidating at first,' Katie says. 'This is quite advanced science and the people working on it are seriously clever. I did eventually feel part of the team, though. It was good to know they valued my contribution and respected me. They didn't pay me but I was expected to show up on time and do an eight-hour day, just like everyone else.' There is no resentment in Katie's comments, however. She believes she has a head start on some of her fellow students in having had an authentic taste of life as a scientist.

D Tariq Bashir

Tariq Bashir won a placement with medical scientists working on new ways to treat malaria. 'It's such an important thing,' says Tariq. 'So many people around the world are affected by malaria, and if we could come up with solutions, it would make such a difference.' Tariq regards himself as fortunate to be interested in a subject that attracts a lot of attention in the media at large, as well as scientific circles. It means the research is well-funded, and scientists involved have the money and time to dedicate to students like Tariq. It also means the competition for student places tends to be stiff, however. 'I did lots of preparation before I applied', Tariq says. 'I read all the research I could. Some of it went over my head, of course, but I asked a friend of my dad's, who's a doctor, to simplify some of it. But I think the malaria team were impressed that I invested time finding out about what they're doing.'

PAPER 1 Reading and
Use of English

PAPER 2 Writing ▶ Part 1
Part 2

PAPER 3 Listening

PAPER 4 Speaking

Essential tips

▶ You don't need to have had experience of working from home to be able to answer this question well. Think of times from your own experience (e.g. when you were at school or university) of the advantages and disadvantages of being able to stay at home.

You **must** answer this question. Write your answer in **220–260** words in an appropriate style on the separate answer sheet.

1 Your class has attended a lecture by a careers tutor about the advantages of joining a company whose employees work online from home. You have made the notes below.

> **The advantages of working from home:**
>
> • no travelling
> • flexibility
> • comfort

> **Some opinions expressed after the lecture:**
>
> 'There are too many distractions.'
> 'I could work whatever part of the day I wanted.'
> 'You would miss the company of fellow workers.'

Write an **essay** for your tutor discussing **two** of the advantages in your notes. You should **explain which advantage you think is more important**, and **provide reasons** to support your opinion.

You may, if you wish, make use of the opinions expressed after the lecture, but you should use your own words as far as possible.

PAPER 1 Reading and
Use of English

PAPER 2 Writing ▶ Part 1
Part 2

PAPER 3 Listening

PAPER 4 Speaking

Write an answer to **one** of the questions **2–4** in this part. Write your answer in **220–260** words in an appropriate style on the separate answer sheet. Put the question number in the box at the top of the page.

2 You are on a planning committee. You hope to bring a music festival to your town. Write to the mayor explaining why a music festival would be good for your town, where it would be held, and what kinds of events there would be. Acknowledge that there may be some disadvantages. Outline what these might be, and how you would try to avoid them.

Write your **proposal.**

3 You work for a hotel chain and have been sent to a holiday resort where your company plans to open a new hotel. You have been asked to report on the leisure facilities of the resort. Write your report, giving information on:

• sports and recreational opportunities
• cinemas and theatres
• cafés and restaurants

Write your **report.**

4 You recently witnessed a car accident. Nobody was seriously hurt, but there was a disagreement about who caused the accident and you had to make a statement to the police, which was an interesting experience. Write a letter to a friend describing:

• the events leading up to the accident
• the accident itself
• the reaction of the drivers and passers-by
• your experience with the police

Write your **letter.**

Essential tips

Question 2

▶ What style would be appropriate for this report? Bear in mind that the report is written for the mayor, and needs to be formal as well as persuasive.

▶ Remember to give a balanced set of ideas in the proposal. Mention problems as well as benefits, before arriving at a set of recommendations that considers both sides of the argument.

Question 3

▶ Remember the overall purpose of this report is to comment on the resort's facilities, with the view of setting up a new hotel there. Bear this in mind throughout your report, as this will help you focus your argument, and avoid making any unnecessary points.

Question 4

▶ Begin by giving a general description of the event. We usually start with general overviews, explaining the situation, before moving to smaller, specific descriptions. Bear in mind the reader is a personal friend, so this should not be a formal-sounding report. Try to make it interesting by adding your own comments on what happened.

PAPER 1 Reading and
         Use of English

PAPER 2 Writing

PAPER 3 Listening ▶ Part 1
                       Part 2
                       Part 3
                       Part 4

PAPER 4 Speaking

Essential tips

Question 2: Does the woman list possible future benefits of the job for Keith's career?

Question 4: Read the wording of the options in this question carefully. What does Rusty say about the purpose of having a samba referee?

Question 6: All the options may appear possible, but listen carefully to what both speakers actually agree on.

🎧 **Track 9**

You will hear three different extracts. For questions **1–6**, choose the answer (**A**, **B** or **C**) which fits best according to what you hear. There are two questions for each extract.

Extract One

You hear two people talking about a job that the man may apply for.

1   What does Keith think is the main disadvantage of the job?
    A   It involves working at weekends.
    B   He will have to use his own car.
    C   The basic pay is not very good.

2   Annie is enthusiastic about the job because
    A   it should lead to a good career for Keith.
    B   Keith is particularly well qualified for it.
    C   it will enable Keith to work from home.

Extract Two

You hear part of an interview with Rusty Upshaw, a bossaball referee.

3   According to Rusty, bossaball is played
    A   on trampolines and sand.
    B   on inflatables.
    C   on trampolines and inflatables.

4   Rusty believes that the samba referee
    A   enhances the attraction of the sport.
    B   distracts the crowd from the game.
    C   keeps the crowd under control.

Extract Three

You hear two people talking about cooking.

5   What does Ricky say about his work as a chef?
    A   Being well organised is the key to success in this profession.
    B   It pays for a chef to specialise in one kind of cooking.
    C   Good chefs have an interest in food from an early age.

6   Both people say they enjoy cooking because it
    A   gives pleasure to friends.
    B   requires total concentration.
    C   helps them maintain good health.

PAPER 1 Reading and
          Use of English

PAPER 2 Writing

PAPER 3 Listening ▶
                        | Part 1 |
                        | **Part 2** |
                        | Part 3 |
                        | Part 4 |

PAPER 4 Speaking

Essential tips

Question 7: What kinds of constructions are built these days? Do you need to include an article in your answer? Is an adjective necessary?

Question 9: From the structure of the sentence you can see that an adjective is needed here. If the wheels of a vehicle don't match so that it can't be used for practical purposes, what sort of function might the vehicle have?

Question 12: What kind of word might complete the phrase: 'The Parisii came to Britain from . . .'? It could be the name of a place: a city, country etc. Remember that you will hear the word or words you want, but not in the same context as in the question.

🎧 **Track 10**

You will hear a writer talking about a biography she has written. For questions **7–14**, complete the sentences with a word or a short phrase.

AN ANCIENT CHARIOT

The chariot was found at a site where (**7**) ....

is being built.

It was buried in a limestone chamber with (**8**) ....

a man's inside it.

The chariot's wheels don't match, suggesting it had a

(**9**) .... function.

The remains of a large number of (**10**) .... were also

discovered near the chariot.

The chamber was probably the tomb of the (**11**) ....

of a tribe.

The Parisii came to Britain from (**12**) ....

Until the discovery of the chariot, it was not known that the Parisii had lived

so far (**13**) ....

It is hoped that the chariot can be moved to (**14**) ....

PAPER 1 Reading and
Use of English

PAPER 2 Writing

PAPER 3 Listening ▶

PAPER 4 Speaking

Part 1
Part 2
Part 3
Part 4

Essential tips

Question 15: The question refers to Reilly's main concern. Listen out for a phrase which has a similar meaning to, my 'main concern'.

Question 17: To prepare for this question, think how you would explain the situations in the options. In the recording you will hear one of these situations expressed in different words.

Question 20: Think about what would motivate you to buy a product, and then think of other ways that the speakers could express the different options.

🎧 **Track 11**

You will hear part of an interview with Fergus Reilly, a marine scientist, about the non-profit organisation he works for: Sustainable Fishing. For questions **15–20**, choose the answer (**A**, **B**, **C** or **D**) which fits best according to what you hear.

15 Fergus Reilly says he is mainly concerned about
   A   the size of the industries involved in processing the fish.
   B   the number of stages the fish pass through before being sold.
   C   the methods used by the fishing industry to maximise their catches.
   D   the financial motivation for the industry to continue over-fishing.

16 According to Reilly, how is Sustainable Fishing going about its campaign?
   A   It is increasing the amount of publicity in the media for the work it does.
   B   It is improving consumers' knowledge about the fish they are buying.
   C   It is persuading supermarkets to offer less endangered species for sale.
   D   It is encouraging suppliers to research into the sustainability of fish stocks.

17 What does Reilly say about the situation for the more popular fish species?
   A   It has proved impossible to convince people of the rate of their depletion.
   B   Scientists are under increasing pressure to rescue them from final collapse.
   C   The growing number of people in the world is adding to their vulnerability.
   D   Their survival depends on the fishing industry agreeing to unpopular controls.

18 The condition of fish sold in supermarkets is in question because
   A   customers are not reliably informed about when it was caught.
   B   it often has to travel a long distance after it has been landed.
   C   it may be sold as fresh when it has been previously frozen.
   D   retailers fail to check the word of salesmen about its age.

19 How does Sustainable Fishing find out what happens to fish after they are caught?
   A   It puts pressure on fishing companies to supply the information.
   B   It funds retailers to trace the supply chain and send back reports.
   C   It receives updates from environmental groups around the world.
   D   It makes use of technology to follow the fish's progress at all stages.

20 In order to motivate consumers to buy sustainably caught fish, retailers can
   A   display advertisements about the need to maintain healthy oceans.
   B   go into schools to give talks about the serious threat to fish stocks.
   C   bring down the price by preparing fish for sale without waste.
   D   employ chefs to create affordable dishes that are easy to cook.

Essential tips

Questions 21–25: Since you will probably not hear most of the key words in the options, you need to be prepared for words and expressions with a similar meaning. For example, instead of saying 'at school' (option A), the speaker might refer to a type of school, a certain class at school, the name of a school etc. Similarly, a speaker may use a word for a certain relative (option B), such as 'aunt', or even a description of who that person is, such as 'my sister's husband'.

Questions 26–30: Think about how someone might describe an activity to convey the idea that it is 'very dangerous' (option A), perhaps by saying what sort of accident might happen. What kind of language could be used to express this? And consider different ways of expressing the idea of 'spirit of cooperation' (option F): what would we call a 'group' in a sport?

Track 12

You will hear five short extracts in which people talk about children's free-time activities.

While you listen, you must complete both tasks.

TASK ONE

For questions **21–25**, choose from list **A–H**, the person who is speaking.

A   Our child began this activity at school.

Speaker 1 ⬚ 21

B   A relative was indirectly responsible for our child taking up this activity.

Speaker 2 ⬚ 22

C   A newspaper article sparked off interest in this activity.

Speaker 3 ⬚ 23

D   We encouraged our child to take up this activity.

Speaker 4 ⬚ 24

E   Our child began this activity as a result of a medical condition.

Speaker 5 ⬚ 25

F   A television programme inspired our child to take up this activity.

G   Our child became interested in this activity while staying with friends.

H   The idea for this activity came from reading about it.

TASK TWO

For questions **26–30**, choose from list **A–H** what view each speaker is expressing.

A   This activity is very dangerous.

Speaker 1 ⬚ 26

B   Our child's physical condition has improved.

Speaker 2 ⬚ 27

C   We were opposed to this activity at first.

Speaker 3 ⬚ 28

D   Our child takes this activity too seriously.

Speaker 4 ⬚ 29

E   We didn't understand what the activity entailed at first.

Speaker 5 ⬚ 30

F   This activity develops a spirit of co-operation.

G   This activity has become fashionable recently.

H   Our child has benefited socially.

Essential tips

Part 1: Think about the vocabulary you need for this topic. You should also consider which tenses are appropriate. For instance, you might say that your father *comes from* a certain city, using the present tense. But, if you want to say when he left that city, you could use a past tense. When you describe how long he has been living in that city, you will probably need to use the present perfect continuous.

Part 2: To describe how people might feel in a certain situation, or what might have happened, you need expressions that express possibility. For example, *he might be feeling*. However, to describe something that has happened, you will need to use appropriate past tenses.

Part 3: An emotion or an abstract concept can be interpreted in different ways. The concept of 'pride' can be positive or negative, for example, so you should be prepared to consider different aspects of the idea you have to talk about. Remember that the point here is not to convince the examiner or the other candidate of your opinion, but to show you can express your views convincingly, and reach a conclusion in an appropriate manner.

Part 4: In this part, you are asked to talk about actual events, or situations and to give your opinion. After answering the question, you may go on to talk more generally about the subject, but you should always show that you have understood the question, first.

Part 1 (2 minutes)

The examiner will ask you a few questions about yourself and about a general topic. For example, the examiner may ask you:

- Would you tell me something about the members of your family?
- Where are the members of your family from?
- Which people from your extended family do you have most contact with?

Part 2 (4 minutes)

You will each be asked to talk on your own for about a minute. You will each be given three different pictures to talk about. After your partner has finished speaking, you will be asked a brief question connected with your partner's photographs.

Departing (compare, contrast and speculate)

Turn to pictures 1–3 on page 175 which show people departing.

(*Candidate A*), it's your turn first. Here are your pictures. They show **people departing**.

I'd like you to compare and contrast **two** of the pictures and say **why you think the people are leaving, and how they might be feeling.**

(*Candidate B*), **in which picture does the departure seem most exciting? Why?**

Exhaustion (compare, contrast and speculate)

Turn to pictures 1–3 on page **176** which show people feeling tired.

Now, (*Candidate B*), here are your pictures. **They show tired people.**

I'd like you to compare and contrast **two** of these situations, and say **why the people might be tired. What kind of exhaustion – mental or physical – do they feel, and why?**

(*Candidate A*), **which type of exhaustion do you find most difficult to get over? Why?**

Part 3 (4 minutes)

Look at page 177 which gives some examples of things people are proud about.

Pride (discuss, evaluate and select)

Here are some different things people are proud about and a question for you to discuss.

First, you have some time to look at the task.

(*Pause 15 seconds*)

Now talk to each other about **why people feel proud about these things.**

Now you have about a minute to decide **which situation gives the most pride.**

Part 4 (5 minutes)

The examiner will encourage you to develop the topic of your discussion in Part 3 by asking questions such as:

- When was the last time you felt proud of something you had achieved?
- Do you think there are forms of pride that can be harmful?
- Would someone who never felt proud of himself or herself be unhappy?
- Are there times when you feel proud of other people? Can you give an example?

For questions **1–8**, read the text below and decide which answer (**A, B, C** or **D**) best fits each gap. There is an example at the beginning (**0**).

Mark your answers **on the separate answer sheet**.

Example:

0 **A** band **B** range **C** scale **D** scope

0	A	B	C	D

Raising awareness

In cities around the world, a wide (**0**) …….. of schemes is being instigated to promote environmental awareness. 'It's just as easy to (**1**) …….. of litter properly as it is to drop it on the streets,' says city councillor Mike Edwards. 'It's a question of encouraging people to do so as a (**2**) …….. of course. Once the habit is ingrained, they won't even (**3**) …….. they are doing it. After all, think what we've achieved with recycling in the home. People have become accustomed to it, so it doesn't (**4**) …….. to them that they're spending any additional time in the process. Only if they have to carry this waste for some appreciable distance to find a suitable container do they feel they are (**5**) …….. .

A quirky, (**6**) …….. gimmick might be enough to change behaviour. With this in (**7**) …….., the city of Berlin is introducing rubbish bins that say *danke*, *thank you* and *merci* when someone drops an item of rubbish into them. It might just (**8**) …….. the trick in this city, too.

1	**A** dispose	**B** discard	**C** dump	**D** dispense
2	**A** principle	**B** system	**C** matter	**D** duty
3	**A** notice	**B** remark	**C** comprehend	**D** appreciate
4	**A** concern	**B** occur	**C** impress	**D** strike
5	**A** inconvenienced	**B** sacrificed	**C** complicated	**D** imposed
6	**A** light-hearted	**B** mundane	**C** subjective	**D** intense
7	**A** context	**B** thought	**C** spirit	**D** mind
8	**A** serve	**B** do	**C** make	**D** play

For questions **9–16**, read the text below and think of the word which best fits each gap. Use only **one** word in each gap. There is an example at the beginning (**0**).

Write your answers **IN CAPITAL LETTERS on the separate answer sheet**.

Example: 0 H A V E ☐☐☐☐☐☐☐☐☐☐☐☐☐☐☐☐

Emotion in books

Something appears to (**0**) …….. happened to the emotional content of books published in the UK. Researchers from the University of Bristol analysed the frequency with (**9**) …….. 'mood' words – those reflecting anger, disgust, fear, joy, sadness and surprise – were used in as (**10**) …….. as 5 million books between 1900 and 2000. (**11**) …….. to one of the researchers, Dr Alberto Acerbi, 'the average book published in 1900 has 14% more emotional content than the average book in 2000.' In (**12**) …….. words, 'a book with 1,000 emotional words in 1900 would have 877 in 2000.'

In (**13**) …….. to this decline in emotional content, the research team found that some interesting differences between British books and those published in the USA have developed since the 1960s. (**14**) …….. having more emotional content than their British counterparts, American books now contain more content-free words. These are words that carry (**15**) …….. or no meaning on their (**16**) …….., such as *and* or *but*, and articles like *the*.

What is the significance of these changes? The researchers say that further work is needed to deal with this question adequately.

PAPER 1 Reading and ▶
        Use of English

PAPER 2 Writing

PAPER 3 Listening

PAPER 4 Speaking

Part 1
Part 2
Part 3
Part 4
Part 5
Part 6
Part 7
Part 8

For questions **17–24**, read the text below. Use the word given in capitals at the end of some of the lines to form a word that fits in the gap **in the same line**. There is an example at the beginning (**0**).

Write your answers **IN CAPITAL LETTERS on the separate answer sheet**.

Example: | 0 | N | O | T | O | R | I | E | T | Y | | | | | | | |

The black widow spider

The black widow spider's (**0**) .... is not without	**NOTORIOUS**
foundation. However, an element of exaggeration	
has led to certain (**17**) .... regarding its evil nature.	**CONCEPT**
Firstly, while it is indeed one of the most venomous	
species of spider, its venom being 15 times stronger	
than that of the prairie rattlesnake, its bite injects such	
a small amount of venom in (**18**) .... that it is unlikely	**COMPARE**
to kill humans. In fact (**19**), ... are rare.	**FATAL**
Black widows bite only if they are touched or their	
web is threatened, and only the adult female is poisonous.	
The female is (**20**) .... by nature, and has been known to	**SOLITUDE**
kill and eat the male after mating. Such (**21**) .... are rare,	**OCCUR**
but they explain how the spider got its name – and its	
reputation.	
Nevertheless, the (**22**) .... effects of this spider's bite	**PLEASE**
should not be (**23**) ...., and if you live in a certain climate	**ESTIMATE**
and have a fireplace in your home, it is advisable to take	
(**24**) .... Black widow spiders often inhabit wood piles,	**CAUTION**
so you should wear gloves when handling firewood.	

PAPER 1 Reading and
         Use of English

PAPER 2 Writing

PAPER 3 Listening

PAPER 4 Speaking

Part 1
Part 2
Part 3
Part 4
Part 5
Part 6
Part 7
Part 8

For questions **25–30**, complete the second sentence so that it has a similar meaning to the first sentence, using the word given. **Do not change the word given.** You must use between **three** and **six** words, including the word given. Here is an example (**0**).

Example:

0   Jane regretted speaking so rudely to the old lady.

MORE

Jane .... politely to the old lady.

Example: | **0** | WISHED SHE HAD SPOKEN MORE |

Write **only** the missing words **IN CAPITAL LETTERS on the separate answer sheet**.

---

25   This novel stands a very good chance of winning the book prize.

HIGHLY

It is .... win the book prize.

26   'You really must stay and have dinner with us!' Laura said to us.

STAYING

Laura .... for dinner.

27   If you need me, call me any time, night or day.

MATTER

Call me if you need me, ... be.

28   I don't want to be disturbed at all this morning!

ACCOUNT

On .... disturbed this morning!

29   If Mark hadn't told Bella about that letter, we wouldn't have argued.

FOR

Had .... telling Bella about that letter, we wouldn't have argued.

30   We're going to miss the start of the film if we don't hurry.

TIME

Unless we hurry, the film .... we get there.

PAPER 1 Reading and ▶
          Use of English

PAPER 2 Writing

PAPER 3 Listening

PAPER 4 Speaking

Part 1
Part 2
Part 3
Part 4
Part 5
Part 6
Part 7
Part 8

You are going to read a magazine article. For questions **31–36**, choose the answer (**A**, **B**, **C** or **D**) which you think fits best according to the text.

Mark your answers **on the separate answer sheet**.

Are you a 'slumper'?

Amanda Stevens cured her bad posture – and her chronic back pain – with the Alexander technique.

Many people will have heard of the Alexander technique but have only a vague idea what it is about. Until earlier this year, I didn't have the faintest idea about it – and saw no reason to think I should. But, hunched over a computer screen one day, I noticed that the neck and backache I regularly suffered were more painful than usual. I was brought up to think that the preferred way of dealing with aches and pains is to do nothing and hope they'll go away, but I eventually allowed myself to be dragged along by a friend of mine to talk to an osteopath who had performed wonders on her. After examining me, the osteopath said: 'I can treat the symptoms by massaging your neck and upper back. But you actually have bad posture. That is what you need to get sorted out. Go off and learn the Alexander technique.'

I had regularly been told by friends and family that I tend to slouch in chairs but had been under the impression that bad posture was something one was born with and could do nothing about. With hindsight, it's hard to believe just how far off the mark I was. Dentists and car mechanics, among others, tend to develop bad posture from leaning over patients or engine bays. Those of us who are mothers often stress and strain their necks and backs lifting and carrying children, and those who sit in front of computers all day are almost certainly not doing our bodies any favours.

After a little searching online, I found an Alexander technique teacher, Teresa Stirling, in my area of town and booked a first appointment. Three months later I am walking straighter and sitting better, while my neck and back pain are things of the past. I feel taller, too, which I may be imagining, but the technique can increase your height by up to five centimetres if you were badly slumped beforehand.

The teaching focuses on the neck, head and back. It trains you to use your body less harshly and to carry out the sorts of movements and actions that we do all the time with less effort. There is very little effort in the lessons themselves, which sets apart the Alexander technique from pilates or yoga, which are exercise-based. A typical lesson involves standing in front of a chair and learning to sit and stand with minimal effort. You spend some time lying on a bench with your knees bent to straighten the spine and relax your body while the teacher moves your arms and legs to train you to move them correctly.

The key is learning to break the bad habits accumulated over years. Try, for example, folding your arms the opposite way to normal. It feels odd, doesn't it? This is an example of a habit the body has formed which can be hard to break. Many of us carry our heads too far back and tilted skywards. The technique teaches you to let go of the muscles holding the head back, allowing it to resume its natural place on the summit of our spines. The head weighs four to six kilos, so any misalignment can cause problems for the neck and body.

The Alexander technique teaches you to observe how you use your body and how others use theirs – usually badly. Look how a colleague slumps back in a chair with his or her legs crossed. That puts all sorts of stresses and strains on the body. Even swimming can harm the neck. The Alexander technique can teach you to swim better, concentrating on technique rather than clocking up lengths.

So who was Alexander and how did he come up with the technique? Frederick Matthias Alexander, an Australian theatrical orator born in 1869, found in his youth that his voice was failing during performances. He analysed himself and realised his posture was bad. He worked on improving it, with dramatic results. He brought his technique to London 100 years ago and quickly gathered a following that included some very famous people. He died in 1955, having established a teacher-training school in London, which is thriving today.

So if you are slouching along the road one day, feeling weighed down by your troubles, give a thought to the Alexander technique. It could help you walk tall again.

31 What does the writer suggest in the first paragraph?
- **A** She had been reluctant to seek treatment for her back problems.
- **B** She was initially sceptical about the Alexander technique.
- **C** She had little faith in the osteopath's methods.
- **D** She was wrong to follow her friend's advice.

32 What does the writer say about bad posture in the second paragraph?
- **A** She had thought that it only affected people in certain occupations.
- **B** She had been told that she would inevitably suffer as a result of it.
- **C** She had misunderstood what the causes of it were.
- **D** She had developed it after having children.

33 What principle of the Alexander technique does the writer identify in the fourth paragraph?
- **A** A person's natural movements shouldn't be altered.
- **B** The Alexander technique shouldn't be attempted without supervision.
- **C** Familiar physical actions shouldn't be performed in a strenuous manner.
- **D** The Alexander technique shouldn't be combined with other types of exercise.

34 What does the writer say about bad habits in the fifth paragraph?
- **A** They are a consequence of actions we perform.
- **B** They inevitably cause physical pain.
- **C** They develop in early childhood.
- **D** They can be difficult to change.

35 What does the writer suggest about Frederick Alexander?
- **A** He was keen to make a name for himself.
- **B** He managed to recover his vocal powers.
- **C** He developed a form of exercise for actors.
- **D** He needed to leave home to develop his technique.

36 What is the writer's main purpose in the article?
- **A** To explain the widespread occurrence of back pain.
- **B** To suggest that back problems can be remedied.
- **C** To explain how debilitating backache can be.
- **D** To challenge common ideas about back pain.

PAPER 1 Reading and ▶
             Use of English
PAPER 2 Writing
PAPER 3 Listening
PAPER 4 Speaking

Part 1
Part 2
Part 3
Part 4
Part 5
Part 6
Part 7
Part 8

You are going to read four writers' contributions to a debate about hosting the Olympic Games. For questions **37–40**, choose from the contributions **A–D**. The contributions may be chosen more than once.

Mark your answers **on the separate answer sheet**.

Hosting the Olympics – is it a good idea?

Four writers give their views about what an Olympic Games can do for the host country.

A

The Olympics are undoubtedly expensive to stage and none of the Games in recent times have made an immediate profit, but they should be considered a long-term investment. The large infrastructure projects like new roads and transport systems, the new sports venues and cultural facilities, the regeneration of rundown urban areas and the increase in tourism all end up stimulating the economy eventually. The international media focus on the Games can also lift the host country's profile to another level. This has a knock-on effect on attitudes within the host country. International attention and proof of a capacity to rise to the challenge can pull the country together, make it feel good about itself and put it in a position to compete in the modern world.

B

Weighing up the pros and cons of hosting an Olympics is a complex business. Research suggests that few former hosts have experienced long-term economic gains. Indeed, certain cities like Montreal and Los Angeles have taken decades to pay off the debts incurred in preparing for and running the two-week-long event, and in cases like these, an unwelcome PR effect of international dimensions seems to come attached. The real benefits are less tangible in that they inspire a local feel-good factor, enhancing a sense of pride in belonging to a city and country that can pull off such a massive and awkward enterprise. There is also the chance for everyone, the younger generations in particular, to observe elite athletes, and therefore sporting excellence, exercise and fitness become cool things to aspire to.

C

For a host city, the Olympic Games are all about 'legacy'. They present an opportunity to showcase, domestically and to the world at large, the notion that the city possesses the know-how and manpower to manage a hugely complex international event, plus an impressive new infrastructure of sports facilities, accommodation and public transport, a vibrant, competent, friendly local population, and historic sites and places of natural beauty for tourists to visit. There is the sporting legacy too, with the greatest athletes from around the world inspiring mass participation, a crucial development when modern lifestyles tend to have a significantly detrimental effect on fitness and health. Critics of the notion of hosting the Olympics often focus on the more easily measurable economic implications which suggest that the Games are not a viable proposition, but the Olympics are not just about money; they are about other aspects of legacy which are at least as significant.

D

Most positive developments that might be associated with hosting the Olympics would happen anyway. The infrastructural investments could be made, incentives for tourists to visit could be offered and trade delegations could be energised. Past experience suggests the financial costs tend to outweigh the benefits anyway, when variables like the absurd bidding process, security and mismanagement are factored in. What of the more intangible spinoffs? First, there is no hard evidence that hosting the Olympics leads to greater public involvement in sports. In fact, studies show sporting activity actually fell in certain Olympic cities once the 'after-party enthusiasm' had worn off. Genuine long-term participation in sports comes from grassroots investment in schools and community facilities rather than glitzy shows. Most Olympic Games are concentrated in one city, usually the capital, and have little impact, economic or otherwise, on other parts of the country. In fact, in some cases, research reveals significant regional resentment about all the attention from government, the media and other organisations being directed at one city. So much for pride in one's country.

Which writer

has a different opinion to the others regarding the economic
impact of hosting the Olympics?

37 ☐

shares writer B's opinion about the implications for sport
in the host country?

38 ☐

expresses a different view to the others about the effect
that hosting the Olympics can have on a national sense of
identity?

39 ☐

takes a similar view to writer A about the likely
consequence for the host country's international reputation?

40 ☐

You are going to read a magazine article. Six paragraphs have been removed from the article. Choose from the paragraphs **A–G** the one which fits each gap (**41–46**). There is one extra paragraph which you do not need to use.

Mark your answers **on the separate answer sheet**.

Close encounters of the wild kind

The rise of wildlife-watching experiences.

Wildlife observation has always proved inspirational for humans. It led Charles Darwin to provide us with a better understanding of how we evolved and it has inspired such everyday innovations as Velcro. US author Peter Matthiessen wrote: 'The variety of life in nature can be compared to a vast library of unread books, and the plundering of nature is comparable to the random discarding of whole volumes without having opened them and learned from them.'

41	

'What is interesting is how much people are willing to pay to be in a wilderness environment,' says Julian Matthews, director of Discovery Initiatives, a company which takes people on small–group trips to more than 35 countries. 'It's still a small part of the tourism industry but it's undoubtedly expanding. There are definitely more and more people seeking wildlife experiences now.'

42	

Matthews recognises the contribution that television has made to our knowledge of nature, but he says 'there's no way to compare seeing an animal in the wild with watching one on TV. While a filmmaker may spend six months shooting an animal and will get closer to it than you ever will, there's no greater pleasure than seeing an animal in its own environment. On film, you're only getting the visuals and the sound. As impressive as they may be, it's not the real thing.' And the good thing is that tourists can now watch wildlife 'live' while helping to protect it – a concept that comes under the broad label of 'ecotourism'.

43	

In practice, this means that many tour operators, guided by ethical policies, now use the services of local communities, train local guides and have close ties to conservation projects. Tour operator Rekero, for example, has established its own school – the Koyiaki Guide School and Wilderness Camp – for Maasai people in Kenya.

44	

Conservation organisations have also realised that tourism can help educate people and provide a valuable source of revenue and even manpower. The World Wildlife Fund, for example, runs trips that give donors the chance to see for themselves how their financial aid is assisting conservation projects in the field, and some organisations even allow tourists to take part in research and conservation.

45	

Similarly, Biosphere Expeditions takes about 200 people every year on what its field operations director, Dr Matthias Hammer, calls an 'adventure with a conscience'. Volunteers can visit six destinations around the world and take part in various activities including snow leopard, wolf and bear surveys and whale and dolphin research.

46	

Of course, going in search of wildlife doesn't always mean you will find it. That sightings of animals in large wild areas don't come automatically is a fact of life. Although potentially frustrating, it makes sightings all the more rewarding when they are made. And the opportunity to do something to help both the environment and local people can only add to the experience.

A He is confident that, if done properly, this combination of tourism and conservation can be 'a win–win situation'. 'People have a unique experience while contributing to conservation directly. Local people and habitats benefit through job creation, research and an alternative income. Local wildlife benefits from our work.'

B While there is indeed much to learn from many species not yet known to science, it's the already opened texts that attract the majority of us, however. And we are attracted in ever increasing numbers.

C As people are able to travel to more extreme places in search of the ultimate wildlife experience, it's worth remembering that you don't have to go to the ends of the earth to catch rewarding glimpses of animals. Indeed, some of the best wildlife-watching opportunities are on our doorstep.

D This growth has been stimulated by the efforts of conservation groups and natural history documentaries. Greater awareness of the planet has led to an increased demand for wildlife tours or the addition of a wildlife-watching component to traditional holidays. People want to discover nature at first-hand for themselves – not just on a screen.

E Despite being an important part of the population there, they have largely been excluded from the benefits brought to the region by tourism. This initiative is a concerted effort to enable them to take up jobs and run programmes themselves.

F Earthwatch is a non-profit international environmental group that does just that. 'Participation in an Earthwatch project is a positive alternative to wildlife-watching expeditions, as we offer members of the public the opportunity to be on the front line of conservation,' says Claudia Eckardt, Earthwatch programme manager.

G It is a term which is overused, but the principle behind it undoubtedly offers hope for the future of many endangered species, as money from tourism directly funds conservation work. It also extends to the consideration of the interests of people living in the places that tourists visit.

PAPER 1	Reading and ▸	Part 1
	Use of English	Part 2
PAPER 2	Writing	Part 3
PAPER 3	Listening	Part 4
PAPER 4	Speaking	Part 5
		Part 6
		Part 7
		Part 8

You are going to read reviews of four psychology books. For questions **47–56**, choose from the books (**A–D**).

Mark your answers **on the separate answer sheet**.

About which book is each following point made?

It is likely to put certain kinds of people off. **47** ☐

It has aims which resemble those in other recently published books. **48** ☐

It offers unnecessary advice to readers. **49** ☐

It makes seemingly original but convincing observations. **50** ☐

It avoids obvious answers to an issue which is familiar to many people. **51** ☐

It may prompt the publication of other books exploring the same subject matter. **52** ☐

It is organised differently from other writing by the same author. **53** ☐

It lacks a clear structure. **54** ☐

It challenges a modern trend in psychology. **55** ☐

It is difficult to understand in places. **56** ☐

Reviews of psychology books

A *Missing Out: In Praise of the Unlived Life* by Adam Phillips

In *Missing Out*, a slim volume peppered with insights that may never have been expressed quite like this before but which make you want to scrawl 'yes' in the margins on almost every page, the psychoanalyst and writer Adam Phillips asserts that we all 'learn to live somewhere between the lives we have and the lives we would like'. For 'modern' people, 'the good life is ... filled to the full'; we seek complete satisfaction. But what we need, argues Phillips, isn't satisfaction but frustration. You can't get instant satisfaction because you can't control people or the world. You can't 'get' other people because no one can be fully understood and neither, of course, can you. But a capacity for tolerating frustration allows us to develop. Appropriately, given the subject matter, this book can be a frustrating read – sometimes you think you're just getting to grips with an idea, only for it to slip away. But, as is often true of Phillips's books, what you do feel when you've finished it is that it offers glimpses of the real, messy and never fully knowable human heart.

B *Together* by Richard Sennett

Together is the second book in a planned trilogy about the skills modern humans need for a happy co-existence. The first addressed the joys of making things with your hands, and the third will be about cities. This one looks at how we can all get along together. Sennett explores the importance of equality and how, in unequal societies, people are less willing to co-operate. He argues that our society is becoming atomised, 'deskilling people in practising co-operation'. The trouble is it all feels atomised itself. Sennett's argument seems to bounce from place to place, and he relies on anecdotes and experience more than data. It aims to be a practical, how-to guide for maximising co-operation, but ends up a sort of unsystematic self-help book: listening is as important a skill as the presentation of your own ideas; discussion need not reach agreement but can teach us new things; assertiveness is valuable, but so is politeness and diffidence. All true, but don't we know it already?

C *Teach Us To Sit Still* by Tim Parks

A few years ago, a number of writers dealt movingly about what it's like to have a serious illness. If *Teach Us to Sit Still* does well, we could be in for a glut of writing by people who don't have much wrong with them, yet still write about it at length. But if they are anything like as good as this, it might not be such a gloomy prospect. A few years ago, Tim Parks couldn't sleep and had serious pains in his side. Medical tests all came back negative, but the pain persisted. So, he embarked on a sceptical exploration of the possible causes of and cures for his woes. He tried out an array of theories and therapies. The intensity of Park's search makes for a less than relaxing read, and, in all probability, there will be readers who fail to make it past the first couple of chapters. Parks, an innovative and prolific novelist, writes wonderfully however, and despite the subject matter, a layer of wit runs through it. Parks eventually achieves some relief through special breathing exercises and meditation, but uncovers no magic formulas.

D *The Antidote* by Oliver Burkeman

Should we all be striving for happiness? Should we think positively? Should we try to ignore any difficult thoughts, feelings, or situations that arise? Many self-help books these days would shout 'Yes!' Oliver Burkeman isn't so sure. A leading writer in what could be called the 'anti-self-help self-help' genre – which happily seems to be swelling – Burkeman's work, as represented in *The Antidote*, is not about positive thinking, finding partners, and getting promotions at work and doesn't offer facile instructions for living a happy, easy life. Rather, it uses research to suggest that we reconsider our assumptions and find new ways of thinking and being. *Help! How to Become Slightly Happier*, his previous book, comprised a series of short sections, each a page or two long, which presented an idea fairly quickly. *The Antidote* has just eight chapters and each one explores a subject like success and failure in detail. So what are his conclusions? Well, one is that we have to stop searching for firm answers and quick fixes.

You **must** answer this question. Write your answer in **220–260** words in an appropriate style on the separate answer sheet.

1 Your principal has suggested a project in which groups of students spend three days on a survival exercise, living in a remote place where they have to organise their own shelter, food and heat. You have made the notes below.

> **The reasoning behind this proposal:**
>
> - self-sufficiency
> - insight into different living conditions
> - teamwork

> **Some opinions expressed by students:**
>
> 'It could be dangerous.'
>
> 'Three days is too short to gain any new insight.'
>
> 'Participants would need considerable preparation.'

Write an **essay** discussing **two** of the arguments in your notes. You should **explain which argument you think is more important** and **provide reasons** to support your opinion.

You may, if you wish, make use of the opinions expressed in the discussion, but you should use your own words as far as possible.

Write an answer to **one** of the questions **2–4** in this part. Write your answer in **220–260** words in an appropriate style on the separate answer sheet. Put the question number in the box at the top of the page.

2 You are a regular contributor to an online magazine called *Film Scene.* You have been asked to write a review of two films which you saw recently, and of which most people had great expectations. You enjoyed one of the films, but found the other one very disappointing.

   Write your **review.**

3 You have been in your first job for a few months. A friend is about to start work and is feeling nervous about it. She wants your advice about how to prepare for the world of work, what to expect and how to behave. Write an email telling her about your experiences and giving her tips on how to cope.

   Write your **email.**

4 Your class is doing a project on endangered species, and you have recently visited a zoo where green spaces have been created for rearing rare animals in captivity. Write a report on green spaces for wildlife in the area where you live, and describe what could be done to create more green spaces.

   Write your **report.**

Track 13

You will hear three different extracts. For questions **1–6**, choose the answer (**A**, **B** or **C**) which fits best according to what you hear. There are two questions for each extract.

Extract One

You hear part of an interview with a woman who has changed her lifestyle.

1   The idea for buying an olive farm came from
    A   a contact in Greece.
    B   Kathy's husband.
    C   a site on the internet.

2   Kathy says she had expected to
    A   miss her home and family in Britain.
    B   find life in Greece more difficult.
    C   feel nostalgic about her old job.

Extract Two

You hear part of a radio discussion in which two teachers are talking about teaching poetry.

3   The man feels that generally poetry
    A   is not taken seriously by teachers.
    B   is not a popular subject to teach.
    C   makes for an uninspiring lesson.

4   The woman's main argument is that
    A   teachers should encourage students to respond to poetry in their own way.
    B   students need guidance if they are to understand and appreciate poetry.
    C   only the poet can give us a valid interpretation of his or her work.

Extract Three

You hear two people talking about an unusual kind of competition.

5   According to Jake, he stopped at the pub
    A   out of curiosity.
    B   to eat something.
    C   to meet someone.

6   The object of the competition is to
    A   tell the most convincing lie.
    B   tell the funniest anecdote.
    C   tell the most obvious tall story.

PAPER 1 Reading and
Use of English

PAPER 2 Writing

PAPER 3 Listening ▶

PAPER 4 Speaking

Part 1
Part 2
Part 3
Part 4

Track 14

You will hear part of a talk by a the director of a sports academy. For questions **7–14**, complete the sentences with a word or a short phrase.

THE WATERMAN SPORTS ACADEMY

The Waterman Sports Academy offers training in several sports, including
swimming and (**7**) ....

Helen coached a girl who wanted to compete in the
(**8**) ....

Her interest in sports medicine dates back to the time when her
(**9**) .... suffered a back injury.

To be successful in a particular sport, an athlete must have
the right (**10**) ....

Helen says that fitness is important, even in sports like
(**11**) ....

She stresses that a (**12**) .... is vital in physical
development.

Athletes who do not have the latest (**13**) ....
are handicapped in competitions.

In Helen's opinion, the most important factor for success is having the
right (**14**) ....

Track 15

You will hear part an interview with Jon Kennedy, an engineer who works on oil rigs. For questions **15–20**, choose the answer (**A**, **B**, **C** or **D**) which fits best according to what you hear.

15 What does Jon Kennedy say about his present job?
   A His work on accident prevention is the most interesting part of it.
   B He would prefer to spend less time doing paper work in the office.
   C He is annoyed at the level of confidentiality his company demands.
   D The location of the rig is inconvenient for workers taking shore leave.

16 Where oil workers are concerned, Jon feels
   A the industry could make an effort to attract a wider range of recruits.
   B college graduates should be more open-minded about a career in the industry.
   C it is regrettable that some engineers feel discouraged about entering the industry.
   D the industry is important because of the opportunities offered to unskilled workers.

17 Jon expresses pride in the drill ship because
   A it is able to withstand extreme weather.
   B it drills wells at maximum subsea depths.
   C it is the newest ship to have been constructed.
   D it cost more to build than other ships of its type.

18 What does Jon say about arriving on the ship?
   A He enjoys meeting up with his co-workers again.
   B He looks forward to getting down to work.
   C He always finds the flight out very exciting.
   D He listens carefully to the safety briefing.

19 Jon says the workers on the rig
   A come to him when they need advice on any problem.
   B are polite to him because he has a high-ranking position.
   C have little time to relax because their jobs are very demanding.
   D don't know each other well because they belong to different companies.

20 What does Jon say gives him particular enjoyment in his current job?
   A developing systems that increase safety for the rig's personnel
   B dealing with emergencies that could be expensive for his company
   C saving money by identifying potential failure in the rig's equipment
   D devising technology to improve the efficiency of the drilling gear

Track 16

You will hear five short extracts in which people talk about their experiences at the theatre.

While you listen, you must complete both tasks.

TASK ONE

For questions **21–25**, choose from list **A–H**, what each speaker says about the show he or she enjoyed most.

A   The atmosphere was intimate.

Speaker 1	21

B   I loved the period costumes.

| Speaker 2 | 22 |

C   The play was very moving.

| Speaker 3 | 23 |

D   I saw the play a couple of times.

| Speaker 4 | 24 |

E   The play had a large cast.

| Speaker 5 | 25 |

F   I went along reluctantly.

G   The star of the show was very talented.

H   The show was performed by a foreign company.

TASK TWO

For questions **26–30**, choose from list **A–H** the view each speaker has about why theatre is an interesting medium.

A   The thrill of watching big stars is unforgettable.

Speaker 1	26

B   You can get carried away by the performance.

| Speaker 2 | 27 |

C   The theatre can be a communal experience.

| Speaker 3 | 28 |

D   It is interesting to learn from the cast.

| Speaker 4 | 29 |

E   Ideas can be conveyed with stunning force.

| Speaker 5 | 30 |

F   Each performance is a unique experience.

G   You sometimes feel transported to a different era.

H   The theatre can surprise and stimulate the audience.

Part 1 (2 minutes)

The examiner will ask you a few questions about yourself and about a general topic. For example, the examiner may ask you:

- What do you enjoy doing when you go away for a holiday?
- How would you describe the best holiday you have ever had?
- What sorts of things can spoil a holiday for you?

Part 2 (4 minutes)

You will each be asked to talk on your own for about a minute. You will each be given three different pictures to talk about. After your partner has finished speaking, you will be asked a brief question connected with your partner's photographs.

> **Sports** (compare, contrast and speculate)

Turn to pictures 1–3 on page 178 which show people taking part in different sports.

(*Candidate A*), it's your turn first. Here are your pictures. They show **people taking part in different sports**.

I'd like you to compare and contrast **two** of the pictures and say **what kind of training each of these sports requires. What are the advantages and disadvantages of taking part in a team sport, as opposed to an individual sport?**

(*Candidate B*), **which of these sports would you find most enjoyable? Why?**

> **Accommodation** (compare, contrast and speculate)

Turn to pictures 1–3 on page 179 which show different homes.

Now, (*Candidate B*), here are your pictures. **They show places where people live**.

I'd like you to compare and contrast **two** of these homes, and say **what you think would be the advantages and disadvantages of living in each one, and what might be the impractical aspects of living there.**

(*Candidate A*), **which of these homes do you think is the most practical? Why?**

Part 3 (4 minutes)

Look at page 180 which gives some examples for reducing the use of cars in a city.

> **Transport** (discuss, evaluate and select)

Here are some different ideas for reducing the use of cars in a city and a question for you to discuss.

First, you have some time to look at the task.

(*Pause 15 seconds*)

Now talk to each other about **how practical each idea is.**

Now you have about a minute to decide **which idea is most likely to improve a city.**

Part 4 (5 minutes)

The examiner will encourage you to develop the topic of your discussion in Part 3 by asking questions such as:

- Should private cars be banned from city centres? (Why? / Why not?)
- What do you think could be done in your area to encourage people to use public transport?
- Some cities encourage people to take passengers in their cars to reduce congestion. Do you think this is a good idea, and would it work in your area? (Why? / Why not?)

For questions **1–8**, read the text below and decide which answer (**A, B, C** or **D**) best fits each gap. There is an example at the beginning (**0**).

Mark your answers **on the separate answer sheet.**

Example:

| 0 | A | rises | B | strikes | C | arrives | D | hits |

| 0 | A | B | C | D |

Mountain rescue in Scotland

Last year, over 200 climbers were rescued from the mountains of Scotland by local teams, who go out in all weathers whenever disaster (**0**) .... Many of these people are volunteers, giving their time and energy freely and, on (**1**) ...., putting themselves in danger. They will risk life and (**2**) .... in an emergency when they are (**3**) .... on upon to rescue foolhardy or unlucky climbers. A whole (**4**) .... of things can go wrong up in the mountains, from sudden, violent storms with virtually zero visibility to unforeseen accidents, and many walkers and climbers owe a huge (**5**) .... of gratitude to the rescue teams!

While rescue teams often work for little or no pay, there are still considerable costs (**6**) .... in maintaining an efficient service. Equipment such as ropes and stretchers is of (**7**) .... importance, as are vehicles and radio communications devices. Although some of the costs are borne by the government, the rescue teams couldn't operate without (**8**) .... from the public. Fortunately, these tend to be very generous.

1	**A** situation	**B** event	**C** moment	**D** occasion
2	**A** limb	**B** blood	**C** bone	**D** flesh
3	**A** pulled	**B** called	**C** summoned	**D** required
4	**A** scope	**B** extent	**C** host	**D** scale
5	**A** recognition	**B** liability	**C** debt	**D** claim
6	**A** implied	**B** involved	**C** featured	**D** connected
7	**A** lively	**B** main	**C** essential	**D** vital
8	**A** grants	**B** allowances	**C** donations	**D** aids

For questions **9–16**, read the text below and think of the word which best fits each gap. Use only **one** word in each gap. There is an example at the beginning (**0**).

Write your answers **IN CAPITAL LETTERS on the separate answer sheet**.

Example: | 0 | A | S | | | | | | | | | | | | | | | | | | | | | |

The ubiquitous shopping mall

It started, (**0**) ...., many modern trends have, in the United States, but it has now spread to many parts of the world. Many towns and cities no (**9**) .... have a genuine centre. Instead, a shopping mall somewhere on the outskirts serves some of the functions of an urban centre. Here, shops and banks are all crowded together, (**10**) ...., especially for those who use a car, is very convenient. After (**11**) .... parked in the basement car park, people can do all their shopping inside the mall, and then load up the car and drive home. (**12**) .... is no need even to go outside, so it doesn't matter what the weather's (**13**) ....

So why should anyone possibly object (**14**) .... the growing number of shopping malls springing up in and around our cities? (**15**) .... of the main reasons is that when most shops are concentrated in malls, it leaves city and town centres deserted and lifeless. Another is that malls all tend to look very similar, (**16**) .... the result that many towns and cities are losing their individual characters.

For questions **17–24**, read the text below. Use the word given in capitals at the end of some of the lines to form a word that fits in the gap **in the same line**. There is an example at the beginning (**0**).

Write your answers **IN CAPITAL LETTERS on the separate answer sheet**.

Example: | 0 | D | A | I | L | Y | | | | | | | | | | | | | | | |

Blogging in the modern day

The earliest blogs tended to be personal accounts of	
(**0**) …….. events. Very soon, however, many types emerged	**DAY**
including critical news commentaries, often well-informed	
and (**17**) …….. expressed. With many millions of bloggers	**ELOQUENCE**
now writing on almost every (**18**) …….. subject each day,	**CONCEIVE**
the traditional media cannot afford to ignore them or	
treat them with (**19**) …….. . Their ubiquity means they have	**RESPECT**
become increasingly (**20**) ……..., as can be seen in the number	**INFLUENCE**
of 'official' news stories that are (**21**) …….. or called into	**CREDIT**
question by bloggers, and also the numerous stories	
initiated through blogs.	
Most large media organisations have now (**22**) ……..	**CORPORATE**
some form of blogging into their news services, but	
independent bloggers still have a freedom unavailable	
to mainstream journalists. They bypass editors and	
publishers, who tend to distort stories. The material	
on blogs is raw, (**23**) …….. by editors, and often harsh and	**MODIFY**
direct in its criticism of the way news is reported by the	
traditional media. Thus, bloggers act as a kind of media	
watchdog, able to check facts and verify or, alternatively,	
(**24**) …….. information in a way that mainstream journalists	**PROOF**
are often unable to.	

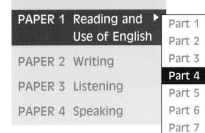
For questions **25–30**, complete the second sentence so that it has a similar meaning to the first sentence, using the word given. **Do not change the word given.** You must use between **three** and **six** words, including the word given. Here is an example (**0**).

Example:

0 Jane regretted speaking so rudely to the old lady.

MORE

Jane .... politely to the old lady.

Example: | **0** | WISHED SHE HAD SPOKEN MORE |

Write **only** the missing words **IN CAPITAL LETTERS on the separate answer sheet**.

---

25 'Mr Brown, a holiday would do you good,' said Dr Mansley.

FROM

'Mr Brown, you .... a holiday,' said Dr Mansley.

26 We were never aware at any moment that something was wrong.

TIME

At .... that something was wrong.

27 If Gary hadn't had that accident, he would have become a professional football player.

FOR

If it .... , Gary would have become a professional football player.

28 We get on very well with Laura's parents.

TERMS

We .... Laura's parents.

29 This wardrobe is so big that I don't believe only one person assembled it.

HAVE

This wardrobe is so big that it .... together by only one person.

30 Someone snatched Sue's bag at the concert.

HAD

Sue .... at the concert.

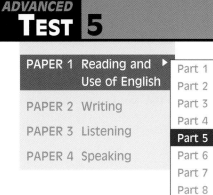

You are going to read a newspaper article. For questions **31–36**, choose the answer (**A**, **B**, **C** or **D**) which you think fits best according to the text.

Mark your answers **on the separate answer sheet**.

The land under the sea

Underwater maps reveal a hidden history

Ten thousand years ago, as the last ice age drew to a close, sea levels around the world were far lower than they are today. Much of the land under both the North Sea to the east of Britain and the English Channel which now separates France and Britain was part of a huge region of forests and grassy plains, where herds of horses and reindeer roamed free and people lived in villages by the lakes and rivers. Then the climate gradually became warmer (a phenomenon certainly not confined to our own age!) and the water trapped in glaciers and ice caps was released. This ancient land was submerged in the resulting deluge and all that remains to tell us that it was once lush and verdant – and inhabited – is the occasional stone tool, harpoon or mammoth tusk brought up from the seabed by fishing boats.

Now the development of advanced sonar technology, known as *bathymetry*, is making it possible to study this flooded landscape in extraordinary detail. A special echo sounder is fixed to the bottom of a survey vessel, and it makes wide sweeps across the seabed. While previous technology has only been able to produce two-dimensional images, bathymetry can now deploy computers, satellite-positioning equipment and special software to create accurate and remarkably detailed maps. For the first time, an ancient riverbed leaps out of the three-dimensional image, complete with rocky ledges rising up from the bottom of the valley. The sites of pre-historic settlements can now be pinpointed, and it is also possible to see in stunning detail the sunken shipwrecks that litter this part of the seabed.

According to archaeologist Dr Linda Andrews, this technological development is of huge significance. 'We now have the ability to map the seabed as accurately as we can map dry land,' she says. She is, however, scathing about the scale of financial support for such projects. 'We have better images of Mars and Venus than of two-thirds of our own planet! Britain is an interesting case. It's been a a maritime nation for much of its history, and the sea has had such a massive influence on it, and in view of this, it's an absolute scandal that we know so little about the area just off the country's shores!'

Once bathymetric techniques have identified sites where people might have built their homes and villages, such as sheltered bays, cliffs with caves and the shores of freshwater lakes, divers can be sent down to investigate further. Robot submarines can also be used, and researchers hope they will find stone tools and wood from houses (which survives far longer in water than on dry land) as proof of human activity. The idea shared by many people in Britain of their country as a natural island kingdom will be challenged by these findings: Britain has been inhabited for about 500,000 years, and for much of this time, it has been linked on and off to continental Europe. It remains to be seen how far this new awareness is taken on board, however.

In fact, the use of bathymetry scanners will not be limited to the study of lost landscapes and ancient settlements. It will also be vital in finding shipwrecks. Records show that there are about 44,000 shipwrecks off the shores of Britain, but there is good reason to believe that the real figure is much higher. In addition, commercial applications are a real possibility. Aggregates for the construction industry are becoming increasingly expensive, and bathymetry scanners can be used to identify suitable sites for quarrying this material. However, mapping the seabed will also identify places where rare plants and shellfish are living. Government legislation could prevent digging at such sites, either to extract material for a profit or to make the water deeper. This is significant in view of the plans to dredge parts of the English Channel to provide deeper waterways for massive container ships.

31 What point is made in the first paragraph about the area now under the sea?

- **A** The fact that it was populated has only recently been discovered.
- **B** It was created by the last ice age.
- **C** Ancient man-made objects have been found there.
- **D** It was flooded, drowning the inhabitants.

32 How does the new sonar technology work?

- **A** It has an echo sounder placed on the seabed.
- **B** It produces two-dimensional images of the sea floor.
- **C** It makes use of a number of different devices.
- **D** It bases its calculations on the location of archaeological sites.

33 How does Dr Andrews feel about the lack of accurate maps of the waters around Britain?

- **A** outraged
- **B** resigned
- **C** astonished
- **D** amused

34 In the fourth paragraph, the writer suggests that a better understanding of the settlements on the seabed may

- **A** inspire more people to take an interest in archaeology.
- **B** modify the attitudes of the British to their country's history.
- **C** provide confirmation about the need to deal with climate change.
- **D** alter the perception people in other countries have about Britain.

35 Quarrying is mentioned in the final paragraph to show that

- **A** there are ways of obtaining funds for research.
- **B** underwater surveys should be completed as soon as possible.
- **C** damage to the seabed has not been recorded accurately so far.
- **D** there are potentially practical benefits for industry.

36 The use of bathymetry scanners may help to

- **A** preserve the marine environment.
- **B** promote the clearing of the English Channel.
- **C** identify new species of plants and animals.
- **D** obtain approval to look for shipwrecks.

PAPER 1 Reading and ▶ Part 1
         Use of English   Part 2

PAPER 2 Writing   Part 3
                         Part 4
PAPER 3 Listening   Part 5

PAPER 4 Speaking   **Part 6**
                         Part 7
                         Part 8

You are going to read extracts from four reviews of a book about the way children are brought up. For questions **37–40**, choose from the reviews **A–D**. The reviews may be chosen more than once.

Mark your answers **on the separate answer sheet**.

Kith: the riddle of the childscape by Jay Griffiths

Four reviewers comment on Jay Griffiths' new book.

A

In this new book, Jay Griffiths draws the familiar but erroneous conclusion that traditional societies and tribes treat nature and children better than modern ones. She is no anthropologist, writing more like a romantic poet about nature and people's identification with the place they grow up in. To justify her admiration for tribal practice, she cites a 2007 UNICEF report that ranked the UK lowest among 21 industrialised countries for the well-being of its children. No analysis of this finding is provided, however. Instead, a single idea of lost childhood freedom is dressed up in excessively poetic, at times, absurd language, and applied to various cultures. According to Griffiths, what children in Britain and similar countries lack is access to nature and the freedom to express their true selves in it. The idea of 'kith', an attachment to your 'home territory' is an interesting one, but the claims she makes about children's development are too often illogical and unsupportable.

B

In a 2007 UNICEF report, the UK came last among 21 industrialised countries for the well-being of its children. Jay Griffiths' question is: why do they feel so unhappy? Her main answer, passionately and eloquently expressed, is that they are 'imprisoned' indoors in front of their TV or computer screens and have lost contact with their kith – the woods, mountains, rivers, streams and wilds of their home territory. There's definitely something in this idea, but the trouble is that Griffiths pursues it in ways that simply don't hold up. Part of the problem is that she regards children as originally innocent and good, and that these characteristics are suppressed by the restrictions imposed on them. As parents have known for millennia, however, children are far more complex than that. She is also guilty of selective deployment of evidence. That same UNICEF report found that children in the UK are healthier and safer than ever before, for example.

C

Jay Griffiths is a self-confessed romantic, believing in the innate purity of children and a need for them to be close to nature, mystery and risk and be gloriously free. She warns us, however, that children in the West today are caged indoors and deprived of their 'kith', a natural domain of woodland, play, solitude, animals, adventure and time to daydream. It's a fascinating proposition, fluently and vividly delivered. But this book is also deeply frustrating. Griffiths ignores all the science that shows that children are, in fact, far from being the simple innocents of romantic tradition. She also fails to provide convincing evidence for her assertion that children in Euro-American cultures are less happy than other children. She refers to a UNESCO report on children's well-being in the UK, Spain and Sweden to support her argument about the importance of the outdoors. That report, however, finds that well-being depends on many factors like time with family, good relationships with friends, involvement in creative and sporting activities, as well as being outdoors.

D

In Euro-American culture, argues Griffiths, infants often lack closeness with their parents and wider families, which leaves psychological scars. Simultaneously, older children are controlled, denied access to natural spaces and pushed through a school system designed to produce employees but not psychologically rounded citizens. Parents refuse to let children play outdoors for fear of over-hyped risks, and in so doing, deny children access to the outer worlds of private, unwatched play so vital to their psychological development. The natural playgrounds of childhood, the fields and woods, have been lost to most children. The result, as the UNICEF surveys of well-being that Griffiths, quotes reveal, is a generation of children who are unhappy and unfulfilled. Her warning message is made particularly compelling by the rare vitality and admirable energy in Griffiths' writing.

Which scientist

has a different opinion from the others about
Griffiths' style of writing?

| 37 | |

shares reviewer A's view of the way Griffiths
develops her ideas about the treatment of children?

| 38 | |

expresses a different view from the others about
the use Griffiths makes of data gathered internationally
about children?

| 39 | |

has a similar opinion to reviewer B about Griffiths'
depiction of children's basic nature?

| 40 | |

PAPER 1 Reading and ▸
         Use of English

PAPER 2 Writing

PAPER 3 Listening

PAPER 4 Speaking

Part 1
Part 2
Part 3
Part 4
Part 5
Part 6
Part 7
Part 8

You are going to read a newspaper article in which a zoology student talks about her experience of doing practical research in an area of rainforest. Six paragraphs have been removed from the article. Choose from the paragraphs **A–G** the one which fits each gap (**41–46**). There is one extra paragraph which you do not need to use.

Mark your answers **on the separate answer sheet**.

Fieldwork in the rainforest of Ecuador – the experiences of a zoology student

When I was at school, I was a huge fan of TV wildlife programmes, and at a certain point I realised that somehow the natural world would have to be part of my life. So here I am a few years later, in the tropical rainforest of eastern Ecuador, a novice field scientist. The word scientist evokes various images, typically perhaps ones of laboratories and white coats, test tubes and lab rats. But what does it mean to be a field scientist?

41

I am currently spending a year at a small scientific research station in a remote patch of the Ecuadorian rainforest belonging to the Kichwa community of San José de Payamino. It is glorious – everything you would expect a tropical rainforest location to be, and a world away from my university in the UK. The air is hot and thick, the trees are densely packed, and everywhere is teeming with life.

42

The local people own the land and govern themselves, but the Ecuadorian government also provides for them: a school complete with computer room and satellite internet, for instance. Each year, they vote for a new president and vice-president, who organise the democratic community meetings. Each family has a *finca* in the forest: a wooden home on stilts.

43

But my normal life here as a work experience student revolves mainly around my personal research, which is a biodiversity study of frogs. I am trying to establish exactly which species are here, where and when I can find them, and what condition they are in.

44

For most of the time, I am just crawling along looking at leaves. Much of field research is like this. It isn't all finding new species and being transfixed by exotic wildlife behaviour. Have you ever seen the behind-the-scenes footage at the end of many nature documentaries, where it turns out a cameraman has been sitting in a tree for three days waiting for a bird to dance? Research is like this – laborious and monotonous – but it can be rewarding too.

45

Being a field scientist basically means being an academic, collecting data and publishing scientific papers. It's interesting but it doesn't pay well, and getting started can be tough. When I was looking for work experience, there were plenty of openings with pharmaceutical companies, but very few matching my desire to explore and investigate wildlife.

46

This is one reason I count myself lucky to be involved in this project. It's largely funded by my university, so I can afford it. Then, by the end of this year, I will have acquired valuable skills, and I am hopeful that the experience will facilitate my progression into post-graduate study.

A To do this, I walk slowly along several paths in the forest, accompanied by a local guide, and at night equipped with a torch. When I spot what I'm looking for, I feel an intense adrenaline rush. Will I manage to capture it? Have I collected this particular species yet?

B Because of this, and having experienced fieldwork, I've decided it's definitely something I would like to do as a career. Once this year is over, I will ask my lecturers to advise me what to do next.

C This morning, for example, a half metre square of mushrooms sprouted on the dirt floor of my kitchen. My favourite time here is in the early evenings. It's finally cool enough to be comfortable, and the nocturnal creatures begin their nightly cacophony, while the setting sun paints the trees orange.

D The reality is, however, that to make your way you need to build up a range of contacts and a portfolio of work. Many of the initial work opportunities that do exist are voluntary – in fact, you often have to pay to join a scheme. A student job where you are paid expenses, let alone a basic salary, is quite rare.

E By and large, they work outdoors, and are interested in pretty much everything from discovering new species to the effect of obscure parasites on ecosystems. They explore and investigate, aiming to understand what they observe. Just two years into my undergraduate zoology degree, I don't quite qualify as one yet, but hopefully I'm heading that way.

F They have their own traditions, too. One day, a local lady was bitten by a lethal snake; whilst I administered shots of anti-venom to her, the local traditional healer, was applying plant remedies to the wound and attempting to suck the venom from it. At least one of the treatments must have worked because she recovered.

G And the thing is to imagine being the person that has made a discovery – the person who first questions something, investigates and then contributes to the vast catalogue of information that is science. I find this concept inspirational.

You are going to read an article in which people talk about their experiences of job interviews. For questions **47–56**, choose from the people (**A–D**).

Mark your answers **on the separate answer sheet**.

Which person mentions the following?

establishing how the interview will be conducted	47
the importance of keeping to the point	48
a relaxed atmosphere in the workplace	49
an abrupt ending to an interview	50
taking responsibility for past errors	51
appearing to have rehearsed responses	52
preparing inquiries to put to a prospective employer	53
awareness of body language	54
revealing what motivates you	55
advantages in being honest about your weaknesses	56

Tell us something about yourself

Being interviewed for a job can be a stressful experience.
We asked four people what they learnt from being in that situation.

A My first interview for a job taught me a great deal. I was applying for the position of junior account executive in an advertising company, which involves dealing with clients on a face-to-face basis. It follows that you have to be good at interpersonal skills, and unfortunately, that's not the impression I gave. Like a lot of people, I tend to babble when I'm nervous. The interviewer began by asking me to say something about myself, and I started talking about my hobbies. But I got carried away and went off at a tangent, which made a bad impression. The other lesson I learnt was that if you are asked to talk about things you aren't good at, you really shouldn't be evasive. You could mention something that can also be a strength. For example, being pedantic is not always a bad thing in certain circumstances, and you should explain how you cope with that deficiency, but you have to say something.

B In my present job, I have to interview applicants, and I can offer a few general tips. Firstly, a candidate should not learn a speech off by heart; you will come across as insincere. Secondly, it is crucial to understand what the interviewer wants you to talk about. For instance, an interviewer might ask about a situation where your supervisor or manager had a problem with your work. Now, what the interviewer is really after is to see how you react to criticism, and the best thing is to say that you tried to learn from this. Finally, don't try to conceal your real character. Many years ago, an interviewer asked me at the end of our talk if I had any questions. I was very keen to get the job, so I asked what opportunities there were for promotion. I wondered if perhaps I had been too direct, but I later discovered that employers like you to seem eager and ambitious.

C I remember one interview I attended with a company that makes ice cream and other dairy products. I turned up in a smart business suit and tie, only to find that my prospective employers were in jeans! They believed in being casual: no private offices, everyone ate in the same canteen, people all used first names with each other. I realised I should have done more research. Needless to say, I didn't get the job. On another occasion, as the interview was drawing to a close, I was asked if I had anything to say. I was so relieved it was over that I just smiled and blurted out: 'No thanks!' I later realised this was a mistake. A candidate should decide in advance on at least ten things to ask the interviewer: it's not necessary to ask more than two or three questions, but you need to have some in reserve in case the question you wanted to ask is answered in the course of the interview.

D Preparation is of extreme importance; things like finding out what form the interview will take. Will there be any sort of written component, for instance, and will you be talking to one person or a panel? And of course, you need to prepare answers to those awkward questions designed to find out more about your character. For example, you might be asked about your most important achievement so far; don't answer this in a way that makes you seem swollen-headed or complacent, as this will suggest that you don't learn easily. Actually, it's not so much what people say that makes them seem arrogant as the way they sit, how they hold their heads, whether they meet the interviewer's eye, so bear that in mind. Another question interviewers sometimes ask, to find out how well you work in a team, is about mistakes you have made. You should have an example ready and admit that you were at fault, otherwise it looks as though you are the kind of person who shifts the blame onto others. But you should also show that you learnt from the mistake and wouldn't make it again.

PAPER 1 Reading and
         Use of English
PAPER 2 Writing   ▶ Part 1
                            Part 2
PAPER 3 Listening
PAPER 4 Speaking

You **must** answer this question. Write your answer in **220–260** words in an appropriate style on the separate answer sheet.

1 Your class has attended a lecture on ways for the government to boost students' interest in science. You have made the notes below.

> **Methods for encouraging an interest in science:**
>
> - TV programmes
> - improved teaching facilities
> - career opportunities

> **Some opinions expressed in the discussion:**
>
> 'Not many young people watch science programmes on TV.'
>
> 'It is expensive to provide laboratories with new equipment.'
>
> 'The government cannot guarantee career opportunities.'

Write an **essay** for your tutor discussing **two** of the methods in your notes. You should **explain which method you think is more important**, and **provide reasons** to support your opinion.

You may, if you wish, make use of the opinions expressed in the discussion, but you should use your own words as far as possible.

PAPER 1 Reading and
Use of English

PAPER 2 Writing ▶
                          Part 1
                          Part 2

PAPER 3 Listening

PAPER 4 Speaking

Write an answer to **one** of the questions **2–4** in this part. Write your answer in **220–260** words in an appropriate style on the separate answer sheet. Put the question number in the box at the top of the page.

2 You have just spent a weekend with a friend you hadn't seen since you were at school together many years ago. Write to your friend saying what the reunion meant to you, what you particularly enjoyed doing during the weekend, and what plans you have for meeting in the future.

Write your **letter**.

3 Your company requires you to wear formal dress to work. There is a proposal to introduce a 'dress-down' day, that is one day at the end of the working week when employees can wear informal clothes. Your manager has asked you to write a report on the advantages and disadvantages of this proposal.

Write your **report**.

4 Your student magazine has asked you to write a review of the latest film in a popular series. Say what is good and bad about the film, and whether it lives up to the earlier films in the series.

Write your **review**.

Track 17

You will hear three different extracts. For questions **1–6**, choose the answer (**A**, **B** or **C**) which fits best according to what you hear. There are two questions for each extract.

Extract One

You hear part of a radio programme in which a man is being interviewed about an unusual sport.

1   According to Chris, cheese-rolling takes place
    A   at only one venue in the world.
    B   on muddy ground.
    C   once a year.

2   Which statement best sums up how Chris feels about cheese-rolling?
    A   It's too dangerous.
    B   It's worth the risks.
    C   It requires training.

Extract Two

You hear two students on a business course talking about a book they are studying.

3   Sue found the book worth reading because it included
    A   case studies of successful enterprises.
    B   advice on how to negotiate a contract.
    C   the legal aspects of setting up a company.

4   What criticism of the book do both speakers express?
    A   Some important information was omitted.
    B   Some of it was badly organised.
    C   It used too much jargon.

Extract Three

You hear two people talking about yawning.

5   According to the woman, until recently, yawning was thought to
    A   be simply a sign that we were tired.
    B   help us breathe more deeply.
    C   promote alertness.

6   Research suggests that contagious yawning is a way of
    A   maintaining alertness in a group.
    B   expressing understanding in a group.
    C   communicating with each other.

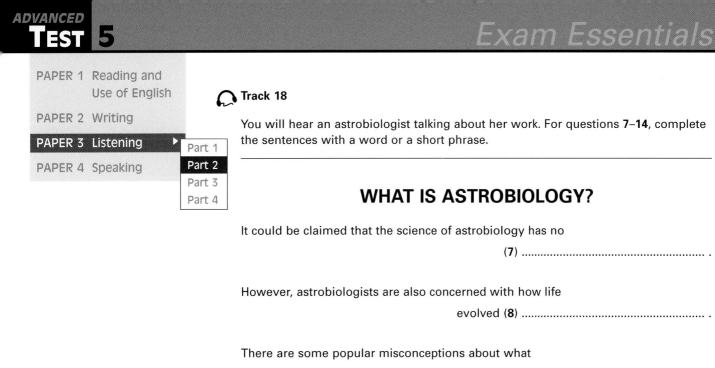

Track 18

You will hear an astrobiologist talking about her work. For questions **7–14**, complete the sentences with a word or a short phrase.

WHAT IS ASTROBIOLOGY?

It could be claimed that the science of astrobiology has no

(**7**) ....

However, astrobiologists are also concerned with how life

evolved (**8**) ....

There are some popular misconceptions about what

(**9**) .... might look like.

For much of the Earth's history, single-celled (**10**) ....

were the only life forms in existence.

Multi-cellular life evolved during the (**11**) ....

known as the Cambrian era.

Then, about (**12**) .... years ago, human-like

creatures evolved.

Life on other planets will probably be (**13**) ....

life on Earth.

Human beings might not have evolved if (**14**) ....

had not become extinct.

Track 19

You will hear part of a radio interview with Pete Birtwhistle, a playwright. For questions **15–20**, choose the answer (**A**, **B**, **C** or **D**) which fits best according to what you hear.

15 What was Pete's attitude to the theatre before he started writing?
   A   He felt it had little relevance to his life.
   B   He didn't feel qualified to judge it.
   C   He thought it would be boring to watch a play.
   D   He preferred comedies to tragedies.

16 How did he feel about leaving his previous job?
   A   He felt very relieved.
   B   He was anxious about his health.
   C   He worried how others would see him.
   D   He was very depressed.

17 What was the most difficult aspect of writing his first play?
   A   disciplining himself to write every day
   B   coming up with a suitable story
   C   allowing the characters to develop
   D   finding an appropriate ending

18 What is the biggest impact that writing has had on Pete's life?
   A   It has made people respect him more.
   B   It has enabled him to express himself.
   C   It has opened up new professional opportunities.
   D   It has allowed him to appreciate other plays.

19 How does Pete choose the theme of a new play?
   A   He looks around for a challenging theme.
   B   He looks for a subject that is in the news.
   C   He looks for a theme that he understands.
   D   He thinks about issues that affect society.

20 How does Pete feel about writing for films?
   A   enthusiastic
   B   worried
   C   cautious
   D   intimidated

🎧 **Track 20**

You will hear five short extracts in which people talk about tracing their ancestors.

While you listen, you must complete both tasks.

TASK ONE

For questions **21–25**, choose from list **A–H**, the person who is speaking.

A	One of my ancestors went abroad to find adventure.	Speaker 1	21
B	A relative ran away from home when he was young.	Speaker 2	22
C	I am descended from immigrants.	Speaker 3	23
D	A family tradition turned out not to be true.	Speaker 4	24
E	At one time the family was wealthy.	Speaker 5	25
F	My great-grandmother came from a rich family.		
G	A relative emigrated to Australia.		
H	My great-great-grandfather changed his name.		

TASK TWO

For questions **26–30**, choose from list **A–H** what view each speaker is expressing.

A	I get angry at the thought of their suffering.	Speaker 1	26
B	Learning the truth caused considerable bitterness.	Speaker 2	27
C	I have become more curious about the story.	Speaker 3	28
D	The whole thing made us feel quite embarrassed.	Speaker 4	29
E	I was delighted to make contact with my relatives.	Speaker 5	30
F	The story saddened me.		
G	I am very proud of my ancestor.		
H	I was disappointed at first.		

Part 1 (2 minutes)

The examiner will ask you a few questions about yourself and about a general topic. For example, the examiner may ask you:

- When and how did you start learning English?
- In what ways is knowing a foreign language useful to you now?
- How do you expect language skills to be important to you in the future?

Part 2 (4 minutes)

You will each be asked to talk on your own for about a minute. You will each be given three different pictures to talk about. After your partner has finished speaking, you will be asked a brief question connected with your partner's photographs.

Groups (compare, contrast and speculate)

Turn to pictures 1–3 on page 181 which show people in groups.

(*Candidate A*), it's your turn first. Here are your pictures. They show **people in groups**.

I'd like you to compare **two** of the pictures and say **what the advantages are of doing these things in groups.**

(*Candidate B*), **do you enjoy doing things in a group? Why? / Why not?**

Experience (compare, contrast and speculate)

Turn to pictures 1–3 on page 182 which show different skills.

Now, (*Candidate B*), here are your pictures. **They show people with different specialist skills.**

I'd like you to compare **two** of these skills, and say **how difficult it might be to acquire these skills.**

(*Candidate A*), **which of these skills would take the longest time to acquire? Why?**

Part 3 (4 minutes)

Look at page 183 which gives some situations where there is a need for time management.

Time management (discuss, evaluate and select)

Here are some different situations where time management is necessary and a question for you to discuss.

First, you have some time to look at the task.

(*Pause 15 seconds*)

Now talk to each other about **why time management is necessary in each situation.**

Now you have about a minute to decide **which situation would benefit most from better time management.**

Part 4 (5 minutes)

The examiner will encourage you to develop the topic of your discussion in Part 3 by asking questions such as:

- Do you think it is a problem if someone is often late for appointments and meetings? (Why? / Why not?)
- Which aspects of modern life, where time is managed badly, do you find most annoying?
- Does modern life make us too anxious about punctuality? (Why? / Why not?)
- When was the last time you were late, and what caused you to be late?

For questions **1–8**, read the text below and decide which answer (**A**, **B**, **C** or **D**) best fits each gap. There is an example at the beginning (**0**).

Mark your answers **on the separate answer sheet**.

Example:

0 **A** define   **B** generate   **C** adopt   **D** cause

0	A	B	C	D

A new look at the Middle Ages

The Institute for Medieval Studies is holding a series of lectures to (**0**) …….. interest in a period of European history which is all too often (**1**) …….. . It is hoped that these lectures will (**2**) …….. some of the misconceptions that (**3**) …….. to this day about the long and eventful span of time between the sixth and the 15th centuries.

It is true that Europe was (**4**) …….. by the plague in the latter part of the 14th century, and that living (**5**) …….. for the majority of people were appalling by modern standards, and life (**6**) …….. was low. The peasants suffered under a brutal feudal system and the (**7**) …….. of learning was open only to a small minority.

However, these negative aspects of medieval life cannot be properly evaluated unless they are viewed in the broader (**8**) …….. . The Middle Ages were also a period of great achievements in architecture, science, technology, art and trade, and the lectures will explore the more progressive and enlightened features of the age, as well as its darker aspects.

1	**A** neglected	**B** abandoned	**C** subdued	**D** deserted
2	**A** respond	**B** refuse	**C** rectify	**D** revive
3	**A** insist	**B** persist	**C** consist	**D** resist
4	**A** injured	**B** eliminated	**C** wounded	**D** ravaged
5	**A** states	**B** circumstances	**C** conditions	**D** situations
6	**A** estimate	**B** forecast	**C** prediction	**D** expectancy
7	**A** pursuit	**B** chase	**C** desire	**D** quest
8	**A** background	**B** setting	**C** context	**D** environment

For questions **9–16**, read the text below and think of the word which best fits each gap. Use only **one** word in each gap. There is an example at the beginning (**0**).

Write your answers **IN CAPITAL LETTERS on the separate answer sheet**.

Example: | 0 | I | N | | | | | | | | | | | | | | | | | | | | |

Speed limits

Engineers have succeeded (**0**) .... developing a sophisticated system for limiting the speed that cars and other vehicles can reach. Known (**9**) .... 'intelligent speed adaptation', or ISA, it is a concept for (**10**) .... there is considerable support. It also has many opponents, however. ISA involves fitting a vehicle with a communications box that knows (**11**) .... fast the vehicle is legally permitted to travel on a particular section of road, and automatically regulates the car's speed. It therefore becomes impossible for a vehicle fitted with (**12**) .... a device to exceed the speed limit.

The communications box could have other uses too. In (**13**) .... to encourage the reduction of traffic, various cities around the world, Singapore and London (**14**) .... them, have introduced congestion zones requiring motorists to pay to enter central areas. At present, (**15**) .... time a vehicle enters the zone, its number plate is photographed and checked against a list, but this system is costly and (**16**) .... from foolproof. The ISA communications box could be easily adapted for this purpose and would be cheaper.

While ISA has its opponents, eventually governments are likely to require a version of it on all vehicles.

PAPER 1	Reading and Use of English ▶	Part 1
		Part 2
		Part 3
PAPER 2	Writing	Part 4
		Part 5
PAPER 3	Listening	Part 6
		Part 7
PAPER 4	Speaking	Part 8

For questions **17–24**, read the text below. Use the word given in capitals at the end of some of the lines to form a word that fits in the gap **in the same line**. There is an example at the beginning (**0**).

Write your answers **IN CAPITAL LETTERS on the separate answer sheet**.

Example: | 0 | C | E | L | E | B | R | A | T | I | O | N | | | | | | |

The origins of Halloween

Nowadays, Halloween is a popular (**0**) …….. which people enjoy in many parts of the world. It is a time when young people in particular dress up as witches or ghosts and have parties.   **CELEBRATE**

Halloween (**17**) …….. about 2,000 years ago with the   **ORIGIN**
Celts, however. These people were the (**18**) …….. of   **INHABIT**
an area that includes Britain, Ireland and Brittany. They
relied on the land for their (**19**) …….., and this meant that   **LIVE**
they were at the mercy of (**20**) …….. weather conditions,   **PREDICT**
especially during the winter.

The Celtic new year began on 1 November, which
also marked the beginning of winter, a period (**21**) ……..   **TRADITION**
associated with death. On the eve of the new year, it was
believed that the barriers between the worlds of the living
and the dead were (**22**) …….. withdrawn, and it was possible   **TEMPORARY**
to communicate with spirits. The Celts believed that the
spirits offered them (**23**) …….. and protection, and their   **GUIDE**
priests were (**24**) …….. able to predict the future on this night. **REPUTE**

Halloween is very different now, of course, but it is interesting
to consider what it once was.

PAPER 1	Reading and Use of English	▶	Part 1
			Part 2
PAPER 2	Writing		Part 3
			Part 4
PAPER 3	Listening		Part 5
			Part 6
PAPER 4	Speaking		Part 7
			Part 8

For questions **25–30**, complete the second sentence so that it has a similar meaning to the first sentence, using the word given. **Do not change the word given.** You must use between **three** and **six** words, including the word given. Here is an example (**0**).

Example:

0   Jane regretted speaking so rudely to the old lady.

   MORE

   Jane .... politely to the old lady.

Example: | **0** | WISHED SHE HAD SPOKEN MORE |

Write **only** the missing words **IN CAPITAL LETTERS on the separate answer sheet**.

---

25   They believe that Mario failed his exam because he was nervous.

   DOWN

   Mario's failure in his exam .... the fact that he was nervous.

26   'Why didn't I ask Linda for her phone number?' thought Sam.

   ASKED

   'If .... Linda for her phone number!' thought Sam.

27   We didn't think Mr Mason was going to recover, so it was a relief when he did.

   PULLED

   We were relieved when Mr Mason .... we didn't think he would.

28   'I really don't like what the press are saying about me!' said Tina.

   OBJECTED

   Tina .... about her by the press.

29   'I don't mind you staying out late, but your father does,' Robbie's mother told him.

   RATHER

   'It's .... minds you staying out late,' Robbie's mother told him.

30   They think that students vandalised the school last night.

   WAS

   It is .... by students last night.

PAPER 1   Reading and ▸
          Use of English

PAPER 2   Writing

PAPER 3   Listening

PAPER 4   Speaking

| Part 1 |
| Part 2 |
| Part 3 |
| Part 4 |
| **Part 5** |
| Part 6 |
| Part 7 |
| Part 8 |

You are going to read a newspaper article. For questions **31–36**, choose the answer (**A**, **B**, **C** or **D**) which you think fits best according to the text.

Mark your answers **on the separate answer sheet**.

Learning to run

An article published in the prestigious scientific journal *Nature* sheds new light on an important, but hitherto little appreciated, aspect of human evolution. In this article, Professors Dennis Bramble and Daniel Lieberman suggest that being able to run was a crucial element in the development of our species. According to the two scientists, humans possess a number of anatomical features that make them surprisingly good runners. 'We are very confident that strong selection for running – which came at the expense of the historical ability to live in trees – was instrumental in the origin of the modern human body form,' says Bramble, a biology professor at the University of Utah.

Traditional thinking up to now has been that the distinctive, upright body form of modern humans has come about as a result of the ability to walk, and that running is simply a by-product of walking. Furthermore, humans have usually been regarded as poor runners compared to such animals as dogs, horses or antelopes. However, this is only true if we consider running at high speed, especially over short distances. Even an Olympic athlete can hardly run as quickly as a horse can gallop, and can only sprint for 15 seconds or so. Horses, antelopes and greyhounds, on the other hand, can run at top speed for several minutes, clearly outperforming us in this respect. But when it comes to long-distance running, humans do astonishingly well. They can maintain a steady pace for many kilometres, and their overall speed is at least on a par with that of horses or dogs.

Bramble and Lieberman examined 26 anatomical features found in humans. One of the most interesting of these is the nuchal ligament, a band of tissue that extends from a ridge on the base of the skull to the spine. When we run, it is this ligament that prevents our head from pitching back and forth or from side to side. Therefore, we are able to run with steady heads, held high. The nuchal ligament is not found in any other surviving primates, although the fossil record shows that *Homo erectus*, an early human species that walked upright, much as we do, also had one. Then there are our Achilles tendons at the backs of our legs, which connect our calf muscles to our heel bones – and which have nothing to do with walking. When we run, these tendons behave like springs, helping to propel us forward. Furthermore, we have low, wide shoulders, virtually disconnected from our skulls, an anatomical development which allows us to run more efficiently. Add to this our light forearms, which swing out of phase with the movement of our legs to assist balance, and one begins to appreciate the point that Bramble and Lieberman are trying to make.

But what evolutionary advantage is gained from being good long-distance runners? One hypothesis is that this ability may have permitted early humans to obtain food more effectively. 'What these features and fossil facts appear to be telling us is that running evolved in order for our direct ancestors to compete with other carnivores for access to the protein needed to grow the big brains that we enjoy today,' says Lieberman. Some scientists speculate that early humans may have pursued animals for great distances in order to exhaust them before killing them. Running would also have conferred an advantage before weapons were invented: early humans might have been scavengers, eating the meat and marrow left over from a kill by lions or other large predators. They may have been alerted to the existence of a freshly killed carcass by vultures, and the faster they got to the scene of the kill, the better.

'Research on the history of human locomotion has traditionally been contentious,' says Lieberman. 'At the very least, I hope this theory will make many people have second thoughts about how humans learned to run and walk and why we are built the way we are.'

31 What does the writer say in the first paragraph about the human ability to run?
- **A** It is worse than our body shape might indicate.
- **B** It developed in combination with other human activities.
- **C** It has always been more important than being able to climb trees.
- **D** It was once overlooked as a determining factor in human evolution.

32 What comparison does the writer make in the second paragraph?
- **A** Humans run as well as horses and dogs at certain distances.
- **B** Humans are better runners than most other animals.
- **C** Humans don't need to run as fast as many animals.
- **D** Humans cannot run for as long as we might think.

33 What does the writer say about the nuchal ligament?
- **A** It can only be found only in modern primates.
- **B** It enables us to run in the manner that we do.
- **C** It forces us to look in the direction we're running.
- **D** It makes us run on two legs rather than four.

34 What does the writer suggest in the third paragraph?
- **A** We could run better if we had stronger arms.
- **B** We could walk without using our calf muscles.
- **C** Our Achilles tendons are an adaptation for running.
- **D** The shape of our shoulders affects the position of our heads.

35 Which conclusion is drawn about early humans in the fourth paragraph?
- **A** They followed birds to avoid dangerous situations.
- **B** They evolved as a result of their hunting skills.
- **C** They developed big brains for running.
- **D** They were unable to kill large animals.

36 According to the final paragraph, what does Professor Lieberman hope to do?
- **A** Dispel any remaining doubts about the nature of the human body.
- **B** Inform people of the real reason why humans are able to run and walk.
- **C** Cause people to reconsider previously held ideas about human anatomy.
- **D** Prove conclusively that humans did not always walk in an upright position.

PAPER 1 Reading and
        Use of English

PAPER 2 Writing

PAPER 3 Listening

PAPER 4 Speaking

Part 1
Part 2
Part 3
Part 4
Part 5
Part 6
Part 7
Part 8

You are going to read extracts from four reviews of a film called *The Great Gatsby*. For questions **37–40**, choose from the reviews **A–D**. The reviews may be chosen more than once.

Mark your answers **on the separate answer sheet**.

The Great Gatsby

Four reviewers comment on **The Great Gatsby** *directed by Baz Luhrmann.*
The film is based on a novel by F. Scott Fitzgerald.

A

Four previous film versions of *The Great Gatsby* have fallen short of the book's brilliant portrayal of a society succumbing to greed, and, unfortunately, Baz Luhrmann's attempt fares little better. F. Scott Fitzgerald's short, lean, subtle novel conjures up disillusion, pain and tragedy as the main characters' relationships unfold, but this sense is largely drowned out by the lavish excess, the fancy camerawork and the general superficiality in this film. Surprisingly, the soundtrack mixing 1920s orchestral pieces with hip hop and modern pop works a treat and is likely to appeal to younger audiences, as is the very strong cast of actors who give some excellent performances, almost in spite of the over-the-top direction. Whether this will prompt them to go back and read the novel, as some have suggested, is highly questionable, however.

B

As other commentators have pointed out, F. Scott Fitzgerald's great novel, revealing the emptiness and pain that lies behind the pursuit of power and wealth, is a concise, elegant, almost understated work. There is no reason, however, why a film of the same story shouldn't take on a different style and this is what Baz Luhrmann does, largely to good effect. Creating huge cinematic set pieces out of 1920s upper-class life, he plays up the fake, the superficial and the decadent. The narrative is unchanged but rather squeezed in, but then it is rather slight in the novel anyway; Fitzgerald's lyrical prose and characterisation are what make it compelling. The decision to mix contemporary pop with music from the 1920s, has a certain logic to it, given Luhrmann's visual approach, but for some reason the mix feels uneasy rather than complementary. There may be an element of wanting to attract teenage viewers – nothing wrong with that, of course.

C

F. Scott Fitzgerald's classic 1925 novel, *The Great Gatsby*, tells the story of a man who ruthlessly chases wealth, ultimately in pursuit of love, only to learn that one can't buy the other. In keeping with his previous films, director Baz Luhrmann's version is a loud confection of colour, lights and noise from start to finish. Its musical soundtrack is a mix of period pieces, contemporary rap and dance tunes which somehow hang together and support the excesses of the parties, car chases and general hysteria. The narrative structure of the novel exposes the artificiality and heartlessness at of the American dream – that of acquiring great wealth from nothing – but the film's overblown nature drowns this message out. The great hope is that all the noise and visual excitement will persuade younger viewers to try reading the novel – which would be a very positive consequence.

D

Baz Luhrmann used modern pop music to energise William Shakespeare's *Romeo and Juliet* and also 19th-century Paris in his film *Moulin Rouge* to great effect. In his version of *The Great Gatsby*, the same strategy merely serves to distance the audience from the human drama they should be engaged with. With his exaggerated operatic style, Luhrmann is the wrong director to shoot F. Scott Fitzgerald's small but perfectly formed novel. It's not that he makes substantial changes to the narrative of the film; the original has a thin plot anyway, and the film is largely faithful to it. It's more that all the noise, flashing lights and dizzying crowd scenes typical of Luhrmann overwhelm both the tragedy and the subtlety characteristic of the original. Audiences, especially perhaps younger ones, will undoubtedly be attracted by the visual and auditory glamour, but they will miss out on what makes the novel great.

Which reviewer

expresses a different view from the others about
the film's potential impact on younger audiences?

37 ▢

takes a similar view to reviewer C on the appropriacy
of the music that goes with the film?

38 ▢

shares reviewer B's opinion about the film's storyline?

39 ▢

has a different opinion from the others about the way
the film is directed?

40 ▢

PAPER 1	Reading and ▶	Part 1
	Use of English	Part 2
PAPER 2	Writing	Part 3
		Part 4
PAPER 3	Listening	Part 5
		Part 6
PAPER 4	Speaking	**Part 7**
		Part 8

You are going to read a newspaper article. Six paragraphs have been removed from the article. Choose from the paragraphs **A–G** the one which fits each gap (**41–46**). There is one extra paragraph which you do not need to use.

Mark your answers **on the separate answer sheet**.

Energy-efficient design

If you consider yourself to be particularly environmentally friendly, there is a community which may interest you. Here, in a large, multi-home development known as BedZED, you can find architecture which is truly green. Buildings come with thick windows and walls, which regulate the temperature at a comfortable level throughout the year. The south-facing windows collect heat and light from the sun, as do solar panels fitted onto the exterior. Not only that, but BedZED is stylish, and every flat comes with a private garden.

41

As far as countries in the West are concerned, the buildings that people live and work in consume far more energy than transport, for example. However, architecture need not consume so much energy, nor produce so much in the way of CO_2 emissions. The intelligent design of the housing at BedZED housing demonstrates that buildings can be made environmentally friendly, without particularly high costs or advanced technology.

42

And indeed, the BedZED community – which has some 84 homes – is really rather cost-effective because of economies of scale: the more homes you build, the less you pay proportionately for the materials and construction of each individual home. This, as well as all the other benefits, is why BedZED is receiving more and more attention.

43

The technology used in the BedZED design could be implemented far more than it currently is, across different forms of architecture. It is neither a challenge,

nor costly to install solar panels, triple-glazed windows, or to insulate floors and walls better. Indeed, according to some estimates, it would be easy to reduce the energy consumption of most of our buildings by up to 20% if we just used more effective design.

44

In large part, the drive for these changes has come from Europe. Here, governments are becoming more concerned about the dangers of relying too much on our current energy and aware of the need to meet energy-reduction goals. Many governments have given financial incentives for using energy-efficient design in the construction industry, and have also tightened regulations. Moreover, a European Union directive now requires house builders to present evidence of how they are meeting energy-efficiency guidelines.

45

It also seems that governments are becoming more involved in the research and development of environmentally friendly designs. At one laboratory in California, a team has experimented with architectural designs such as windows which become darker on sunny days, thereby reducing the amount of heat coming into the home. This would, in theory, offer significant savings for people who make heavy use of air-conditioning in hot, sunny climates. Interesting initiatives have been taken elsewhere, too.

46

We still have not reached a situation in which the general public fully accepts such measures. From a marketing perspective, it can still be difficult to convince customers that energy efficient products are worthwhile. However, as energy prices rise, this is sure to change.

A Indeed, according to one researcher from the European Commission in Brussels, who works on energy efficiency, it would be possible to achieve a great deal simply by using existing technologies.

B Governments elsewhere in the world are playing their part too. In the US, the Energy Star programme provides standards for the energy efficiency of consumer products, from home construction to computers and kitchen appliances. This has resulted in energy-efficient products becoming commonplace, and indeed, an attractive choice for consumers.

C Both of these regions still make every possible attempt to meet energy consumption guidelines as governments around the world attempt to come to grips with the threat of global warming. There seems every likelihood that this project could lead the way–one can only hope that others will follow.

D In India, for example, a New Delhi-based non-profit organisation has helped to create systems whereby small villages can use waste products from farming, and convert them into power. And in Sweden, there is research into how heat from the ground can be used to provide hot water or heating for homes.

E Although it might seem like a state-of-the-art paradise for the super-rich, it's actually an estate of affordable housing built between 2000 and 2002 in a suburb of London. It can't be said that the people who live here are all eco-warriors, but they are part of a growing tendency to find buildings which use less energy.

F This essentially, means finding out how to increase efficiency in the least complicated manner possible. BedZED, for example, was planned so that even if the homes need more energy, despite their eco-friendly designs, there is still a power plant based on the site. This plant, which uses waste materials, can meet any remaining energy demands from residents.

G Recently, this has been coming from Asia in the form of Indian and Chinese visitors. Also, more zero-energy communities are under construction elsewhere in the UK, as well as in the USA.

You are going to read a newspaper article in which people talk about changes in their careers. For questions **47–56**, choose from the people (**A–D**).

Mark your answers **on the separate answer sheet**.

In which section of the article are the following mentioned?

the unexpected demands of the business | **47** |

a cautious approach to doing business | **48** |

an established network of contacts | **49** |

taking advantage of modern communications | **50** |

realising an ambition | **51** |

the cost of setting up a business | **52** |

plans to branch out | **53** |

the competitive nature of a business | **54** |

the need to update knowledge | **55** |

helping people to fill in official forms | **56** |

A change in direction

It is becoming increasingly common for people to change careers at some point in their lives. Four people describe their experiences of changing direction.

A I used to work in the accounts department of a large engineering company before it was taken over by a bigger corporation. I found the new management style hard to adjust to, so I looked for something else. I'm interested in maths and my wife suggested I try teaching, but I figured I'd better not stray far from what I was familiar with. I knew a change in the way self-employed people complete their tax returns was due to be introduced, and I had an idea for some software showing people how to go about it. So, I teamed up with a programmer I knew, with me writing the content and him doing the technical side. It proved much more successful than I'd anticipated, and we've gone on to produce more software showing people how to manage their finances. I've deliberately kept the operation small-scale. I work from home and the outlay for office equipment was low. People say I should expand, but that brings all sorts of new challenges and I like things as they are.

B Two years ago, I felt like a change. I'd been teaching physical education to secondary school students for eight years. I wanted to continue in something to do with sports, so I became an independent personal trainer. It's worked out well. I have agreements with gyms around the city to use their facilities, and I train adults – individuals and small groups. Luckily, I had a ready-made clientele, in the shape of former colleagues and people they recommended me to. Any personal trainer worth their salt should attend training courses on a regular basis to familiarise themselves with the latest developments in sports science – there's lots of really good research these days about things like running techniques, nutrition and rehabilitation from injury. It interests me but also knowing this stuff is good for my reputation. As long as my clients enjoy and can afford my sessions, I can't ever see myself being short of work. If anything, the number of people wanting help to get fit is only likely to increase.

C I studied sociology at university and when it was over, I didn't know what to do next. Several other people on my course started to work for local government services and it looked as though that was a possibility for me. Then, I heard about a new project to re-landscape a park in the city – there were gardening jobs going. I thought: 'That's it!' I can't say I'd dreamed of becoming a gardener, but I'd always thought that working outdoors would be brilliant. I now run my own landscape gardening company and employ three other people. I still spend most of my time in parks and gardens doing physical work, but I also have to manage the business. At first, I was surprised at how much paperwork I had to deal with. Completing forms and things like that is very time-consuming, and I'm thinking of hiring someone to do it. I've also been invited to write articles about gardening for a couple of magazines and websites, and I definitely want to do more of that in the future.

D I worked for an advertising agency for about ten years, but the sector's very cut-throat, and when we got a new boss he decided to make his mark by getting rid of a few people, myself included. Once I got my breath back, I decided to go freelance rather than join another agency. It occurred to me that a lot of companies need not only an advertising campaign but also a consultant, an independent expert to give them an honest view of their situation. I do almost all my work from home, using email, video conferencing and other online tools. It's satisfying as well as being financially rewarding. One advantage, of course, is that I have control over my own time, which wasn't the case before. For example, if there are forms or other tedious paperwork to deal with, I can usually put it off to another day, or even pay someone to do it for me. Like most self-employed people, I work very hard, but I knew it would be like this, and I don't mind it.

You **must** answer this question. Write your answer in **220–260** words in an appropriate style on the separate answer sheet.

1 Your class has attended a seminar discussing the possibility that your school should be sponsored by companies in the neighbourhood. You have made the notes below.

> **Reasons for commercial sponsorship of your school:**
>
> • generous funding
> • professional management
> • local involvement

> **Some opinions expressed in the discussion:**
>
> 'Finance cannot be guaranteed.'
>
> 'The companies will influence the teaching curriculum.'
>
> 'It's good to encourage children to contribute to the local environment.'

Write an **essay** for your tutor discussing **two** of the reasons in your notes. You should **explain which reason you think is more important** for the school to consider, and **provide reasons** to support your opinion.

You may, if you wish, make use of the opinions expressed in the discussion, but you should use your own words as far as possible.

PAPER 1 Reading and
Use of English

PAPER 2 Writing ▶ Part 1
Part 2

PAPER 3 Listening

PAPER 4 Speaking

Write an answer to **one** of the questions **2–4** in this part. Write your answer in **220–260** words in an appropriate style on the separate answer sheet. Put the question number in the box at the top of the page.

2   Your class has had a discussion on the role of education in preparing young people for work, and you agreed to write a report on the discussion for your teacher.

These are the questions that were discussed:

- Is it better to specialise with a view to becoming an expert in one field, or should students have as broad an education as possible?
- What do employers want from someone they hire?

Write your **report**.

3   You are working as an entertainments assistant in a summer camp for children aged 8–15. Write an email to your friend at home who is thinking about doing a similar job about the highs and lows of the experience, describing the work, your relationship with the children and your social life.

Write your **email**.

4   The music section of a national newspaper has announced a competition, and is inviting customers to write a review of a live concert they have been to. Reviews must mention aspects of the concert they enjoyed, and also ones they found disappointing. You have decided to enter the competition, and write about a concert you have been to recently.

Write your **review**.

Track 21

You will hear three different extracts. For questions **1–6**, choose the answer (**A**, **B** or **C**) which fits best according to what you hear. There are two questions for each extract.

Extract One

You hear an interview with a head teacher about the environmental policy at her school.

1   Some students are currently helping to
   A   source organic food for the school canteen.
   B   reduce the school's fossil-fuel consumption.
   C   develop a system for recycling rubbish.

2   According to the teacher, one positive outcome of the program is that
   A   the school gets valuable publicity for its environmental projects.
   B   the students are motivated to work for the future of the environment.
   C   the parents have become concerned about the environment.

Extract Two

You hear an interview with a man talking about his first day at work.

3   What did Colin find most difficult about his first day at work?
   A   remembering people's names
   B   following his supervisor's instructions
   C   finding his way around the company

4   Who should listeners contact first if they want personal advice?
   A   Colin
   B   the interviewer
   C   the programme producer

Extract Three

You hear two people talking about yawning.

5   According to the woman, until recently, yawning was thought to
   A   be simply a sign that we were tired.
   B   help us breathe more deeply.
   C   promote alertness.

6   Research suggests that contagious yawning is a way of
   A   maintaining alertness in a group.
   B   expressing understanding in a group.
   C   communicating with each other.

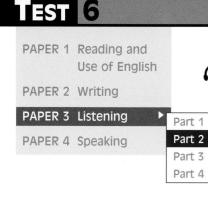

Track 22

You will hear an archaeologist talking about an experience he had in South America. For questions **7–14**, complete the sentences with a word or a short phrase.

AN UNPLEASANT ADVENTURE

The archaeologist's original task was to (**7**) ....

the ruined city and the area around it.

He was then asked to suggest ways to (**8**) ....

It appears that the (**9**) .... air exhaled by visitors is

damaging the walls.

The archaeologist wanted to survey a tomb near the site of a proposed

(**10**) ....

Unfortunately, the tomb had been damaged by flood water from

(**11**) ....

The archaeologist lost his footing on some (**12**) ....

As he fell, he broke his (**13**) ....

He was found when a (**14**) .... heard his shouts for help.

Track 23

You will hear part of a radio interview with Professor Hector Williams, a linguist. For questions **15–20**, choose the answer (**A**, **B**, **C** or **D**) which fits best according to what you hear.

15 What was the assumption behind medieval interest in an artificial language?
   A It would be easy to learn a logical language.
   B The language would be more suited to classification.
   C The universe was constructed on linguistic principles.
   D The language would be a key to understanding the universe.

16 The artificial language based on the names of the notes in the scale
   A had a vocabulary of single-syllable words.
   B could be understood by people in the west.
   C simplified the task of reading music.
   D was intended to be easy to learn and understand.

17 How did Professor Williams feel when he first heard Esperanto spoken?
   A He thought it was a dialect of Italian.
   B He felt it had a pleasant sound.
   C He considered it was successful in its aims.
   D He wanted to know the logic behind it.

18 According to Professor Williams, what is the main objection to an artificial language?
   A It is not very expressive.
   B It cannot be used to talk about the past.
   C It does not have any native speakers.
   D It has a limited vocabulary.

19 What characteristic of Esperanto speakers does Professor Williams find most striking?
   A their optimism
   B their naivety
   C their dedication
   D their elitism

20 Professor Williams considers that no artificial language will ever become universal because
   A the language instinct is fundamental in all human beings.
   B identity and language are strongly linked for most people.
   C it is impossible to invent a completely artificial language.
   D too few people would ever consider learning one.

🎧 **Track 24**

You will hear five short extracts in which people whose jobs involve travelling talk about their work.

While you listen, you must complete both tasks.

TASK ONE

For questions **21–25**, choose from list **A–H**, what job each person has.

A	a musician		
		Speaker 1	**21**
B	a journalist		
		Speaker 2	**22**
C	a sports person		
		Speaker 3	**23**
D	a technical trouble shooter		
		Speaker 4	**24**
E	an ecologist		
		Speaker 5	**25**
F	a sales representative		
G	a translator		
H	an airline pilot		

TASK TWO

For questions **26–30**, choose from list **A–H** what view each speaker is expressing.

A	I'm pleased if I can settle misunderstandings.		
		Speaker 1	**26**
B	I'm glad to get a break from the office.		
		Speaker 2	**27**
C	I worry about having a negative impact.		
		Speaker 3	**28**
D	I wouldn't be able to tolerate a desk job.		
		Speaker 4	**29**
E	I get bored if I'm not constantly travelling.		
		Speaker 5	**30**
F	I'm happy that I can make friends easily.		
G	I'm excited to go on overseas assignments.		
H	I enjoy communicating when I'm abroad.		

Part 1 (2 minutes)

The examiner will ask you a few questions about yourself and about a general topic. For example, the examiner may ask you:

• What means of transport did you use to get here today?
• What sort of public transport is available in this area?
• Which forms of transport do you prefer, and which do you dislike?

Part 2 (4 minutes)

You will each be asked to talk on your own for about a minute. You will each be given three different pictures to talk about. After your partner has finished speaking, you will be asked a brief question connected with your partner's photographs.

Anxiety (compare, contrast and speculate)

Turn to pictures 1–3 on page 184 which show people feeling anxious.

(*Candidate A*), it's your turn first. Here are your pictures. They show **people in stressful situations**.

I'd like you to compare **two** of the pictures and say **what might be making the people anxious**.

(*Candidate B*), **which situation would you least like to be in? Why?**

Achievement (compare, contrast and speculate)

Turn to pictures 1–3 on page 185 which show different skills.

Now, (*Candidate B*), here are your pictures. **They show people who have achieved something.**

I'd like you to compare **two** of the pictures, and say **what you think these people have achieved and what difficulties they might have had in reaching their goals**.

(*Candidate A*), **which person do you think might be most proud of their achievement? Why?**

Part 3 (4 minutes)

Look at page 186, which shows situations where you need to consider appearance.

Appearance (discuss, evaluate and select)

Here are some different situations where your appearance is important and a question for you to discuss.

First, you have some time to look at the task.

(*Pause 15 seconds*)

Now talk to each other about **why your appearance is important in each situation**.

Now you have about a minute to decide in **which situation it's most important to have a good appearance**.

Part 4 (5 minutes)

The examiner will encourage you to develop the topic of your discussion in Part 3 by asking questions such as:

• In what sort of situations do you think someone's appearance is most important?

• Do you think it is possible to ignore fashion? (Why? / Why not?)

• To what extent do you judge a person by his or her appearance?

• How important is appearance to someone who cares what other people think?

For questions **1–8**, read the text below and decide which answer (**A, B, C** or **D**) best fits each gap. There is an example at the beginning (**0**).

Mark your answers **on the separate answer sheet**.

Example:

| 0 | **A** frequent | **B** common | **C** general | **D** normal |

| 0 | A | **B** | C | D |

Vanilla surprise

Vanilla is such a (**0**) …….. flavour that it comes as a surprise to learn that it is also one of the world's most expensive crops. The vanilla plant is (**1**) …….. to the Americas. Its flowers grow in (**2**) …….. , and in nature they are pollinated by hummingbirds and bees. The (**3**) …….. seed pods resemble oversized French beans, and develop their (**4**) …….. flavour and fragrance during the curing process. After harvesting, the beans are treated with heat or hot water and are placed in the sun every day for many weeks. When they have (**5**) …….. to a fifth of their original size, they are divided according to size and quality.

Like other spices that we (**6**) …….. for granted today, vanilla has a fascinating history. In the 16th century, the Spanish imported the spice to Europe. However, attempts to grow vanilla in other locations (**7**) …….. with failure: the plants would not produce pods, and it was only when a way was found to pollinate the flowers artificially that the commercial exploitation of this valuable crop (**8**) …….. under way.

1	**A** resident	**B** local	**C** native	**D** inhabitant
2	**A** series	**B** bouquets	**C** bands	**D** bunches
3	**A** deriving	**B** resulting	**C** producing	**D** arising
4	**A** distinctive	**B** appetising	**C** tasteful	**D** potential
5	**A** concentrated	**B** shrunk	**C** sunk	**D** lessened
6	**A** give	**B** make	**C** do	**D** take
7	**A** resulted	**B** hit	**C** met	**D** finished
8	**A** got	**B** started	**C** came	**D** began

For questions **9–16**, read the text below and think of the word which best fits each gap. Use only **one** word in each gap. There is an example at the beginning (**0**).

Write your answers **IN CAPITAL LETTERS on the separate answer sheet**.

Example: 0 | O | F | | | | | | | | | | | | | | | | | | | | |

Ancient cartoons

The technique of telling a story through a sequence (**0**) …….. pictures, though associated with modern cartoons, was in fact in use about 500 years ago. The British Library in London has some wonderful examples of these early cartoons, all of (**9**) …….. were produced to order for wealthy clients. (**10**) …….. makes this art form so interesting is that it flourished in one small part of Europe – Flanders, today a region of northern Belgium – (**11**) …….. to die out as printing was developed.

Many of the tiny pictures were (**12**) …….. larger than a postage stamp. They were painted by hand in books about the size of a modern paperback. The artists, (**13**) …….. skills were rewarded by high salaries, worked slowly, and the buyers sometimes had to wait years for the work to be completed. In the (**14**) …….. of one four-volume example, the buyer waited for well (**15**) …….. a decade.

The cartoons show a variety of subjects, but episodes from history were popular, (**16**) …….. were fairy tales.

PAPER 1 Reading and ▸ | Part 1
Use of English | Part 2
| Part 3
PAPER 2 Writing | Part 4
| Part 5
PAPER 3 Listening | Part 6
| Part 7
PAPER 4 Speaking | Part 8

For questions **17–24**, read the text below. Use the word given in capitals at the end of some of the lines to form a word that fits in the gap **in the same line**. There is an example at the beginning (**0**).

Write your answers **IN CAPITAL LETTERS on the separate answer sheet.**

Example: | 0 | C | R | E | A | T | O | R | | | | | | | | | | | |

Sir Arthur Conan Doyle

Famous the world over as the (**0**) …….. of Sherlock Holmes, **CREATE**
Sir Arthur Conan Doyle was born in Edinburgh in 1859
into an Irish family who were (**17**) …….. in the art world. **INFLUENCE**
Arthur probably inherited the ability to tell stories from
his mother, who was a source of (**18**) …….. to him. **INSPIRE**

Thanks to the (**19**) …….. of some relatives, Arthur was **GENEROUS**
able to study medicine at Edinburgh University. He
was a bright student, but (**20**) …….., and his zest for **REST**
adventure led him to accept a contract as ship's
surgeon. Returning home, he completed his (**21**) …….. **MEDICINE**
studies in 1881, and eventually settled in the south
of England.

It is believed that Doyle based Holmes' character on
one of his university tutors, Dr Joseph Bell, whom
he regarded with (**22**) …….. for his powers of logic. **ADMIRE**
The first Sherlock Holmes story was received with
such (**23**) …….. that Doyle was encouraged to write more. **ENTHUSE**
In 1893 he killed off his hero in order to concentrate on
writing what he saw as more serious work, but this
caused a public (**24**) …….., and he was forced to bring **CRY**
Holmes back to life.

For questions **25–30**, complete the second sentence so that it has a similar meaning to the first sentence, using the word given. **Do not change the word given.** You must use between **three** and **six** words, including the word given. Here is an example (**0**).

Example:

0 Jane regretted speaking so rudely to the old lady.

MORE

Jane .... politely to the old lady.

Example: | **0** | WISHED SHE HAD SPOKEN MORE |

Write **only** the missing words **IN CAPITAL LETTERS on the separate answer sheet**.

---

25 Sally showed absolutely no fear when climbing the wall.

DISREGARD

Sally showed .... own safety when climbing the wall.

26 The identity of the murderer was never discovered.

NEVER

The police .... was.

27 'It's not a good idea to call Leo just yet,' Valerie told me.

AGAINST

Valerie advised .... for a while.

28 It was only after I left the office that I realised I had forgotten the file.

DID

Only after leaving .... I had forgotten the file.

29 If I lose this match, people will never let me forget it!

LIVE

If I lose this match, I .... down!

30 Internal Affairs are investigating allegations of police fraud.

INTO

Allegations of police fraud .... Internal Affairs.

PAPER 1 Reading and ▶
              Use of English

PAPER 2 Writing

PAPER 3 Listening

PAPER 4 Speaking

Part 1
Part 2
Part 3
Part 4
Part 5
Part 6
Part 7
Part 8

You are going to read a newspaper article. For questions **31–36**, choose the answer (**A**, **B**, **C** or **D**) which you think fits best according to the text.

Mark your answers **on the separate answer sheet**.

Saving the big birds

At first glance, why anyone would want to save California condors is not entirely clear. Unlike the closely related Andean condors with their white neck fluff or king vultures with their brilliant black-and-white colouring, California condors are not much to see. Their dull black colour – even when contrasted with white underwings – featherless head and neck, oversized feet and blunt talons are hardly signs of beauty or strength. Their appeal begins to become evident when they take flight. With a nine-and-a-half-feet wingspan and a weight of up to 28 pounds, California condors are North America's largest fully flighted birds. In the Americas, only Andean condors are bigger. California condors can soar almost effortlessly for hours, often covering hundreds of miles a day – far more than other birds. Only occasionally do they need to flap their wings – to take off, change direction or find a band of warm air known as a thermal to carry them higher.

When it was discovered that the condor population was becoming dangerously small, scientists and zookeepers sought to increase condor numbers quickly to preserve as much of the species' genetic diversity as possible. From studying wild condors, they already knew that if a pair lost an egg, the birds would often yield another. So the first and sometimes second eggs laid by each female in captivity were removed, artificially incubated, and the chicks raised using hand-held puppets made to look like adult condors. Such techniques quickly proved effective.

Despite these achievements, the effort to save California condors continues to have problems. Survival rates of captive-hatched condors released to the wild are, for some people, too low, and some have had to be recaptured after they acted foolishly or became ill. As a result, the scientists, zookeepers and conservationists who are concerned about condors have bickered among themselves over the best ways to rear and release the birds.

Some of the odd behaviour on the part of these released birds is hard to explain. At times they landed on people's houses and garages, walked across roads and airport runways, sauntered into park visitor centres and takeaway restaurants, and took food offered by picnickers and fishermen. None are known to have perished by doing so, though. More seriously, one condor died from drinking what was probably antifreeze. Others died in collisions with overhead electrical transmission wires, drowned in natural pools of water, or were killed by golden eagles and coyotes. Still others were shot by hunters and killed or made seriously ill from lead poisoning. Some just disappeared. Most recently, some of the first chicks hatched in the wild died after their parents fed them bottle caps, glass shards, pieces of plastic and other man-made objects that fatally perforated or blocked their intestines. These deaths may be due to the chicks' parents mistaking man-made objects for bone chips eaten for their calcium content.

Mike Wallace, a wildlife specialist at the San Diego Zoo, has suggested that some of the condors' problems represent natural behaviour that helps them survive as carrion eaters. The real key to successful condor reintroduction, he believes, lies in properly socialising the young birds as members of a group that follow and learn from older, preferably adult birds. That, he argues, was missing from earlier condor releases to the wild. Typically, condors hatched in the spring were released to the wild that autumn or winter, when they were still less than a year old. Especially in the early releases, the young condors had no adults or even older juveniles to learn from and keep them in their place. Instead, the only other condors they saw in captivity and the wild were ones their own age. Now, condor chicks at several zoos are raised in cave-like nest boxes. The chicks can see older condors in a large flight pen outside their box but cannot interact with them until they are about five months old. Then the chicks are gradually released into the pen and the company of the social group. The group includes adult and older juvenile condors that act as mentors for younger ones. It is hoped that this socialisation programme will help the birds adapt to the wild when they are released.

31 What does the writer say is the Californian condor's most impressive feature?
    A The height at which it can fly.
    B The range of colours it displays.
    C The way it glides through the air.
    D The similarity it has to the Andean condor.

32 In the initial stage of the conservation programme,
    A eggs were taken from the nests of wild condors.
    B female condors were captured and studied carefully.
    C scientists and zookeepers tried to create genetic diversity.
    D condors were encouraged to produce more eggs.

33 What does the writer say in the third paragraph about the attempts to save
Californian condors from extinction?
    A Freed condors have tried to return to the places where they were born.
    B There is disagreement about the breeding methods employed.
    C The majority of birds reintroduced into the wild have died.
    D Attempts to breed condors in captivity have failed.

34 In the fourth paragraph, the writer says that some of the condors released into
the wild
    A adapted surprisingly quickly to their new surroundings.
    B displayed a tendency to seek out human contact.
    C died from ingesting too much fast food.
    D kept altering their eating habits.

35 According to Mike Wallace, there will be fewer problems
    A if young condors are taught appropriate behaviour by mature birds.
    B if the chicks are surrounded by older birds when they hatch.
    C if young condors are trained not to eat so much carrion.
    D if the chicks are kept in special boxes for five months.

36 The main purpose of the article appears to be
    A to evaluate the need to preserve the California condor.
    B to gain support for the California condor conservation project.
    C to examine developments in the California condor conservation
       programme.
    D to analyse factors surrounding the California condors' failure to adapt to
       the wild.

PAPER 1 Reading and ▶ | Part 1
Use of English | Part 2
PAPER 2 Writing | Part 3
| Part 4
PAPER 3 Listening | Part 5
| **Part 6**
PAPER 4 Speaking | Part 7
| Part 8

You are going to read extracts from four reviews of a book about memory. For questions **37–40**, choose from the reviews **A–D**. The reviews may be chosen more than once.

Mark your answers **on the separate answer sheet**.

Moonwalking with Einstein: the art and science of remembering everything by Joshua Foer

Joshua Foer spent a year training his memory. Four reviewers comment on the book he wrote about his experiences.

A

Brain-training, particularly memory-training, is a large industry and Joshua Foer consults some of its best-known gurus in his quest to become a 'warrior of the mind'. While not a self-improvement manual from that stable, this book details various time-honoured memorisation techniques largely derived from the ancient Greeks and Romans, and presents some intriguing portraits of memory champions able to perform apparently supernatural feats of recall. After a year's hard training, Foer himself becomes an elite memoriser, winning the US Memory Championships. He also supplies a useful, reader-friendly guide to 'memory' in history and an introduction to psychological and neuroscientific research on memory. At times, it feels a little too friendly, with the science in particular deserving a linguistically more formal and detached approach. It is good, however, to be reminded of what we are all capable of if we only put our minds to it.

B

Joshua Foer describes the year he spent training to compete in the US Memory Championships, and of what he learned about memory – how it works, its historical role in society and in education, and how techniques can be acquired to transform someone with an average memory into an outstanding mental athlete. It's a delight to travel with Foer into the geeky, largely male subculture of the competitive memorisers, and his account of the neurological functions of memory, delivered in clear, lively prose, is generally sound and up-to-date, with one notable exception. The idea that all our past experiences are stored in the brain, waiting to be retrieved, is now largely disputed by scientists. Foer's book is a reminder of how extraordinary our minds can be.

C

Joshua Foer admits his normal recall is no better than average. After a year of dedicated training, however, he won the US Memory Championships, and broke the speed record for memorising the order of a shuffled pack of cards. It's an entertaining story, which Foer combines with lucid, accessible explanations of a complex subject – the function and operation of memory in the human brain. Foer is not a neuroscientist, but his treatment of the subject is balanced and faithful to the science, apart, that is, from suggesting that all memories are permanently retained, though not always re-activated; studies now suggest that memory is very much subject to change. If a self-help, brain-training guide is what you are after, look elsewhere, but there are interesting accounts here of ancient memorisation methods, some of which have been in use for thousands of years.

D

As Joshua Foer rightly points out, the 'art of memory' has a long and noble history. In fact, until recently, memorisation was central to education, learning and authority. Now, it is largely disdained as a waste of time, and we externalise our memories into books and digital records. In training for the US Memory Championships, Foer employed techniques that have been known and used for thousands of years, and he developed his skills to the point that he became national champion. Sadly, what these competitive memorisers have to memorise is utterly trivial – sequences of playing cards, long lists of unfamiliar words, random numbers. In the sections of the book that deal with the history and science of memory, Foer proves he has a gift for communicating quite complex ideas in a manner that is palatable without being patronising. It's a pity that so much of the book is taken up with the dreary world of mental athletes, who perform tricks to store pointless information.

Which reviewer

expresses a different attitude to the others regarding
Foer's descriptions of memory?

`37` [ ]

takes a similar view to reviewer B about the accuracy
of Foer's account of how memory works?

`38` [ ]

expresses a different view from the others about
Foer's writing style?

`39` [ ]

shares reviewer C's opinion of how useful Foer's book
is for people who want to acquire better memory skills?

`40` [ ]

PAPER 1 Reading and ▸   Part 1
          Use of English   Part 2
PAPER 2 Writing   Part 3
                            Part 4
PAPER 3 Listening   Part 5
                            Part 6
PAPER 4 Speaking   **Part 7**
                            Part 8

You are going to read a magazine article. Six paragraphs have been removed from the article. Choose from the paragraphs **A–G** the one which fits each gap (**41–46**). There is one extra paragraph which you do not need to use.

Mark your answers **on the separate answer sheet**.

All this jazz

What makes someone give up a stable career for the uncertainy of playing the saxophone in a jazz band? Walter Williams finds out.

I'm sitting backstage with Marjorie Anderson in a small theatre in the French town of Villeneuf. In a few minutes she will walk on stage with the jazz band she plays with, Les Jazzistes. They have been together for two years now, slowly but steadily building up a loyal following, and there is little doubt that tonight's gig will be a success.

| 41 |

Yet she is clutching her saxophone like a petrified child. 'I'm scared of the audience,' she says. 'You've got to be kidding,' I tell her. 'No,' she says with a snort. 'I freeze up when I look at them.'

| 42 |

Marjorie lives in France and plays the sax professionally. She has a distinctive technique, honed to perfection by hours of practice and, some would claim, plays with added passion by virtue of the fact that she has made huge sacrifices in order to devote herself to jazz. In addition to being a fine musician, she's a vet by training: two careers not normally associated with each other.

| 43 |

It was probably something in her childhood. She grew up in Sydney, Australia, and was something of a child prodigy – as a flautist. She played with a youth orchestra, but then abruptly decided that music was not for her. 'I auditioned for a prestigious orchestra, but nothing came of it.' Her sense of rejection at the time was overwhelming. 'I was very thin-skinned in

those days,' Marjorie admits. 'I felt threatened every time someone commented on my playing or my technique.'

| 44 |

However, it emerged a decade later that contentment of this sort was not what Marjorie really yearned for. Her brother treated her to a week in Paris for her 35th birthday, and they went to a club whose lively jazz scene has been attracting a demanding clientele for over 70 years. The effect on Marjorie was immediate; it was as if she was hearing music for the first time.

| 45 |

'I moved here because it hit me that for 35 years, I'd never been in touch with my inner self, with my needs and desires,' she told me. 'Oddly enough, I didn't consider taking up the flute again. It was the saxophone that grabbed my attention. It was so much more expressive in terms of my own essential being.'

| 46 |

I ask her if she has any regrets about dropping out to follow her dreams. She says no, but that she feels a bit guilty. 'I realise playing the sax in a band isn't saving the world. Sometimes I feel I ought to be doing something more useful.' Being a musician leaves Marjorie little time for much else. Nevertheless, she has decided to reinvent herself yet again – as a writer this time. In fact, she has just finished her autobiography, entitled *Why Not Try It?* It's a question many readers, envious of her courage, will find uncomfortable.

A To help her with this, she reaches for her sunglasses. Wearing them throughout her appearance in front of this small crowd – maybe 250 people – is one of the methods she uses to control her nerves.

B Marjorie refused to let such a minor problem daunt her. Soon she was playing music again, this time with renewed determination to be one of the best sax players in the world. Then, without any warning, she developed a fear of performing in public that nearly paralysed her. It was time to take action.

C 'I thought I'd gone to heaven,' she says. 'It was a turning point. The experience told me I had to hear and play more music, and really live before it was too late.' This was the moment when she decided to make a radical change in her life.

D As if this combination wasn't unusual enough, five years ago, she suddenly decided to sell her thriving vet practice in Australia and moved to France – without knowing a word of French. What would make someone abandon her entire life and take up playing music at the age of 35?

E Her new-found stagefright was the other curious factor about this return to public performance. Marjorie believes her terror is related to the sense that she is baring her soul when she performs. 'The other thing I do to make myself less scared is stand completely still on stage,' she explains.

F So she went to college instead, and trained as a vet. She threw herself into her profession, channelling her energy into building up a practice. 'I became stronger psychologically because I was successful in my career,' she says. 'I see it as a positive thing. I was satisfied with my life.'

G It is an enviable position to be in, especially for someone who, like Marjorie, has managed to make a living in a notoriously precarious profession. What is more, she has done it in a country a long way from her place of origin.

You are going to read an article in which four scientists talk about the emotional side of their work. For questions **47–56**, choose from the people (**A–D**).

Mark your answers **on the separate answer sheet**.

Which scientist

acknowledges the role another scientist has had in the development of their career? **47** ☐

draws a parallel between significant and less well-known scientific findings? **48** ☐

points out how unimpressed by reputation scientists tend to be? **49** ☐

mentions the desire scientists have to achieve a major breakthrough? **50** ☐

says that certain aspects of their work can be tedious? **51** ☐

comments on the impact discussion can have on the generation of new ideas? **52** ☐

draws attention to a common misconception? **53** ☐

mentions the satisfaction derived from thinking about the value of their work? **54** ☐

mentions a reconciliation with a colleague? **55** ☐

describes the anxiety involved in switching from one field of study to another? **56** ☐

Scientists and their emotions

A Steven Greene, biologist

Not long ago, I had a long argument with a fellow biologist about a particular set of experiments. Things got pretty loud and heated, and harsh words were said. A week later, we sent mutually apologetic texts and made up.

This sort of thing doesn't find its way into scientific papers. We have to present our data, analysis and interpretation in a way that allows another scientist to understand each step. I am sometimes jealous of artists for whom sharing and explaining the emotional journey of a piece of work is celebrated. The absence of a natural forum for scientists to describe their emotions in their work can lead to the erroneous view that we don't have any. In fact, we usually make a huge emotional investment in our work.

Science is not for the faint-hearted. I remember attending a talk years ago, at which the speaker, a distinguished biologist, was continually challenged by the audience. At one point, a fierce debate broke out at which the speaker was a mute bystander. This lack of deference is by no means exceptional.

B Catherine Edwards, oceanographer

Writing a proposal is where most new science begins these days and it's set out like a business case. After all, your fabulous new idea needs money: equipment, salaries, overheads. The funding bodies are tough to impress. So the excitement of having a big new idea is only the first step.

The first proposal I ever wrote was for a three-year project. Initially, writing about why my research topic mattered cheered me up no end. It's easy to forget the bigger picture when you're working on details, and it was reassuring to be reminded of the importance of my research subject.

Working out the project details was fiddly and time-consuming. Then it slowed down even more, to a dull plod, as I checked and rechecked things. This was my idea and I desperately wanted it to be good, to deserve funding. Months after the deadline, an email told me my project would be funded. My idea wasn't rubbish! Others wanted it too!

C Dominika Gajewska, neuroscientist

While doing my postgraduate studies in psychology, I got temporarily side-tracked by the question of why certain serious psychological problems that afflict some people always seem to emerge at the end of adolescence. You can make it through childhood and adolescence and then suddenly become affected. Does something happen in brain development during adolescence that acts as a trigger? As I read the existing literature, I became increasingly frustrated that there didn't seem to be many answers.

I talked to my psychology professor, an expert on child development, and she said: 'Why don't you fill the gap yourself? Apply for funding and start some new research in developmental neuroscience focusing on human adolescence?'

As she said those words, I remember feeling excited and slightly apprehensive. It wasn't until then that I realised it was exactly what I wanted to do – move into a subject that was rather unknown territory to me. I was taking a risk by moving into developmental work with so little experience, but my mentor's encouragement made all the difference. Ten years later, I'm pleased with the outcome.

D Arif Shah, chemist

In a lab recently, a student of mine excitedly showed me a flask containing a dark solution. She shone a torch and it lit up, in a vivid bright green. 'Fluorescence,' I said. The glow attracted a small crowd. Although not a research-changing observation, it sparked off excited speculation. What was the structure? How was the light being generated? What spectrums and measurements should be recorded to understand the observation?

That buzz was a faint echo of the moment, over 200 years ago, when the pioneering chemist Humphry Davy first electrolysed molten potash and was rewarded with a spray of brilliant flashing droplets of potassium. Davy apparently danced round the room in delight.

Few of us are likely to come close to a discovery of that importance, though it's something many yearn for. There is, however, something profoundly pleasurable in going over results and observations with students and colleagues. The unexpected turns up in little ways in day-to-day research and each time a miniature brainstorming session ensues, where adjustments are made to the way research is going.

PAPER 1 Reading and
         Use of English
PAPER 2 Writing ▶ **Part 1**
                     Part 2
PAPER 3 Listening
PAPER 4 Speaking

You **must** answer this question. Write your answer in **220–260** words in an appropriate style on the separate answer sheet.

1 The government wants to economise on local library services. Your class has attended a seminar held by a government representative. You have made the notes below.

Methods of economising:

- reduced hours
- library closures
- voluntary assistants

Some opinions expressed in the discussion:

'Most libraries already have inconvenient opening hours.'

'Libraries are an important educational resource.'

'It's important to have trained librarians.'

Write an **essay** discussing **two** of the methods in your notes. You should **explain which method you think is more important** for the local government to consider and **provide reasons** to support your opinion.

You may, if you wish, make use of the opinions expressed in the discussion, but you should use your own words as far as possible.

PAPER 1 Reading and
Use of English

PAPER 2 Writing ▶ Part 1
Part 2

PAPER 3 Listening

PAPER 4 Speaking

Write an answer to **one** of the questions **2–4** in this part. Write your answer in **220–260** words in an appropriate style on the separate answer sheet. Put the question number in the box at the top of the page.

2   There has been a fire in your home. No one was hurt, but there was a lot of damage. Write to your insurance company describing what happened, the reason for the fire, and asking about payment for your temporary accommodation.

Write your **letter**.

3   You would like to promote healthy eating in your college, and believe one way to do this is to get students interested in cookery. You write to your principal proposing a weekend *Festival of Cookery* in the college. Explain how this could be organised and suggest ideas for making the festival exciting and fun.

Write your **proposal**.

4   Your class has just returned from a two-week visit to a school in another country. You stayed with host families and took part in classes and activities at the school. Each participant has been asked to write a report on the experience for the school magazine, saying what was interesting and enjoyable, and if there were any difficulties.

Write your **report**.

Track 25

You will hear three different extracts. For questions **1–6**, choose the answer (**A**, **B** or **C**) which fits best according to what you hear. There are two questions for each extract.

Extract One

You hear a man and a woman talking about the sport of karting (racing small motor vehicles).

1   When the man goes to an event, he
   A   drives a kart.
   B   maintains machines.
   C   helps manage the races.

2   The woman thinks that karting
   A   is a good way to learn driving skills.
   B   is a growth area for sports companies.
   C   is too expensive for most people to afford.

Extract Two

You hear part of a radio programme in which an interior designer is giving advice on colour in the home.

3   According to Eugene, orange
   A   calms and reassures you.
   B   stimulates and inspires you.
   C   is a natural cure for insomnia.

4   The interviewer believes that the living room is difficult to decorate because of
   A   the need to consider several other factors.
   B   the paintings on the wall.
   C   the need to be sociable.

Extract Three

You hear a conversation between a man and a woman about something that has just happened.

5   What experience is the man describing?
   A   He knocked down an old man with his car.
   B   He was involved in a head-on collision with a lorry.
   C   He hit another car while trying to avert an accident.

6   The man thinks the police
   A   may prosecute the lorry driver.
   B   are unlikely to take action against the old man.
   C   will hold the old man responsible for the accident.

PAPER 1 Reading and
         Use of English

PAPER 2 Writing

PAPER 3 Listening ▶
                           | Part 1
                           | **Part 2**
                           | Part 3
                           | Part 4

PAPER 4 Speaking

Track 26

You will hear part of a talk by a writer who has written a book about bread. For questions **7–14,** complete the sentences with a word or short phrase.

OUR DAILY BREAD

Supermarket (**7**) .... believe that baking bread on the premises attracts customers.

About (**8**) .... of bread in Britain is no longer baked in the old-fashioned way.

In the past, it took (**9**) .... for the yeast to ferment.

Nowadays, the fermentation process is faster, and less
(**10**) .... is used.

Unless salt is added, bread baked in the modern way is
(**11**) ....

Calcium propionate can be sprayed on the bread to prevent it from going
(**12**) ....

The speaker believes certain (**13**) .... may be caused by modern bread-making methods.

Supermarkets (**14**) .... on the sale of bread.

🎧 **Track 27**

You will hear part of a discussion between Velma Andrews, a lawyer, and Sergeant William Bailey, a police officer. For questions **15–20**, choose the answer (**A**, **B**, **C** or **D**) which fits best according to what you hear.

---

15 How did William feel the first time he gave evidence in court?
  A humiliated
  B nervous
  C furious
  D indifferent

16 Velma suggests that police officers giving evidence should
  A study the evidence more carefully.
  B ignore the lawyer for the defence.
  C not take comments personally.
  D demonstrate that they are honest and reliable.

17 Velma compares a police officer's evidence to a piece in a jigsaw puzzle because
  A it is unimportant unless it is part of a bigger picture.
  B it may not fit in with the rest of the evidence.
  C the defence lawyer will try to destroy it.
  D the police officer should only talk about his or her evidence.

18 William suggests that lawyers
  A adopt a special manner in the courtroom.
  B can be detached about a case.
  C might actually be close friends.
  D do not take their work seriously.

19 Velma's advice suggests that police officers should
  A never volunteer a personal opinion.
  B not answer a question unless they are sure of the answer.
  C remember they are not really addressing the lawyer.
  D not get into an argument with the judge.

20 William's main concern is that
  A a criminal could get away with his or her crime.
  B a court case could be confusing.
  C young police officers find courts terrifying.
  D police officers might argue with the lawyer.

PAPER 1 Reading and
           Use of English

PAPER 2 Writing

PAPER 3 Listening ▶

PAPER 4 Speaking

    Part 1
    Part 2
    Part 3
    Part 4

Track 28

You will hear five short extracts in which people talk about wind power.

While you listen, you must complete both tasks.

TASK ONE

For questions **21–25**, choose from list **A–H**, the attitude each speaker has towards wind power.

A   Placing wind turbines out at sea is acceptable.

                  Speaker 1 | 21 |

B   We should exploit wind power.

                  Speaker 2 | 22 |

C   Wind turbines are a threat to birds.

                  Speaker 3 | 23 |

D   Wind power has created attractive business
      opportunities for some people.

                  Speaker 4 | 24 |

E   Wind turbines are an unpleasant sight.

                  Speaker 5 | 25 |

F   There are valid objections to situating
      wind turbines offshore.

G   Wind power is grossly inadequate.

H   Wind power is a practical way to generate electricity.

TASK TWO

For questions **26–30**, choose from list **A–H** what each speaker says about the alternatives to wind power.

A   We should consider nuclear power, if it is safe.

                  Speaker 1 | 26 |

B   Hydroelectric power cannot create enough
      energy.

                  Speaker 2 | 27 |

C   Other renewable energy-generating schemes
      would be expensive to set up.

                  Speaker 3 | 28 |

D   Only if various renewable sources are exploited
      collectively will they produce enough energy.

                  Speaker 4 | 29 |

E   Hydroelectric power is a feasible way of generating
      enough electricity for our needs.

                  Speaker 5 | 30 |

F   Wind power cannot completely replace fossil fuels.

G   Nuclear power is the safest alternative to fossil fuels.

H   The best way is to use fossil fuels efficiently.

Part 1 (2 minutes)

The examiner will ask you a few questions about yourself and about a general topic. For example, the examiner may ask you:

• What job do you do, or would you like to do?
• What kind of working environment would suit you best?
• What sort of job would you dislike, and what working conditions would not appeal to you?

Part 2 (4 minutes)

You will each be asked to talk on your own for about a minute. You will each be given three different pictures to talk about. After your partner has finished speaking, you will be asked a brief question connected with your partner's photographs.

> **Respect** (compare, contrast and speculate)

Turn to pictures 1–3 on page 187 which show people showing respect.

(*Candidate A*), it's your turn first. Here are your pictures. They show **people showing respect**.

I'd like you to compare **two** of the pictures and say **what could be prompting the people to show respect, and how the people receiving the show of respect might feel.**

(*Candidate B*), **are the old and the young in your country respectful towards each other?**

> **Partnership** (compare, contrast and speculate)

Turn to pictures 1–3 on page 188 which show different partnerships.

Now, (*Candidate B*), here are your pictures. **They show people in partnerships.**

I'd like you to compare **two** of the pictures, and say **what kind of partnerships they illustrate and say how you think the partners feel about each other.**

(*Candidate A*), **do you prefer to work with a partner or on your own? Why?**

Part 3 (4 minutes)

Look at page 189 which shows some recreational activities.

> **Recreation** (discuss, evaluate and select)

Here are some different things that people do in their spare time and a question for you to discuss.

First, you have some time to look at the task.

(*Pause 15 seconds*)

Now talk to each other about **why people want to do these things.**

Now you have about a minute to decide **which activity is the most enjoyable for most people.**

Part 4 (5 minutes)

The examiner will encourage you to develop the topic of your discussion in Part 3 by asking questions such as:

• Why do you think some people choose to do dangerous recreational activities like mountain climbing?

• Do you think everyone needs some sort of recreational activity? (Why? / Why not?)

• Would it be possible to encourage more children to take up recreational activities other than sports (hobbies, such as collecting stamps, or gardening)?

For questions **1–8**, read the text below and decide which answer (**A, B, C** or **D**) best fits each gap. There is an example at the beginning (**0**).

Mark your answers **on the separate answer sheet**.

Example:

0   **A**   long   **B**   wide   **C**   far   **D**   high

0	A	B	C	D

Mushrooms

In order to maintain a healthy diet, we are encouraged to eat a (**0**) …….. range of fruit, vegetables and other natural foodstuffs. The nutritional (**1**) …….. of such things as carrots, fish and beans are often praised, but mushrooms tend to be (**2**) …….. . Research, however, suggests that they may well be qualified to join the (**3**) …….. of so-called superfoods like broccoli and blueberries.

'They may seem plain,' says dietician Dr Sarah Schenker, but studies have (**4**) …….. that they help reduce the risk of serious illnesses. They contain (**5**) …….. no fat, sugar or salt, and they're a valuable (**6**) …….. of dietary fibre. They also contain many essential vitamins and minerals, and they're good, too, for people wanting to (**7**) …….. down on their calorie intake – adding them to dishes like stews can make you feel fuller, but they're 90% water.

More than 2,500 (**8**) …….. of mushrooms grow in the wild, but, so far, most research has focused on a few types like *shitake*, *maitake* and white button mushrooms. There is clearly much more to discover about this intriguing food.

1	**A** profits	**B** aids	**C** favours	**D** benefits
2	**A** overdrawn	**B** overlooked	**C** overgrown	**D** overseen
3	**A** ranks	**B** grades	**C** rows	**D** files
4	**A** presented	**B** displayed	**C** revealed	**D** exposed
5	**A** virtually	**B** fairly	**C** closely	**D** utterly
6	**A** outset	**B** base	**C** root	**D** source
7	**A** break	**B** cut	**C** pull	**D** let
8	**A** breeds	**B** classes	**C** varieties	**D** bands

For questions **9–16**, read the text below and think of the word which best fits each gap. Use only **one** word in each gap. There is an example at the beginning (**0**).

Write your answers **IN CAPITAL LETTERS on the separate answer sheet**.

Example: | 0 | A | L | L | | | | | | | | | | | | | | | | | | | | |

Independent television

People going to the UK for the first time are often surprised that there are no advertisements at (**0**) …….. on the BBC television channels. Their absence is (**9**) …….. to the fact that the constitution of the BBC forbids it to accept advertising. So, (**10**) …….. does the BBC get the money it needs to keep it going? The answer is that, (**11**) …….. selling BBC programmes to other broadcasters around the world, the BBC is financed from revenue raised by the sale of television licences. The fee for the licences is set by the government, but (**12**) …….. this, the BBC is not state run, and it retains an independence of (**13**) …….. it is very proud. It can be said that the viewers themselves pay for the BBC, since (**14**) …….. single household that owns a television in Britain has to purchase a licence. Some viewers prefer other channels, but a valid licence is obligatory, (**15**) …….. or not you watch the BBC. Failure to buy one is (**16**) …….. the law.

For questions **17–24**, read the text below. Use the word given in capitals at the end of some of the lines to form a word that fits in the gap **in the same line**. There is an example at the beginning (**0**).

Write your answers **IN CAPITAL LETTERS on the separate answer sheet**.

Example: | 0 | H | E | I | G | H | T | | | | | | | | | | | | |

From coin to paper

In 9th-century China, at the (**0**) …….. of the Tang dynasty,   **HIGH**
the government became concerned about the serious
(**17**) …….. of carrying around large amounts of coins in   **CONVENIENT**
order to conduct business (**18**) …….. . Consequently, they   **TRANSACT**
devised a method of paying merchants with money
certificates, which could be exchanged for coin money
on demand at the capital. These certificates had an
unfortunate (**19**) …….. to blow away if there was any wind,   **TEND**
but they were (**20**) …….., so merchants began exchanging   **TRANSFER**
them with each other instead of using coins.

It was not until the Song dynasty that actual paper
money was created. Initially introduced by a group
of merchants and (**21**) …….., each banknote had images   **FINANCE**
of houses, trees and people printed on it. These were
(**22**) …….. by various intricate markings, the identification   **COMPANY**
of which could be made only by the issuing banks. Then,
in 1023, the government decided to (**23**) …….. the banknotes   **DRAW**
and issue government notes in their place. These could be
exchanged for government-issued coins, and so could be
used to buy simple groceries. As a result, the use of paper
money soon became (**24**) …….. .   **SPREAD**

For questions **25–30**, complete the second sentence so that it has a similar meaning to the first sentence, using the word given. **Do not change the word given.** You must use between **three** and **six** words, including the word given. Here is an example (**0**).

Example:

0 Jane regretted speaking so rudely to the old lady.

MORE

Jane .... politely to the old lady.

Example: | **0** | WISHED SHE HAD SPOKEN MORE |

Write **only** the missing words **IN CAPITAL LETTERS on the separate answer sheet**.

---

25 Fatima's warm welcome surprised me.

ABACK

I .... of Fatima's welcome.

26 Tom hates parties, so don't try to persuade him to go.

WORTH

It .... Tom into going to parties because he hates them.

27 'You will have to travel a lot in this job,' the manager told Sofia.

INVOLVE

The manager informed Sofia .... a lot.

28 We would have arrived here late if Ravi's father hadn't taken us to the bus stop.

FOR

Had .... Ravi's father taking us to the bus stop, we would have arrived here late.

29 It is possible that Theresa took your car keys this morning by mistake.

ACCIDENTALLY

Theresa .... your car keys this morning.

30 I didn't recognise Sara until she took off her sunglasses.

ONLY

It .... her sunglasses that I recognised her.

You are going to read a newspaper article. For questions **31–36**, choose the answer (**A**, **B**, **C** or **D**) which you think fits best according to the text.

Mark your answers **on the separate answer sheet**.

Senses that work together

A few years ago, on work experience at Oxford University, I had the privilege of being roped in for an experiment by a research team led by Professor Charles Spence. Sitting in a tiny room in a warren of labs and offices, I was shown a rack of bottles of scent and a computer program that let me play the sound of musical instruments at different pitches. My task was to sniff all the scents, and pick the sound that fitted each one best. Puzzled, I inhaled my first sample – sweet and slightly sickly, like bubble gum. Deep blaring brass seemed instinctively wrong, so I tried out higher, purer sounds and eventually settled on a high piano note. I left not much the wiser about what was going on. But the team was covering new ground in a field known as cross-modal perception.

When we think about how our senses work, we imagine them operating individually: you sniff a flower, and the smell is delivered uninterrupted from nose to brain. However, it's more complicated than that. Our senses mingle more often than we realise, collaborating to help us make sense of the world more easily. We call dull thuds 'heavy' and associate them with large objects, even though the sound itself has no size or weight. This would have helped our ancestors decide whether to run away from predators based on how big they sounded, without stopping to look them over. Most evidence for cross-modal perception comes from studies into sound and vision – not surprising considering how often we use them together. But research that shows other senses crossing over is emerging all the time, and it seems that even sound and smell sometimes form an unlikely pairing.

When two New York researchers, Daniel Wesson and Donald Wilson, began investigating an 'enigmatic' area of the brain called the olfactory tubercle, they were confronted with **this fact**. Originally, they only intended to measure how olfactory tubercle cells in anesthetised mice responded to smell. But during testing, Wesson noticed that every time he clunked his coffee mug down next to the experiment, the mouse cells jumped in activity. In fact, the olfactory tubercle is physiologically well-placed to receive both smell and sound information from the outside world; and so Wesson and Wilson broadened their investigation.

They found that among individual cells, most responded to odour but a significant number were also active when a tone was played. Some cells even behaved differently when smell and sound were presented together, by increasing or suppressing their activity. There may be some evolutionary sense behind the phenomenon – a sound accompanied by an unfamiliar smell could alert you to the presence of a predator.

Of course, mice aren't people, and a handful of firing cells don't always add up to a conscious experience. But Charles Spence's team have been carrying out experiments like the one in which I participated at Oxford University, which seem to show that sounds and smells cross over in human perception, too. Recently, they pulled together a group of people and gave them various drinks to smell. Participants were asked to sniff different samples, and then match them to an appropriate musical instrument and pitch. The results were interesting: piano was regularly paired with fruity scents; musky smells sounded like brass.

Further research found that listening to different sounds can alter your perceptions. Studying taste this time, the team ordered some special toffee and put together 'soundscapes' corresponding to bitterness and sweetness. Participants tasted identical pieces of toffee while listening to each soundscape, and found the toffee more bitter or sweeter, depending on which soundtrack they were listening to.

Studies like this are helping scientists redefine our understanding of the senses, and how the brain integrates them to its advantage. The consequences are worth considering. Could we see collaborations between musicians and chefs to produce sound-enhanced food and drink? Will you be ordering a coffee with a soundtrack to bring out your favourite aromas? Come to think of it, that could be one notion you hope coffee shops chains *don't* get round to.

31 What does the writer suggest about the experiment she was involved in?
   A   The findings that came out of it were disappointing.
   B   Those running it treated her with kindness.
   C   It was conducted in a light-hearted manner.
   D   She had little understanding of its purpose.

32 In the third paragraph the writer is
   A   introducing a new idea into her report.
   B   illustrating a point she has made previously.
   C   making her reservations about something clear.
   D   explaining the background to a particular issue.

33 What point does *this fact* in the third paragraph refer to?
   A   Evidence about the way senses work is hard to obtain.
   B   Sound and vision are relatively easy to study.
   C   There can be a link between sound and smell.
   D   A lot of research focuses on the senses.

34 In Wesson and Wilson's research,
   A   the link between sound and smell in mice was discovered by chance.
   B   the mice were affected in the same way by both sound and smell.
   C   the results confirmed what the researchers had suspected.
   D   the mice used seemed to be afraid of certain sounds.

35 What does the writer say about the experiment described in the seventh paragraph?
   A   The participants were initially reluctant to be involved in it.
   B   Its outcomes failed to support what was found in other experiments.
   C   The associations made between sounds and smells were consistent.
   D   Its purpose was different from that of the experiment she'd taken part in.

36 How does the writer feel about wider implications of the research she reports on?
   A   convinced the findings will have a major impact in the near future
   B   uneasy about how the knowledge acquired might be applied
   C   surprised by developments that have already taken place
   D   excited about forthcoming creative opportunities

You are going to read extracts from four articles written by scientists about the idea of bringing extinct animals back to life. For questions **37–40**, choose from the extracts **A–D**. The extracts may be chosen more than once.

Mark your answers **on the separate answer sheet**.

De-extinction

Developments in genetic science mean that scientists
may be able to bring extinct species back to life. Four scientists give
their views on this topic.

A

Thanks to advances in genetic technology, scientists may eventually be able to revive species we thought were gone forever. The idea is stunning and would revolutionise the way we think about science. Having destroyed countless species over the last 10,000 years, humans could, through science, begin to reverse the damage we have caused. It would deliver a profoundly hopeful message. Knowledge and techniques developed for de-extinction would also be directly applicable to living species that are endangered, so conservation would benefit. Revived species would also help to restore a great deal of ecological richness. Returning certain birds to the forests of North America would bring much greater plant diversity to these areas that are so important for humans, as well as for other wildlife. De-extinction may be difficult to achieve but it would undoubtedly be worth it.

B

Major breakthroughs, such as species revival, would have various consequences, one being that they can restore our faith in science, progress and even in ourselves. Species revival would show that science can be used for good, not simply to feed our lower appetites. We could also apply what we learn from it to efforts to conserve living species. Achieving de-extinction would require considerable time and effort, of course, but the idea that it would divert resources from conservation rests on a false assumption. The truth is that money invested in high-tech solutions would not otherwise be available for the protection of wild environments and species; it would probably go into such activities as plant research for commercial use. What we do need to think through carefully, however, is how we would re-introduce species into nature. The ecosystem of a vanished species will have changed since it last inhabited it, and anyway, its extinction almost certainly resulted from the deterioration of its natural habitat. But we have time to consider this, and it doesn't mean de-extinction isn't worth pursuing.

C

Work on genetic techniques that may help restore species will happen whether we approve of it or not, and the funds required would not alternatively be available for conservation but would instead be directed at some other cutting edge field like medical science. So scientists and the general public alike may as well go along with it. The fact is, it is likely to be widely welcomed and will help create a favourable climate for science. What does concern me is how animals that have been brought back to life could be put into the wild once again. Besides the challenge of recreating conditions within which they might survive – which in many cases would require changing the biodiversity of huge geographical areas, for example – there is the thought that they might pose a serious threat to existing species, either because they could carry diseases or because they invade and destroy habitats for other creatures.

D

Just suppose we managed to bring a species back to life and that it was able to reproduce. What then? It's hard enough introducing zoo-raised species into the wild, let alone ones that are no longer with us and whose disappearance was due to changes in the environments they depended on. Our endeavours to conserve living species and the ecosystems they rely on are already starved of resources. Diverting funds to work on de-extinction would only deprive them further. But the most dangerous aspect of the de-extinction notion is that it reinforces the idea that advanced science can solve all our problems. If we can reclaim extinct species in a laboratory, then why bother protecting forests, wetlands, rivers and oceans? Why worry about endangered species if we can simply keep their DNA and revive them some time later? De-extinction only distracts us from safeguarding out planet's biodiversity for future generations.

Which scientist

has a similar opinion to scientist B about the financial implications of investing in de-extinction?

37

has a different opinion from the others about how attitudes towards science would be influenced by working on de-extinction?

38

expresses a different view from the others about environmental issues associated with de-extinction?

39

shares scientist A's view of how de-extinction research would contribute to other areas of science?

40

PAPER 1 Reading and ▸
         Use of English
PAPER 2 Writing
PAPER 3 Listening
PAPER 4 Speaking

Part 1
Part 2
Part 3
Part 4
Part 5
Part 6
Part 7
Part 8

You are going to read a newspaper article about an extraordinary archaeological discovery in Orkney, an island in the north of Scotland. Six paragraphs have been removed from the article. Choose from the paragraph **A–G** the one which fits each gap (**41–46**). There is one extra paragraph which you do not need to use.

Mark your answers **on the separate answer sheet**.

5,000 year-old temples discovered on the Scottish island of Orkney

North-west of Kirkwall, the capital of Orkney, lies the Ness of Brodgar, a narrow strip of land which separates the island's two largest freshwater lakes. At their edges, the water laps against a green, hilly landscape, peppered with giant stone rings, ancient villages and other archaeological riches.

41

What had escaped their attention was the temple complex of the Ness of Brodgar. Its size and complexity have since left archaeologists searching for superlatives to describe the wonders unearthed there. 'It's a Neolithic site without parallel in western Europe. Yet we previously thought it was just a hill,' says archaeologist Nick Card. 'It's actually entirely man-made, although it covers more than six acres of land.'

42

The people responsible for this architectural marvel arrived on Orkney about 6,000 years ago in the Neolithic (or New Stone) Age. They were the first farmers in Britain, and on Orkney rapidly established a vibrant culture with their giant stone circles, communal tombs, and the buildings at the Ness of Brodgar. The beliefs that underpinned the temple complex are unknown, however, as is the purpose of its great structures.

43

What is clear is that the cultural energy of the farming folk of Orkney dwarfed that of other civilisations at that time. In size and sophistication, the temple complex of Brodgar is comparable with the wonders of ancient Egypt, for example, though much older. The fact that it was built on a small island to the north of

Scotland, makes it all the more remarkable. For many archaeologists, its discovery has revolutionised our understanding of the period.

44

We know that these innovators first reached Orkney on boats from mainland Scotland. They brought cattle, pigs and sheep with them, as well as grain to plant. These early farmers were clearly successful, though life would still have been precarious, with hunting and fishing providing precious supplies of extra protein.

45

Discarded stone tools and pieces of elegant pottery tell us, however, that they lived long and well enough for an increasingly sophisticated society to emerge. Over centuries, small communities coalesced into larger tribal units, and sizeable constructions went up. Many of these – like the huge circles of standing stones and a 5,000-year-old village – have long been acknowledged as highly significant monuments. Eventually, in 1999, they were given World Heritage status by UNESCO, an act that led directly to the discovery of the Brodgar temple complex.

46

The assumption had been that it was a natural feature of the landscape. However, the new investigations indicated quite the opposite. 'The density and extent of what we detected below the surface stunned us,' says Card. Initially, archaeologists thought they had stumbled upon a general site that had been in continuous use for a few thousand years after those early settlers, but it all dated back to Neolithic times. What is more, the quality of workmanship evident in the buildings, carvings and pottery unearthed 'wouldn't be seen again on Orkney almost until modern times'.

A One thing archaeologists are sure of, nevertheless, is that it wasn't a settlement to live in. 'It was a huge ceremonial centre,' says Card, 'but the ideas and views of its builders remain a mystery.'

B The fate of the complex remains a puzzle, on the other hand. About 4,000 years ago, roughly 1,000 years after construction began, it was abruptly abandoned. Whatever the cause, the great temple complex was deserted and forgotten for the next four millennia.

C Evidence for this has been discovered at the site of a Neolithic village: the bones of domesticated animals alongside those of wild deer, whales and seals. Analysis of human bones from the period suggest that few people reached the age of 50 and those who survived childhood usually died in their 30s.

D For decades, researchers have been drawn to this remote place. It was extensively scrutinised until a recent chance discovery revealed that, for all their thoroughness, archaeologists had completely overlooked a Neolithic treasure eclipsing all others on Orkney – and further afield too.

E 'This recognition prompted us to think about the land surrounding the sites we knew,' says Card. 'We decided to survey it to see what else might be found.' Technology, like ground-penetrating radar for pinpointing man-made artefacts hidden underground was used. And the first location selected for this was the Ness of Brodgar.

F And when all the buildings were intact, it must have looked extremely impressive. Two giant walls protected more than a dozen large temples – one measuring almost 25 m square – all linked to outhouses and kitchens by carefully constructed stone pavements.

G 'We need to turn the map upside down when we consider the Neolithic era,' says Card. 'London may be the cultural hub of Britain today, but 5,000 years ago, Orkney was the centre for new ideas. The first grooved pottery, so distinctive of the era, was made here, for example, and then spread southwards.'

PAPER 1 Reading and
        Use of English
PAPER 2 Writing
PAPER 3 Listening
PAPER 4 Speaking

Part 1
Part 2
Part 3
Part 4
Part 5
Part 6
Part 7
Part 8

You are going to read an article in which four people talk about works of art they admire and the artists who created them. For questions **47–56**, choose from the people (**A–D**).

Mark your answers **on the separate answer sheet**.

Which writer

claims they are indifferent to a lot of art?	**47**
refers to artists being associated with a particular subject?	**48**
describes how a work of art gives an insight into a particular period of time?	**49**
points out the widespread impact an artist has had on other artists?	**50**
is impressed by how the style of an artwork suits its subject matter?	**51**
mentions the influence artists have had on their own work?	**52**
admits to ignorance of certain types of art?	**53**
talks about a work of art stimulating a variety of feelings?	**54**
refers to the universality of the subject matter of a particular work of art?	**55**
compares the significance of artists from different times in history?	**56**

Works of art we admire

A **The author Philip Pullman talks about Claude Monet's *The Four Trees* painted in 1891**

What does it mean for a work of art to be great? I think it must signify influence as well as a self-contained perfection of form. I can only talk about western art because, while I can see beauty in, say, a bronze sculpture from the Benin kingdom of West Africa, I have no idea whether it was influential in its own culture, or typical, or what.

So I've chosen a painting by Monet, who changed the way painters in the west saw and depicted light, and light is the subject of every representational painting: light falling on flesh, on stone, on cloth, on water. *The Four Trees*, one of a series of paintings of a stretch of the river Epte in France, is great because it conveys the sense of a bright morning with freshness and brilliance (the delicious golden light on the curve of trees in the distance); and because it's thrilling–I pity anyone who didn't feel a shock of delight at seeing that grid of dark lavenders over pale blue and gold.

B **The actor Kristin Scott Thomas talks about Gustave Caillebotte's *Paris Street: Rainy Day* painted in 1877**

As the title of the painting suggest, it shows a street scene in Paris on a wet day. The brilliant thing about it is its composition. A lamp post in the middle of the painting creates a sharp division, which makes it like a scene from a film. It throws you into the 19th century city with its wide boulevards and grand buildings. On the right, a couple walk towards us. His coat flaps open as if he'd just enjoyed a good lunch. Her arm is linked through his as they watch something beyond the lamp post that surprises him and amuses her but that we cannot see. On the other side of the black post, life is slower, lonelier and wet. The slippery shining cobblestones in the road give me cold toes, and I can smell the damp wool from all those coats. It isn't a cold day, but a miserable, rainy late autumn afternoon. I experience a twinge of envy as I think about this comfortable, affectionate couple going home to tea and a warm fire.

C **The sculptor Cornelia Parker talks about the photographs of Bernd and Hilla Becher from 1988**

Great artists can make you look at the world differently. Think of Monet with his haystacks at the end of the 19th century, or Turner with his sunsets several decades before: once you've seen their paintings, you never look at those things in the same way. That's exactly what Bernd and Hilla Becher have done for industrial architecture in the last 50 years. The German artists spent decades travelling around, obsessively cataloguing those grim, ubiquitous structures – gas-cooling towers, pitheads, pylons – that most of us think of as ugly. In the Bechers' work, they become like people, each with their own character.

I can't look at any such structures in real life without thinking of their photographs. I have several pinned to the walls of my studio. As a sculptor, I'm fascinated by their shape and form. The best works of art allow space for the viewer to bring their own interpretation and the Bechers' photographs always do this.

D **The artist David Hockney talks about Picasso's *Mother and Child (First Steps)* painted in 1943**

There's not much art I don't like, although nowadays a great deal of art doesn't generate strong feelings in me one way or another. I could say the paintings of Fra Angelico in Florence in Italy are my favourite works, or Rembrandt's great drawing, in the British Museum, of a family teaching a child to walk. But why not Picasso's treatment of this theme? It's something that absolutely everybody has experienced and witnessed. Today, thousands of depictions will be made of this all over the world, most with a camera: Uncle Charlie, for example, teaching little Edna to walk, photographed by mum. But most will not be able to show us what Picasso does: the child, both thrilled and frightened; the anxious mother, whose supple hands clasp the child's still awkward fingers. The way Picasso uses Cubist techniques to break up their bodies and present different perspectives allows him to give us that detail. It's abstract but at the same time manages to convey the humanity of the moment in a wonderfully touching manner.

You **must** answer this question. Write your answer in **220–260** words in an appropriate style on the separate answer sheet.

1 Your class has attended a discussion on the methods governments should use to encourage people to take more exercise. You have made the notes below.

<u>**Methods governments could use to encourage people to exercise more:**</u>

- more sports facilities
- education
- media campaigns

Some opinions expressed in the discussion:

'Sports facilities are expensive to create.'

'Schools already do their best.'

'You cannot guarantee results from media publicity.'

Write an **essay** for your tutor discussing **two** of the methods in your notes. You should **explain which method you think is more important**, and **provide reasons** to support your opinion.

You may, if you wish, make use of the opinions expressed in the discussion, but you should use your own words as far as possible.

PAPER 1 Reading and
Use of English

PAPER 2 Writing ▶ Part 1

PAPER 3 Listening ▶ **Part 2**

PAPER 4 Speaking

Write an answer to **one** of the questions **2–4** in this part. Write your answer in **220–260** words in an appropriate style on the separate answer sheet. Put the question number in the box at the top of the page.

2   You belong to a sports club and recently led a trip, funded by the club, for a group of fellow members to watch a major sports event in your capital city. Write a report on the trip for the club committee, saying why you thought the club's money was well spent.

Write your **report**.

3   Your local tourist office is planning to produce a tourist guidebook. It will give the contract for writing the guidebook to someone who is familiar with the local area. You are interested.

Write to the tourist office, saying why you would be suitable for the job. Outline your familiarity with the area, including your knowledge of:

- places of historical interest
- areas of natural beauty
- theme parks and amusement parks.

Write your **letter**.

4   You work on a student newspaper. You have been asked by the editor to write a review of an enduringly popular novel, outlining its most successful features, its shortcomings and the reasons it has remained popular.

Write your **review**.

🎧 **Track 29**

You will hear three different extracts. For questions **1–6**, choose the answer (**A**, **B** or **C**) which fits best according to what you hear. There are two questions for each extract.

Extract One

You hear two college friends discussing a lecture they have just attended.

1 What was the subject of the talk?
   A starting a business
   B preparing for a job interview
   C working abroad

2 They liked the talk because the speaker
   A gave plenty of opportunity for questions.
   B handed out useful information.
   C had a friendly and humorous style.

Extract Two

You hear part of a radio programme in which two people are discussing growing herbs.

3 According to Jerry, herbs are particularly useful
   A in a corner of the garden.
   B when they grow on windowsills.
   C if grown among vegetables.

4 Which of the following is not true about growing herbs?
   A Annual herbs are not used in cooking.
   B Herbs are easy to cultivate.
   C Perennial herbs add flavour to food.

Extract Three

You hear two friends talking about job interviews they recently attended.

5 What did James feel about the experience?
   A He was surprised that only one person interviewed him.
   B He was relieved that the interviewer asked easy questions.
   C He was worried about the number of people being interviewed.

6 Susan thinks she was well prepared for her interview because
   A she had a presentation to show.
   B she did a lot of research on the company.
   C she planned the journey there carefully.

PAPER 1 Reading and
         Use of English

PAPER 2 Writing

PAPER 3 Listening

PAPER 4 Speaking

Part 1
Part 2
Part 3
Part 4

Track 30

You will hear an anthropologist talking about a recent find. For questions **7–14**, complete the sentences with a word or short phrase.

A SIGNIFICANT FIND

Several fossil skulls were dug up in Ethiopia last

(**7**) ....

There were at least (**8**) .... adult skulls and one that

belonged to a child.

It appears that the people these skulls belong to were our

(**9**) .... ancestors.

Anthropologists now believe that *Homo sapiens* is

(**10**) .... from Neanderthals.

The reason why the Neanderthals (**11**) ....

is not known.

The people whose skulls have been found probably used

(**12**) ....

They also lived in (**13**) ...., a factor which probably

helped them to survive.

The early days of human evolution are still (**14**) ....

to modern scientists.

🎧 **Track 31**

You will hear an interview with Marianne Nolan, a surfing champion. For questions **15–20**, choose the answer (**A**, **B**, **C** or **D**) which fits best according to what you hear.

---

15 What does Marianne Nolan say about entering the senior surfing championships?

    A She is pleased to have the chance to learn from experienced surfers.

    B She is realistic about the amount of training that will be involved.

    C She has confidence that she will succeed in the early rounds.

    D She has mixed feelings about competing at such a high level.

16 According to Marianne, women surfers today

    A are prepared to take more risks than they did in the past.

    B are mainly concerned with having a beautiful surfing style.

    C are more likely to think in terms of becoming professional surfers.

    D are determined to achieve the same recognition for their skill as men.

17 In Marianne's opinion, young girls who surf should

    A find creative ways to promote surfing as a sport in top international events.

    B thank previous generations for pioneering surfing as a serious sport for women.

    C push their friends to take up surfing as a way of staying fit and healthy.

    D join surfing clubs that encourage boys and girls to compete with each other.

18 What does Marianne say about being considered a good surfer?

    A She thinks it could lead to sponsorship in the future.

    B It gives her hope that she will win the same title.

    C She feels it is both a burden and a compliment.

    D It surprised her to receive so much publicity.

19 When asked about her future, Marianne says she

    A has been too busy with her sport to make decisions about a job.

    B expects that a career will develop naturally out of her sport.

    C wonders how well she will adjust to having a routine job.

    D has changed the idea she previously had for a career.

20 What lesson does Marianne say she has learned from competitive surfing?

    A Prepare for the unexpected.

    B Be generous to people you defeat.

    C Know when you have reached your limit.

    D Do not let victory make you too confident.

Track 32

You will hear five short extracts in which people talk about holidays that went wrong.

While you listen, you must complete both tasks.

Task One

For questions **21–25**, choose from list **A–H**, the person who is speaking.

A   a working holiday

B   a student exchange trip

C   a sailing holiday

D   a city weekend break

E   a guided walking tour

F   a music course

G   a gastronomic tour

H   a camping holiday

Speaker 1	21
Speaker 2	22
Speaker 3	23
Speaker 4	24
Speaker 5	25

Task Two

For questions **26–30**, choose from list **A–H** what view each speaker is expressing.

A   shame at the way they behaved

B   shock at the cost of the holiday

C   unhappiness with their companions

D   disappointment about the food

E   anger at the condition of their hotel room

F   frustration at the amount of time wasted

G   dissatisfaction with the way the holiday was organised

H   dismay that they had spoilt the holiday for their friends

Speaker 1	26
Speaker 2	27
Speaker 3	28
Speaker 4	29
Speaker 5	30

Part 1 (2 minutes)

The examiner will ask you a few questions about yourself and about a general topic. For example, the examiner may ask you:

• How popular are the cinema and the theatre in your town or region?
• Which do you prefer: going to the cinema, or watching films on television?
• What was the last film that you enjoyed?

Part 2 (4 minutes)

You will each be asked to talk on your own for about a minute. You will each be given three different pictures to talk about. After your partner has finished speaking, you will be asked a brief question connected with your partner's photographs.

> **Stress** (compare, contrast and speculate)

Turn to pictures 1–3 on page 190 which show stressful situations.

(*Candidate A*), it's your turn first. Here are your pictures. They show **people in stressful situations.**

I'd like you to compare **two** of the pictures and say **what is stressful about these situations, which is the more situation, and why.**

(*Candidate B*), **what sort of situation do you find stressful?**

> **Struggling against the elements** (compare, contrast and speculate)

Turn to pictures 1–3 on page 191 which show people struggling against the weather.

Now, (*Candidate B*), here are your pictures. **They show people who have to struggle against the elements.**

I'd like you to compare **two** of the pictures, and say **what kind of problems the people face and how they might be feeling.**

(*Candidate A*), **what sort of struggle against the elements would you find most difficult? Why?**

Part 3 (4 minutes)

Look at page 192 which gives some situations where people are being creative.

> **Creativity** (discuss, evaluate and select)

Here are some different situations where people are engaged in creative activities and a question for you to discuss.

First, you have some time to look at the task.

(*Pause 15 seconds*)

Now talk to each other about **what rewards people get when they do these things.**

Now you have about a minute to decide **which creative activity is the most rewarding.**

Part 4 (5 minutes)

The examiner will encourage you to develop the topic of your discussion in Part 3 by asking questions such as:

• How important is it for people to feel creative in some way?
• Do you feel people get a similar sense of satisfaction from other activities?
• It is sometimes said that everyone has the potential to be creative in some way. Do you agree? (Why? / Why not?)

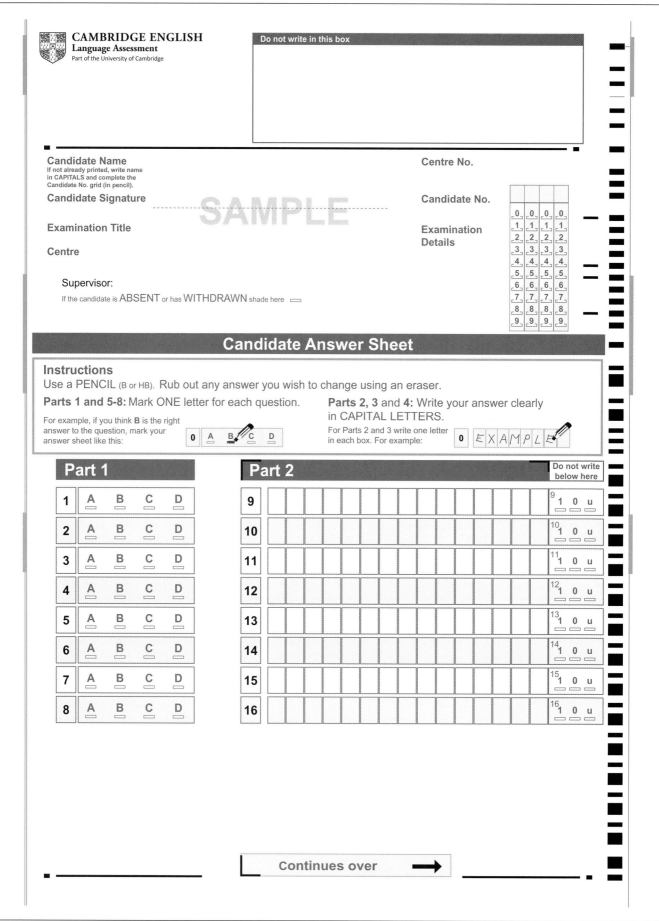

Part 3

17																					17 1 0 u
18																					18 1 0 u
19																					19 1 0 u
20																					20 1 0 u
21																					21 1 0 u
22																					22 1 0 u
23																					23 1 0 u
24																					24 1 0 u

Part 4

25		25 1 0 u
26		26 1 0 u
27		27 1 0 u
28		28 1 0 u
29		29 1 0 u
30		30 1 0 u

Part 5

31	A B C D
32	A B C D
33	A B C D
34	A B C D
35	A B C D
36	A B C D

Part 6

37	A B C D
38	A B C D
39	A B C D
40	A B C D

Part 7

41	A B C D E F G
42	A B C D E F G
43	A B C D E F G
44	A B C D E F G
45	A B C D E F G
46	A B C D E F G

Part 8

47	A B C D E
48	A B C D E
49	A B C D E
50	A B C D E
51	A B C D E
52	A B C D E
53	A B C D E
54	A B C D E
55	A B C D E
56	A B C D E

CAMBRIDGE ENGLISH
Language Assessment
Part of the University of Cambridge

Do not write in this box

Candidate Name
If not already printed, write name
in CAPITALS and complete the
Candidate No. grid (in pencil).

Candidate Signature

Examination Title

Centre

Centre No.

Candidate No.

Examination
Details

Supervisor:
If the candidate is ABSENT or has WITHDRAWN shade here ☐

Test version: A B C D E F J K L M N   Special arrangements: S H

Candidate Answer Sheet

Instructions

Use a PENCIL (B or HB).
Rub out any answer you wish to change using an eraser.

Parts 1, 3 and 4:
Mark ONE letter for each question.

For example, if you think **B** is the
right answer to the question, mark
your answer sheet like this:

0   A☐ B▬ C☐

Part 2:
Write your answer clearly in CAPITAL LETTERS.

Write one letter or number in each box.
If the answer has more than one word, leave one
box empty between words.

For example:

0 N U M B E R   1 2

Turn this sheet over to start.

Part 1

	A	B	C
1	A	B	C
2	A	B	C
3	A	B	C
4	A	B	C
5	A	B	C
6	A	B	C

Part 2 (Remember to write in CAPITAL LETTERS or numbers)

SAMPLE

	1 0 u
7	
8	
9	
10	
11	
12	
13	

Part 3

	A	B	C	D	E	F	G	H
15	A	B	C	D	E	F	G	H
16	A	B	C	D	E	F	G	H
17	A	B	C	D	E	F	G	H
18	A	B	C	D	E	F	G	H
19	A	B	C	D	E	F	G	H
20	A	B	C	D	E	F	G	H

Part 4

	A	B	C	D	E	F	G	H
21	A	B	C	D	E	F	G	H
22	A	B	C	D	E	F	G	H
23	A	B	C	D	E	F	G	H
24	A	B	C	D	E	F	G	H
25	A	B	C	D	E	F	G	H
26	A	B	C	D	E	F	G	H
27	A	B	C	D	E	F	G	H
28	A	B	C	D	E	F	G	H
29	A	B	C	D	E	F	G	H
30	A	B	C	D	E	F	G	H

SAMPLE

TEST 1

▶▶ **PART 2**

Candidate A

Language bank

These people could be …

He/She seems to be …

I imagine …

I suppose …

I'm fairly sure …

I'd say they are probably …

Apparently, …

Judging by the fact that …

Similarly, …

I can't tell who/where/what …

actors
annual tradition
audience
carnival
clown in a circus
costume
masks
on stage
professional
put on a performance
street party
take part (in festival, play, etc.)
theatre

- Why are the people dressed in this way?
- How do you think they are feeling?

▶ 1

▶ 2

▶ 3

▸▸ PART 2

Candidate B

Language bank

This picture shows ...

They must be ...

It might/could be ...

He/She seems to be ...

In contrast to ...

As in the previous picture ...

There are a number of advantages/
disadvantages to working ...

One advantage/disadvantage
would be that ...

I imagine it's very ...

agricultural workers
cheap labour
craft
create something with your hands
executive
exhausting
highly paid/badly paid
indoors/outdoors
job satisfaction
manual labour
mentally/physically exhausting
potter
sophisticated modern office
stressful
suffer from heat/stress
tea plantation
well-equipped office

• **What are the advantages and disadvantages of working in these environments?**

▶▶ **PART 3**
   Candidates A and B

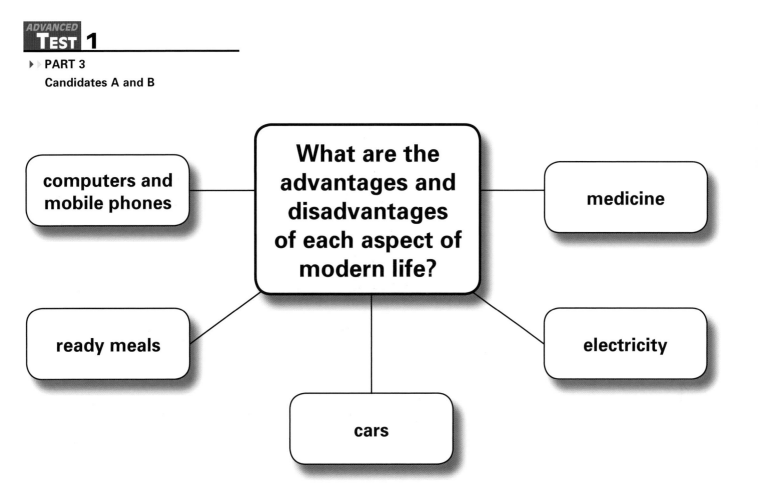

Language bank

The benefits/drawbacks of ... are obvious, I think.

What about the advantages/disadvantages, in your view?

Do the disadvantages outweigh the advantages in your opinion?

It's easy to see the benefits of computers and mobile phones, don't you think?

Mobile phones certainly make it easier to keep in touch, wouldn't you say?

I'm not sure whether there are any health risks associated with heating food in a microwave oven. What do you think?

It's usually more convenient to drive somewhere than to take public transport, but surely the pollution caused by cars is too high a price to pay?

I'd find it difficult to think of any disadvantages connected with electricity.

Perhaps we have to distinguish between electricity itself and the means of generating it.

▶▶ **PART 2**

Candidate A

Language bank

I guess/I imagine ...

He/She appears to be ...

He/She may be ...

He/She looks as though ...

On the other hand, he/she might be ...

To judge from the clothes he/she's wearing, ...

To judge from his/her posture, ...

about to dive
apprehensive
bathing trunks
business suit
concentrate on what you are about to do
diving board
have your arms outstretched
interview for a job
nervous
overcome your fears
wait in the wings
waiting area

- What could the people be anticipating?
- How do you think they are feeling?

▶▶ **PART 2**

Candidate B

Language bank

I can't tell whether the person is a man or a woman. It looks as if/though ...

I can't see the expression on his/her face, but I think he/she must be ...

Perhaps he/she feels ...

It's also possible that he/she ...

If I were him/her, I'd probably feel ...

The landscape/room might make me feel ...

The man looks like he is dressed for cold weather.

The person is dwarfed by the landscape.

Perhaps she's waiting ...

She might simply be looking at something outside.

alone

depressing atmosphere

elderly lady

insignificant

inspiring

lonely

peer through the curtains

remote

rugged

spectacular

suffer from loneliness

tracksuit

uplifting

- **Why are the people alone?**
- **How do you think they are feeling?**

▶ **1**

▶ **2**

▶ **3**

▶▶ **PART 3**
   Candidates A and B

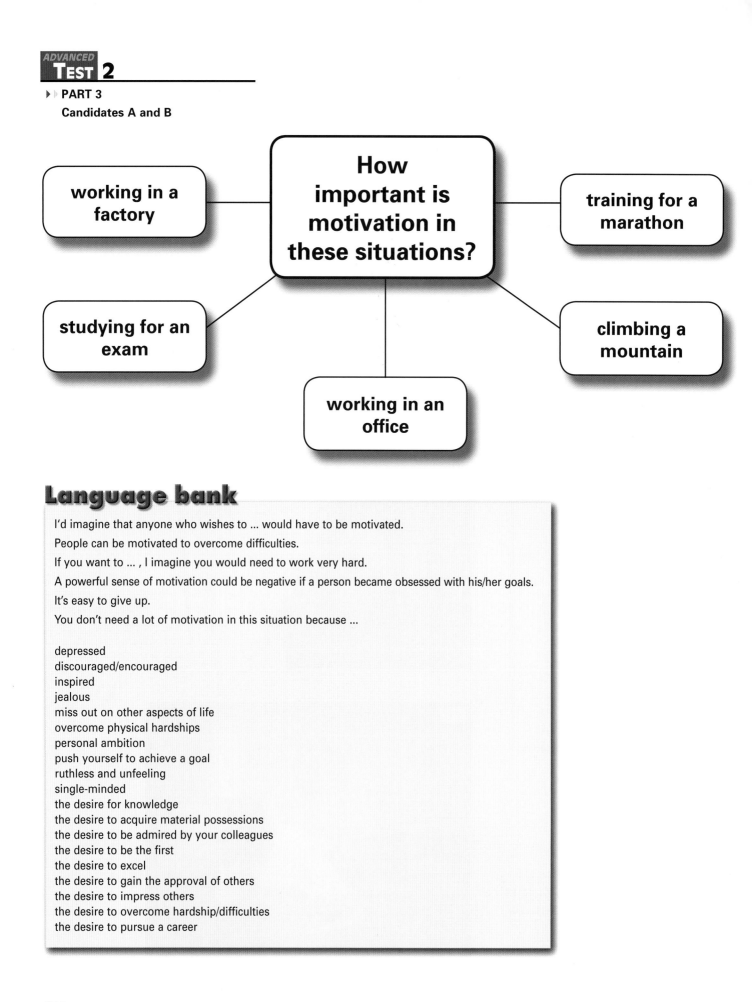

working in a factory

studying for an exam

How important is motivation in these situations?

training for a marathon

climbing a mountain

working in an office

Language bank

I'd imagine that anyone who wishes to ... would have to be motivated.

People can be motivated to overcome difficulties.

If you want to ... , I imagine you would need to work very hard.

A powerful sense of motivation could be negative if a person became obsessed with his/her goals.

It's easy to give up.

You don't need a lot of motivation in this situation because ...

depressed
discouraged/encouraged
inspired
jealous
miss out on other aspects of life
overcome physical hardships
personal ambition
push yourself to achieve a goal
ruthless and unfeeling
single-minded
the desire for knowledge
the desire to acquire material possessions
the desire to be admired by your colleagues
the desire to be the first
the desire to excel
the desire to gain the approval of others
the desire to impress others
the desire to overcome hardship/difficulties
the desire to pursue a career

▶▶ **PART 2**

  Candidate A

Language bank

It looks as if/though ...

They appear to be ...

They must be ...

I would say he/she's probably ...

Perhaps they're going somewhere on holiday.

They're about to leave on a holiday, not a business trip.

Like the man in the second picture, ...

Unlike the man in the second picture, these people are ...

The mode of transport in this case is very different.

about to board a spaceship
about to set off
boot of the car
briefcase
business trip
casual clothes
crew of a spaceship
embark on a journey/mission
family car
intercity train
load the luggage
members of a family
space mission
spacesuit
station platform
suit and tie
suitcase on wheels

- Why might the people be leaving?
- How might they be feeling?

Candidate B

Language bank

He/She looks very tired.

He/She must be feeling exhausted.

This makes me think he/she's been working ...

In all likelihood, ...

Of course, it's also possible that ...

I suppose they feel satisfied as well as exhausted.

In contrast to the previous two images, this picture shows ...

Judging by his/her expression ...

look after a young child
loosen your tie
mental/physical work
renovate a house
rest your head on your hand
stare at a computer screen
stiff muscles
wear a shirt and tie

- **Why might the people be tired?**
- **What kind of exhaustion – mental or physical – is each person feeling, and why?**

▶▶ PART 3
  Candidates A and B

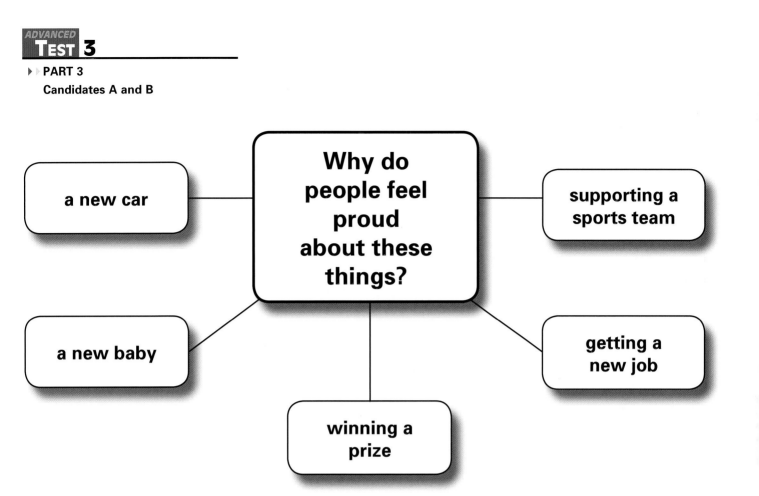

Language bank

achievement
cheer
dedicate yourself to achieving your goal
delighted
feel part of a group
it's natural to be proud of ...
justifiably proud
own an impressive car
parental pride
proud of your child/offspring
public acclaim
satisfied with yourself
trophy
victory
work and save in order to buy something

▸▸ **PART 2**

Candidate A

Language bank

Presumably, this sport appeals to people who ...

It attracts people who are ...

People who are ... are inclined to do this sport.

People who want to excel in this sport must be ...

This sport does not demand the same level of fitness as ...

In contrast to ... , this sport ...

aim
archer
archery
bow and arrow
bull's eye
concentration
co-ordination
head a ball
hit the target
individual/team sport
powerful physique
score a goal
take part in
training and practice
weightlifting

- What kind of training do these sports require?
- What are the advantages and disadvantages of taking part in a team sport, as opposed to an individual sport?

▸ **1**

▸ **2**

▸ **3**

▶▶ **PART 2**
   Candidate B

- What are the advantages of living in each place?
- What are the impractical aspects of living in each home?

Language bank

I should think a home like this would be ...

In contrast to the other buildings, this home ...

The house seems to be made of ...

One advantage/disadvantage of a home like this would be ...

Its location would be a disadvantage in case of illness or other emergencies.

The building itself would be expensive to keep up because ...

It would require a large staff to look after a home like this.

Some people may dislike feeling that their home is just like all the rest.

Privacy might be a problem in a home like this.

cut off from civilisation
flats in an apartment block
high heating and maintenance costs
insulation
isolated
(lack of) privacy
log cabin
mansion
rural/urban environment stately home
unsuitable for domestic purposes

▶ 1

▶ 2

▶ 3

▶▶ **PART 3**

Candidates A and B

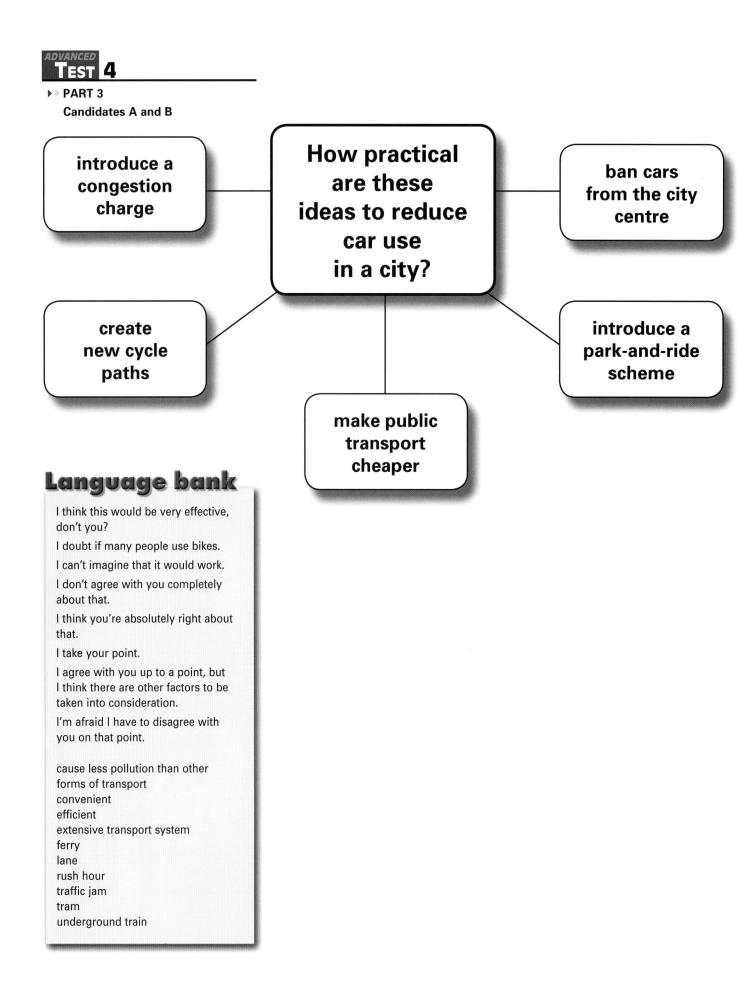

introduce a congestion charge

How practical are these ideas to reduce car use in a city?

ban cars from the city centre

create new cycle paths

introduce a park-and-ride scheme

make public transport cheaper

Language bank

I think this would be very effective, don't you?

I doubt if many people use bikes.

I can't imagine that it would work.

I don't agree with you completely about that.

I think you're absolutely right about that.

I take your point.

I agree with you up to a point, but I think there are other factors to be taken into consideration.

I'm afraid I have to disagree with you on that point.

cause less pollution than other forms of transport
convenient
efficient
extensive transport system
ferry
lane
rush hour
traffic jam
tram
underground train

▶▶ **PART 2**

Candidate A

Language bank

These people are wearing some kind of uniform ...

They're wearing similar clothes.

It's more effective to be part of a large group.

They look as if they're in the army or some branch of the armed forces.

They look as if they're protesting.

They're musicians in an orchestra.

Clearly, they feel part of a group because ...

As far as I can tell, the orchestra is made up of people of different ages.

Presumably, the sense of belonging to a group comes from their shared interest in music.

They may be amateur musicians, but they might also be professionals.

cello players
holding up a sign
military uniform
officers
protest
sharing a sense of danger
string section of an orchestra
taking action
trying to get their point of view across

- **What are the advantages and disadvantages of doing these activities in a group?**

▶ 1

▶ 2

▶ 3

▶▶ **PART 2**

Candidate B

Language bank

The farmer appears to be examining his crops.

He must like working outdoors.

It's not entirely clear from his expression how he feels about ...

He seems to be a teacher.

He may be demonstrating something to his pupils.

Perhaps his experience has led him to conclude that ...

I suppose he's learnt how to use discipline in a class/gain the respect of the children he's teaching.

She seems to be looking after the panda cub.

She must have studied for a long time.

• **How difficult is it to acquire each skill?**

▶ **1**

▶ **2**

▶ **3**

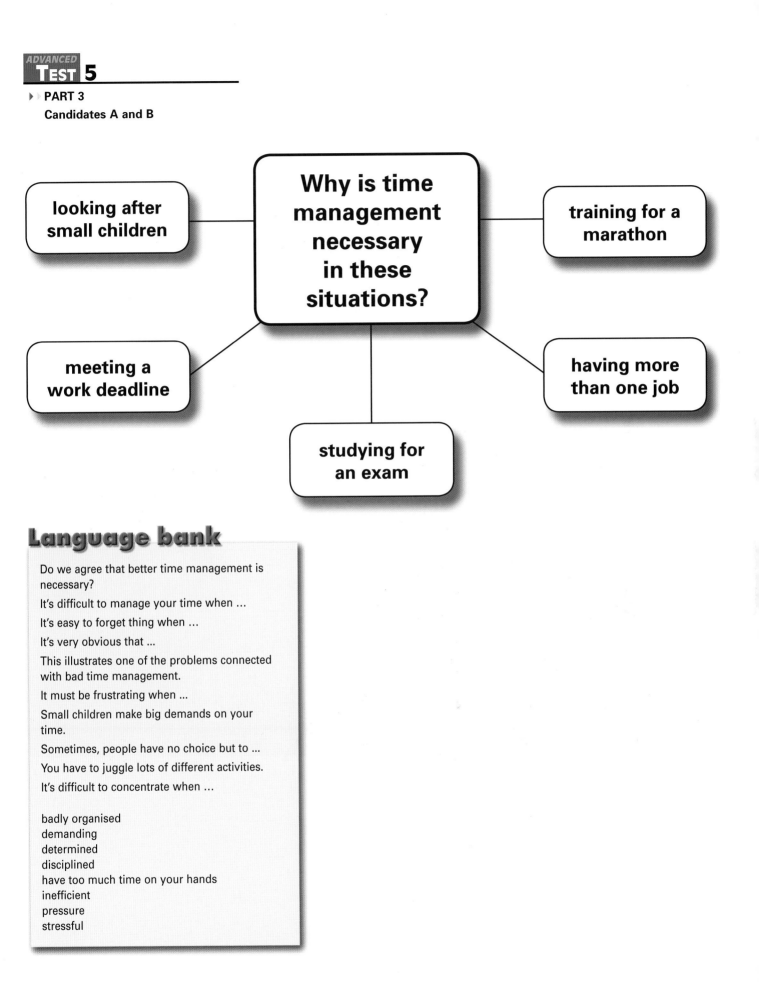

▶ **PART 2**

Candidate A

- **What might be making these people anxious?**
- **Which situation would you least like to be in?**

Language bank

I imagine he/she's anxious about ...

My impression is that he/she ...

My guess would be that he/she ...

Maybe he/she's already ... and is now ...

Whereas, the first picture shows someone worried about ...

This picture depicts someone in a state of anxiety about ...

The person's facial expression shows he/she's anxious or worried.

being told the results
biting her nails
deal with a problem
on board a plane
patient
physician
possible treatment.
take off and landing
waiting nervously

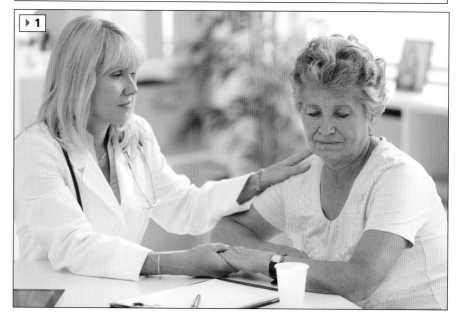

▶ 1

▶ 3

▶ 2

▶▶ **PART 2**

Candidate B

Language bank

It's obvious that he/she ...

I suppose he/she's pleased/relieved that ...

He/She's probably feeling pleased because ...

He/She's happy because he/she's finally managed (to do something).

I would guess that he/she ... for the first time, and he/she's delighted.

He/She's expressing his/her pleasure at this achievement.

It's not entirely clear what/who ...

academic achievement
congratulate someone on his/her promotion
degree/diploma
doing something for the first time
first feeling of independence
graduate from college/university
shake hands on a deal
successful negotiation

- **What have these people achieved?**
- **What difficulties might they have had in reaching their goal?**

▶ **1**

▶ **3**

▶ **2**

▶▶ **PART 3**

Candidates A and B

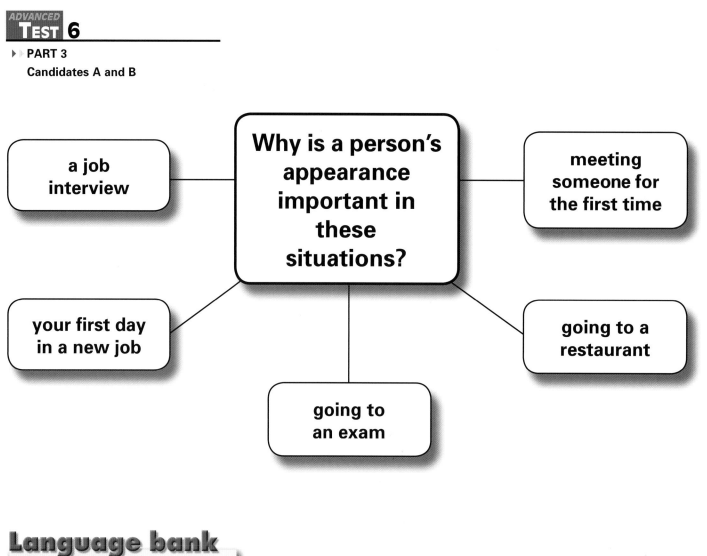

Language bank

The clothes you wear give the impression that you are ...

First impressions are important because ...

It's normal to judge people by their appearance

Some people don't care about convention/fashion.

You can come across as ...

anti-establishment
arrogant
attractive
capable
confident
conservative
efficient
fashion victim
formal event
scruffy

▶▶ **PART 2**

Candidate A

- **What could be prompting people to show respect in these situations?**
- **How might the people receiving the show of respect feel?**

Language bank

She might be her grandmother.

He/She's looking at ... with a friendly but respectful expression.

He/She may respect ... for several reasons.

She may have been brought up to behave respectfully towards older people.

He appears to have made a speech.

I expect an audience is obliged to applaud a speaker out of politeness, but the facial expressions of these men suggest that their respect is genuine.

I know he's a famous politician, but I can't remember his name.

I think the man in the photo is ..., but I'm not sure.

applaud
bow to someone
express your admiration
honour someone for his/her achievements
(lack of) respect for old people
statesman
make a speech
politeness/courtesy is important
politician

▶ 1

▶ 2

▶ 3

▶▶ **PART 2**

Candidate B

- **What kind of partnerships are these?**
- **How do the partners feel about each other?**

Language bank

There's no way of telling whether they're ... or ...

In all likelihood, they're colleagues.

They're wearing ... , so they're probably ...

They must have a great deal of confidence in one another.

Trust would be the basis of their working relationship, I imagine.

In this kind of partnership, I imagine respect for the other person's ability must be crucial.

They obviously have a lot of fun together.

They must enjoy what they do.

building site
buskers
collaboration
colleague
contribution
co-operation
have confidence in someone
intellectual ability
laboratory
lab technician
mutual trust
musician
rely on your colleague
white lab coat

▶ 1

▶ 2

▶ 3

▶▶ **PART 3**
   Candidates A and B

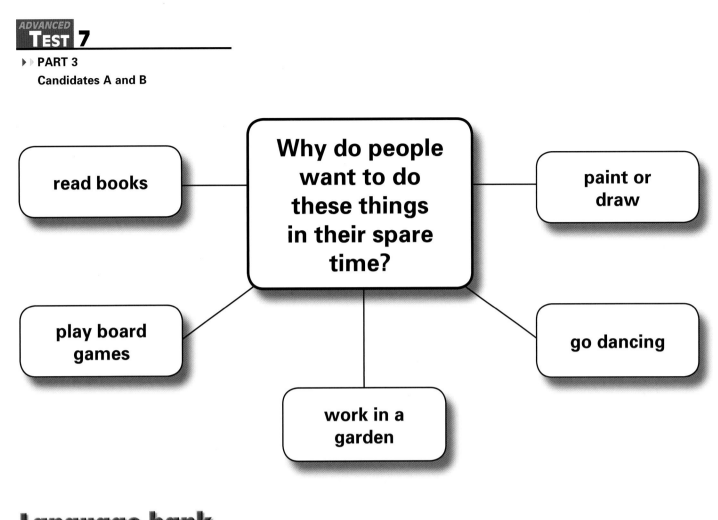

Language bank

This is a physically demanding activity, but I suppose it's a way of relaxing for some people.

Personally, I don't understand why people would choose to ...

This is a solitary/creative/exciting pastime.

It's a very popular thing to do, especially with older people.

It allows you to switch off.

It exercises the mind.

You don't have to think.

artistic
competitive
express yourself
freedom
get away from it all
nature
solitary
spend time with other people
unwind

▶▶ **PART 2**

Candidate A

Language bank

I can't see exactly what they're doing, but I think they're …

It looks as though they're under a lot of stress.

I'd say this kind of stress is due partly to … and partly to …

There's a certain amount of danger involved in work like this.

There's always the danger that something could go wrong.

I think most performers feel nervous before going on stage, and this could be a cause of stress.

assembly line
boring and repetitive
buy/sell shares
conveyor belt
fall behind
high levels of noise
investor
make/lose a fortune
price of shares
stage fright
stock exchange
stockbroker
there's a lot at stake

• **What is stressful about these situations?**
• **Which might be the most stressful and why?**

▶▶ **PART 2**

Candidate B

Language bank

The people in the boat are probably there from choice.

Probably they feel exhilarated, even though there are dangers involved.

They may not have realised how dangerous the situation would be.

They might regret ...

In contrast, they bably has have no alternative but to do battle against the elements.

They might be facing starvation.

They are trying to protect their homes or property against flooding.

(The river) burst its banks.

drown
fishing boat
flood/flooding
in danger of capsising
rough sea
scorching heat
scratch a living from the land
sparse vegetation
starve
stormy
suffer from drought
survive
the soil is parched
water shortage
waves

- **What kind of problems do the people face?**
- **How might they be feeling in their current situation?**

▶ 1

▶ 2

▶ 3

▶▶ PART 3
Candidates A and B

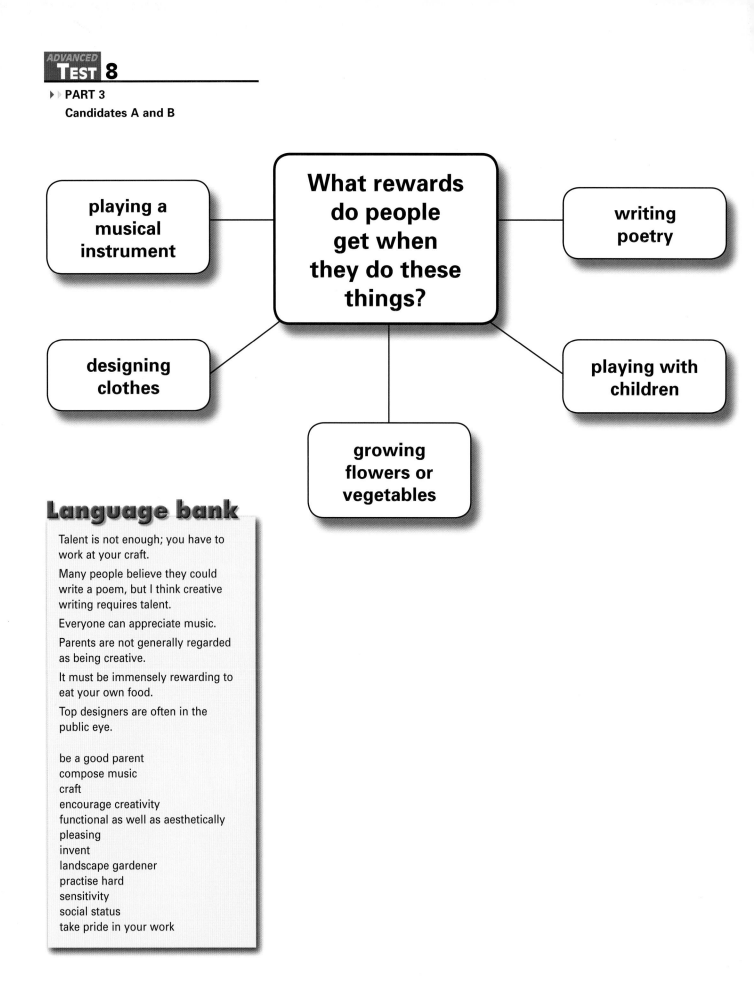

playing a musical instrument

What rewards do people get when they do these things?

writing poetry

designing clothes

playing with children

growing flowers or vegetables

Language bank

Talent is not enough; you have to work at your craft.

Many people believe they could write a poem, but I think creative writing requires talent.

Everyone can appreciate music.

Parents are not generally regarded as being creative.

It must be immensely rewarding to eat your own food.

Top designers are often in the public eye.

be a good parent
compose music
craft
encourage creativity
functional as well as aesthetically pleasing
invent
landscape gardener
practise hard
sensitivity
social status
take pride in your work

Preparing, planning and checking

▶▶ Preparing for the Writing Paper

Producing a piece of writing that fulfils a certain function is a difficult task for anybody, even in their native language. To prepare for the Writing Paper, it goes without saying that you need to have read widely. Then, you need to have studied all the basic text types you may be asked to produce, and understood the basic features that characterise them: layout, organisation, style and register. You should also practise completing writing tasks in the time allowed in the exam. Remember the criteria the examiners will use in awarding marks:

- Has the candidate achieved the purpose stated in the instructions?
- Does the text have a positive general effect on the target reader?
- Does the text cover all the content points?
- Is the text well organised and are ideas linked appropriately?
- Has language been used accurately?
- Does the text exhibit a good range of vocabulary and grammatical structures?
- Is the register appropriate for the task?
- Is the layout appropriate?

Ideally, the pieces of writing you produce should be checked by an experienced teacher who can provide useful feedback. Such feedback can help you compile a list of useful expressions, such as the useful phrases you find with the model answers in this section. You can also learn what sort of mistakes you make habitually so you can avoid them. For instance, if you find that you frequently make mistakes with a certain tense, you should consult a good grammar guide to clear up your confusion.

▶▶ Planning your answer

Perhaps the most useful lesson that experienced writers learn is the importance of planning what to write before they actually begin writing. Most good writers usually write several drafts of a text before they are satisfied with the result. Unfortunately, in the exam you do not have time to produce several drafts, and it would be a serious mistake to try: you only have time for a single draft. But you do have time to make a plan.

Always read the question carefully and make sure you understand the following:

- Who are you writing for?
- What are the points you must include in your answer?
- Does the text type have any particular layout requirements?
- Do you have the necessary vocabulary to answer the question?

Then prepare a plan or outline of what you are going to write. Its purpose is to help you, so it doesn't matter if you change it or cross things out – nobody else is going to read it. But it has to show clearly the different sections of your writing and what points you must include in which section. When you look at the plan closely, you might want to change it; for instance, something might be better in a different paragraph, or you might realise you will be repeating yourself. When you are satisfied with your outline, you will find it much easier to write your text. Planning takes time, so allow a minimum of 15 minutes for it.

▶▶ Checking

Most people make more mistakes than normal under exam conditions, so always allow at least ten minutes at the end to read through your work. Think of your task here as having two parts. First, check that you have answered the question correctly and that you have included all the information that was required. Secondly, check for mistakes in grammar, spelling, punctuation etc. You should by now have had enough experience to know where you often make mistakes – the spelling of certain words, for instance, or a particular type of punctuation.

If you need to correct something, make the correction neatly and legibly. If you need to cross out something you have written, just put one line through the word or words.

1 Essay

▶ ▶ **Exam task – Part 1**

Your class has had a discussion on the advisability of bringing the voting age in your country down from 18 years old to 16 years old. You have made the notes below:

Points made on the advisability of bringing the voting age down to 16 years old:

- young people are good judges
- politicians will think more about young people's needs
- young people will take more interest in politics

Other opinions expressed during the discussion:

'Teenagers already have enough on their plates.'

'Young people don't trust politicians.'

'There aren't enough young people in parliament.'

Write an **essay** for your tutor discussing **two** of the points you made in your notes. You should **explain which point you think is more important** and **provide reasons** to support your opinion.

You may, if you wish, make use of the opinions expressed in the discussion, but you should use your own words as far as possible.

▶ ▶ **Approach**

▶ Here is a straightforward way to write an essay. If you have two main points to make, you can give your essay a clear structure by dividing it into four paragraphs.

Have a title that grabs the attention

Paragraph One – The first paragraph of an essay provides the introduction. It states what is to be discussed and why. Your main points are briefly introduced. This paragraph need not be lengthy.

Paragraph Two – In the second paragraph more background information is provided in greater detail. Your first, often strongest main point is expanded upon. Bring in and refute any arguments against your point of view.

Paragraph Three – The third paragraph provides your second key point, tying it into the theme of your essay. Again, bring in opposing points of view and support your second key point with information and background.

Paragraph Four – The fourth and final paragraph is used to summarise or conclude your essay. It shows how the two key points you have presented compare or relate to each other. It also clearly re-states your initial position from the introductory paragraph.

▶ Add quotations, statistics, facts, examples and other relevant data to support your points.

▶ The tone and register can be formal or semi-formal depending on your treatment of the topic. If your essay is written in a formal register, only bring in informal expressions when you use a direct quotation to support your argument.

▶ Punctuation is important in essays, and can be a powerful tool in expressing subtle or emphatic points. Short sentences make for a punchy style, but get irritating if they are over-used; long sentences need careful use of commas, semi-colons and dashes to achieve flow and rhythm.

▶▶ **Model answer**

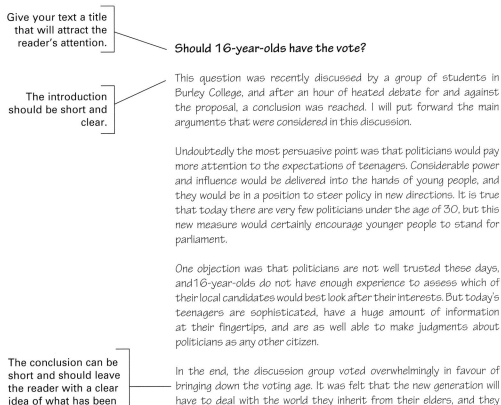

Give your text a title that will attract the reader's attention.

The introduction should be short and clear.

The conclusion can be short and should leave the reader with a clear idea of what has been described or discussed.

Should 16-year-olds have the vote?

This question was recently discussed by a group of students in Burley College, and after an hour of heated debate for and against the proposal, a conclusion was reached. I will put forward the main arguments that were considered in this discussion.

Undoubtedly the most persuasive point was that politicians would pay more attention to the expectations of teenagers. Considerable power and influence would be delivered into the hands of young people, and they would be in a position to steer policy in new directions. It is true that today there are very few politicians under the age of 30, but this new measure would certainly encourage younger people to stand for parliament.

One objection was that politicians are not well trusted these days, and 16-year-olds do not have enough experience to assess which of their local candidates would best look after their interests. But today's teenagers are sophisticated, have a huge amount of information at their fingertips, and are as well able to make judgments about politicians as any other citizen.

In the end, the discussion group voted overwhelmingly in favour of bringing down the voting age. It was felt that the new generation will have to deal with the world they inherit from their elders, and they have the right to a say in the government that will shape that world for them.

Useful phrases

Introduction

I will put forward ...

There are two main points to discuss ...

I am going to discuss the issue of ...

Main body

The most important point is ...

In addition ...

As opposed to that ...

Looking at it from another point of view ...

It is true that ...

Conclusion

In conclusion/To summarise, ...

The outcome is clear that ...

2 Formal letter

▶ ▷ Exam task – Part 2

A colleague of yours, Alice Watson, has applied for a job in the public relations department of a large charity, Poverty Action. You have been asked to write a letter providing a character reference for her. Indicate how long and in what capacity you have worked with her, and how her personal characteristics would make her suited for the job. Here is part of the letter you received from Poverty Action.

> The job of Public Relations Co-ordinator consists mainly of supervising PR work, and entails travelling around the country and working with various people in our large organisation. The successful applicant will need good managerial skills and be committed to the philosophy of our charity.

Write your **letter**.

▶ ▷ Approach

▶ A character reference is almost always addressed to the organisation where someone has applied for a job or a place to study. Generally, you should use the heading line 'To whom it may concern', rather than writing to a specific person. If the exam question asks you to refer to certain characteristics of a person, make sure you do so. You should also imagine what other information may be required, bearing in mind the position the person has applied for.

▶ All character references are formal in style. Generally, you should write at least three paragraphs: introduction, main body and conclusion.

Useful phrases

Introduction

To whom it may concern

I have been asked to write this reference for (Ms Watson).

With reference to your letter of (3rd March) …

I have known (Ms Watson) for the last (four) years …

I was her supervisor/superior in (the publicity department of) …

Main body

(Ms Watson) has always shown great dedication/commitment to her work. She has (excellent managerial skills) …

Her duties/tasks here included …

She proved to be … competent/dependable/efficient/popular with colleagues.

Conclusion

I understand that (Ms Watson) has applied for …

I am certain that (Ms Watson) would be extremely capable …

I have no hesitation in recommending her for …

I should be very happy to supply any further information.

Please do not hesitate to contact me …

▶ ▶ Model answer

This is the standard heading for character references.

To whom it may concern,

State the name of the person for whom you are writing the reference.

Ms Alice Watson

Say how you know the person and explain in what way you worked together.

I have been asked to write this reference for Ms Alice Watson, who worked with me for almost four years in the Head Office of the charity *Children in Need*. I was her immediate superior in the publicity department of that organisation, so I was able to observe her work at close quarters and feel qualified to evaluate her suitability for similar positions.

Explain what sort of jobs the person did, and describe the positive characteristics she showed.

Ms Watson was extremely committed to her work and always performed to the highest standard. Her tasks included checking press releases and writing letters to a wide variety of recipients, and she displayed first-class communication skills. The executives of the organisation found her entirely trustworthy, and she always carried out her work cheerfully and efficiently. At various times of the year our department employed a number of temporary staff in order to send out appeals for donations, and in her dealings with these people Ms Watson exhibited very good managerial skills. She was also popular with the permanent staff, though she never allowed this to interfere with the work that had to be done.

I understand that Ms Watson has applied for the position of Public Relations Co-ordinator, which I imagine entails considerable responsibility. I have no hesitation in recommending her for this position, and I am certain she will prove an excellent and hard-working member of your organisation. Naturally, I would be very happy to supply any further information, so please do not hesitate to contact me if this should be required.

Refer to the person's suitability for the tasks involved in the new job.

Yours faithfully,

Emma Lyons
Public Relations Officer
Children in Need

End the letter formally.

3 Informal letter/email

▶ ▶ **Exam task – Part 2**

You've received a letter from someone who was a good friend at school. Your friend moved to another part of the country and you lost touch with each other. Reply to the letter giving your news and suggesting a meeting.

Now write your **letter**. You do not need to include postal addresses.

▶ ▶ **Approach**

▶ Be careful you understand exactly who you are writing to, and what you must include in your letter. Here, you are writing to an old friend, giving your news, although you haven't communicated for a long time.

▶ You are writing to a friend, so the register should be informal.

Useful phrases

Introduction

It was great/a lovely surprise to get your letter last week.

What a lot's happened in five years!

I was so pleased/sad to hear about …

Main body

As for me, I've been busy with …

It's been an exciting few years.

You won't believe it, but …

My main news is that …

Why don't we get together some time?

It'd be a lot of fun to meet up.

Come and stay one weekend.

Signing off

Text me on (phone number)…

Here's my email address.

Take care of yourself/Look after yourself.

Lots of love/Cheers

▶ ▶ Model answer

Hi Chris,

Begin with an enthusiastic reaction to your friend's letter. In a few words, comment on his/her news.

It was great to get your letter, and such a surprise. I can't believe it's five years since we left school – so much has happened. It seems amazing that you're married and have got a baby boy. Congratulations! But I'm sad to hear your Dad hasn't been well. Please say hello to him from me.

Write a mini biography for yourself. You could have fun with this part, but make it plausible - it's probably best not to go over the top.

It's been an exciting few years for me too. I'm not married yet, but I've got a job I enjoy which involves a lot of travelling. When we left school, and you went off to college, I started work on our local paper. A couple of years ago I was offered a job in the foreign news department of a TV channel, and I'm on the move all the time. It's a steep learning curve for me because I have to keep up with international politics, and know about the geography and economy of different countries (remember I wasn't exactly brilliant at either of those subjects at school!). I think they took me on because I'm not bad at foreign languages.

Anyway, let's get together soon. I've got a week's holiday coming up and I'd love to see you and your family. How does the first week of May sound? I could easily get a train over and spend an afternoon with you.

Text me on 06009 546 385.

All the best to your wife and son. I can't wait to meet them!

Take care.

Mel

As this is a letter to a friend, you can end informally.

4 Report

▶ ▶ **Exam task – Part 2**

An international magazine is investigating tourism in various areas around the world. You have been asked to write a report for the magazine's editors, addressing the following questions:

- How has tourism in your region changed over the last decade?

- What are the reasons for these changes?

- What problems exist and can anything be done to solve them?

Write your **report**.

▶ ▶ **Approach**

▶ Read the question carefully to see whether you should include your own opinions in the report, and if this is the case, make it clear in the report when you are describing objective facts and when you are giving your interpretation. Depending on the task, you may need to describe something, give an account or narrate an event, express an opinion, and possibly compare and contrast.

▶ You can use headings and possibly bullet points or numbered lists to make it easier for the reader to find information quickly. The introduction and conclusion can be short. You are usually asked to write a report for some sort of organisation or publication, so the language you use should be semi-formal or formal. Even if you use bullet points or numbered lists, you should write complete sentences, not just notes. Remember that in formal writing we often use the passive voice.

Useful phrases

Introduction
The following report evaluates/ describes/ presents/provides an account of ...
This report aims to provide an overall view of the situation.
I shall describe the situation below.

Main body
a popular destination easy to reach by
a popular destination
easy to reach by rail/road/air
holidays to (Prague) are widely advertised
overcharging
service in hotels

It is generally accepted that ...
The vast majority of visitors ...
This is probably due to the fact that ...
While data is hard to come by, it is thought that ...

Conclusion
One measure which may improve the situation would be to introduce ...
I am of the opinion that ...
It is my view/opinion that ...
On balance, it appears that ...

▶ ▶ **Model answer**

Give your report a
suitable title.

Tourism in Prague

Introduction
The last decade has seen a dramatic increase in the number of
tourists visiting the Czech Republic in general and Prague in particular.
The following report presents a brief overview.

Write a brief
introduction that
provides a few
important facts and
summarises what your
report is about.

Background
Until 1989, Prague was not a popular destination for tourists from
western Europe due to a number of factors.
- The city was difficult to reach; visitors often had to wait for long
  periods at border crossings.
- There was little information about trips to Prague in foreign travel
  agencies.
- Some people felt nervous about trips to countries in central and
  eastern Europe.

Use bullet points to
provide a list, but
make sure each point
is grammatically the
same; here each point
is a complete sentence.

Changes
All the above factors have changed dramatically: Prague is now easy
to reach by road, rail and air; trips to Prague are widely advertised in
western countries; few visitors feel nervous about visiting a country in
eastern Europe any more.

You can use semicolons
to separate items in a
list, but as with bullet
points, make sure
each item is the same
grammatically.

Criticisms
The majority of visitors to Prague are extremely satisfied on the
whole; however, there are a few complaints about two specific areas:
- taxi drivers acting in a rude manner and, in many cases,
  overcharging.
- hotels providing less than adequate service.

Future development
The city council is at present considering stricter laws relating to
taxi drivers. Moreover, the local tourist authority is reclassifying the
hotels in the city.

Conclusion
While Prague can offer visitors a generally positive experience, there
are some issues which need to be addressed. I am of the opinion that
better regulation of taxi drivers and hotels will solve these problems.

Make sure each section
is clearly separated
from the others.

---

5 Proposal

▸ ▸ **Exam task – Part 2**

You work at a language school that offers summer courses to students from abroad. This year the director of the school wants to hold an introductory weekend for the students. She has asked you to write a proposal for the programme. She doesn't want the weekend to cost the school very much and wants the programme to include:

- information on local facilities
- social events arranged for the students.

Write your **proposal.**

▸ ▸ **Approach**

▸ Writing a proposal is similar, to but not exactly the same as, writing a persuasive essay or producing a report.

▸ A proposal should define a problem or challenge and describe a solution that will persuade a busy, thrifty or sceptical reader to support it. Employ facts, not opinions, to bolster the argument for approval.

▸ Outline your plan or project, demonstrating possible outcomes.

▸ Any discussion of financial or other resources should present a realistic picture of the expense required.

▸ Make the proposal clear and concise, and ensure the presentation is attractive and engaging as well being well-organised and helpful.

▸ A proposal should include the following elements.

Introduction: State the background to the proposal and summarise it. (This allows a decision maker to quickly get the gist of the proposal.)

Project description: Explain why the plan or project is needed, how it will be put into effect and how it will be evaluated.

Budget analysis: If necessary, outline the financial aspects of the plan or project.

Conclusion: Summarise the proposal's main points.

Useful phrases

Introduction
In view of the fact that ...
Considering the fact that ...
At present, the situation is that ...
My experience suggests that ...

Main body
It would be helpful to students to be told ...
It would be of great benefit to students if ...
One possible solution would be to ...
Providing the event is properly organised, it could be of great

assistance to students.
Students could also be ...
You might also like to consider ...
In all likelihood, ...
The chances are ...

Conclusion
Any teething troubles could quickly be overcome ...
In conclusion, I feel (quite) strongly that this is the best way to ...
In spite of/Despite the effort required, this would be a worthwhile step ...

▶ ▶ **Model answer**

Give your proposal a suitable title.

Introductory weekend for foreign students

In the introduction, briefly outline the situation and indicate your position.

Previously the students' introduction to our school and town has been carried out informally, but the summer intake of students has increased to such an extent that a more organised introduction would be very beneficial.

Use simple headings to organise your ideas clearly.

Day 1
This should begin with a welcome from the director, and introduction of members of staff, followed by practical information on using local transport, banks and medical services; and a question-and-answer session.

A coffee break could also include a 'getting-to-know-you session', where students meet each other and their teachers, and are shown round the school.

In the afternoon the school coach could take the students on a tour of the town, so they find out where the local cinema, shopping centres and sports facilities are, and be given information about places of interest.

Use a variety of structures to make suggestions. For example: *would be* and *could also be*.

In the evening it would be a good idea to hold a party with a barbeque and dancing so that students could spend time with their teachers and fellow students in a relaxed atmosphere.

Day 2
A popular idea might be an afternoon coach trip to a local beauty spot.

Budget
The main expenses would be fuel and parking costs for the school coach, and food and music for the party. I think these could be taken out of the school's entertainment fund.

Conclusion
A programme like this would get the summer courses off to a flying start, and give everyone involved a lot of pleasure.

6 Review

▶ ▶ **Exam task – Part 2**

You have been watching a popular series on TV about people taking part in a competition for the best amateur photographer, and you have decided to write a review of it for your college newspaper. Say what was good and bad about the series, and whether you would recommend the second series, which starts soon.

Write your **review.**

▶ ▶ **Approach**

▶ This is for students, so it can be informal and critical.

▶ Start with an attention-grabbing opening.

▶ It can express your personal response, but should be impartial for the most part.

▶ Use the sandwich method – what was good, what was bad, what was good; or the other way round for a negative review.

▶ The review should be informative, bringing in a little background, comparisons with similar programmes.

▶ Finish by summing up your opinions and making your recommendation.

Useful phrases

The thing that struck me most was …

The problem was (it just went on too long).

For the most part …

Broadly speaking, …

All in all, …

To be honest, …

It was the most boring/exciting thing I've watched for ages.

▶ ▶ **Model answer**

The great national TV photo competition

Generally state your
overall opinion.

What a surprise! I loved it!

I was not thrilled when my editor told me to review this photography competition. It was going out every Monday evening for a month. What a waste of an evening, I thought. But from programme one, I was hooked.

Go into details, giving
more information about
your opinion.

I'm not a photographer, but the first thing that struck me was the passion of the photographers. They would put themselves into great danger, hanging off cliffs or creeping up on ferocious animals to get their picture. And all this just for the love of it. Their sheer enthusiasm made you want to rush out and buy a camera.

This was the first series, and it had its faults. Sometimes the pace dragged a bit, and there was too much technical gossip among the contributors. And I have to admit, some of the photos that made it into the later rounds seemed uninspired to me - banal or sentimental.

Give a balanced view,
if possible.

The last three competitors, who were up against each other in the final round, produced some absolutely stunning work. They must have been an inspiration to the millions of other photographers in the country, and proof that the age of the gifted amateur has returned.

The programme's popularity ratings were through the roof, so of course National TV is putting on a second series. They will have listened to criticism and hopefully cut out some of the technical detail. I for one can't wait for it to begin.

Give a general
conclusion or
recommendation.

TEST 1

PAPER 1 Reading and Use of English

▶▶ PART 1

govern (v) to control the actions or behaviour of a person, a system, an organisation, etc.

stimulus (n) something that makes someone or something move or react

fluctuation (n) the process of varying irregularly

impose (v) to force someone or something to behave or react in the way that you want them to

at will (phr) whenever and in whatever way you want

▶▶ PART 2

pursuit (n) an activity such as a sport or hobby

sow the seeds of (phr) to do something that will cause a bad situation in the future

▶▶ PART 3

endeavour (n) an attempt to do something, especially something new or difficult

habitat (n) the place where a particular type of animal normally lives

sanctuary (n) a place where wild animals are protected

▶▶ PART 5

etching (n) a picture formed by cutting lines on a metal plate, piece of glass, stone, etc.

depict (v) to paint; to draw

on a variety of counts (phr) in several ways

sheer (adj) used to emphasise that something is very large, good, etc.

staggering (adj) extremely great or surprising

hold your own (phr) to perform satisfactorily

epoch (n) a period of history

albeit (conjunction) even though; despite

inadvertently (adv) not on purpose; unintentionally

cordon off (phr v) to enclose an area

intimidating (adj) frightening

show up (phr v) to become visible

convey (v) to communicate or make known

preliminary (n) a preparation for an event

rigid (adj) very unwilling to change ideas or behaviour

tentatively (adv) provisionally

aesthetic (adj) concerned with beauty and art

vulnerable (adj) exposed; unprotected

▶▶ PART 6

feasible (adj) possible to do

manned (adj) a vehicle with people working in it

wipe out (phr v) to destroy

precipitate (v) to lead to something to start happening

engulf (v) to surround or cover something completely

▶▶ PART 7

batch (n) a group of things

verdict (n) someone's opinion about something

naive (adj) believing only good things will happen

take off (phr v) to increase or succeed quickly

figure out (phr v) to solve; to understand

budding (adj) (someone who is) starting to do an activity and (will) probably (be) successful at it in the future

down (v) to drink or eat something quickly and finish it off

soundbite (n) a short, quotable statement

asset (n) something or someone that is useful

status quo (n) the way things are now

fiendishly (adv) extremely

preach (v) to give someone advice in a way that they think is boring or annoying

falling-out (n) a quarrel

preservative (n) a chemical that keeps food from going bad

unadulterated (adj) not containing unwanted substances

dash (n) a small amount of something

quirky (adj) unusual, especially in an interesting way

complementary (adj) complementary things go well together, although they are usually different

bust-up (n) a serious quarrel

munch (v) to chew strongly on something

stumbling block (n) an obstacle, something that causes problems and stops you from doing what you want to do

▶▶ PART 8

misconception (n) an idea based on the wrong information or a wrong understanding

coolness (n) glamour or attractiveness for other people

rating (n) measurement of how good something is

immerse (v) become completely involved in

adrenalin (n) substance produced when you are excited

do a degree (n) the qualification of a university course

brief (n) duties and responsibilities in a job

at first hand (phr) experiencing something yourself

blunder (n) mistake

flair (n) natural talent

TEST 2

PAPER 1 Reading and Use of English

▶▶ PART 1

shovel (n) a tool, similar to a spade, with a long handle and a metal plate used for moving earth, snow, etc.

buried (adj) hidden under the ground

feature (n) aspects of a person, place or thing that are important or typical

trial (n) a process of testing something to see if it works

dwelling (n) a house or other building where people live

infallible (n) never wrong; never making mistakes

disclose (n) give information that was previously secret

▶▶ PART 2

all told (phr) in total

insight (n) an understanding of something

▶▶ PART 3

engraver (n) someone who carves, cuts or etches a text, design or picture into a block or surface used for printing

dissect (v) to cut apart or separate

mount (v) to place or fix something on or in a support or setting for display or study

▶▶ PART 5

bewitch (v) to charm; to captivate

ball (n) large, formal party

wand (n) magic stick

convey (n) carry

smitten (adj) very attracted to, or in love

amid (preposition) in or into the middle of; surrounded by

stock (adj) commonly used

spirit (n) a mental disposition characterised by firmness or assertiveness

enduring (adj) lasting; surviving

shortcoming (n) a fault; a deficiency

sibling (n) a person with the same parents as someone else; a brother or sister

show backbone (phr) show that you are a strong character

enlightened (adj) freed from ignorance and misinformation

villain (n) a bad person, especially a criminal

empathise (v) to understand another's feelings, etc.

protagonist (n) main character in a story

make concessions (phr) allow or change something to make a situation less difficult

▶▶ PART 7

linguist (n) a person who knows several languages and their structure; someone who carries out research into languages

conversely (adv) the opposite or reverse of something

forge ahead (phr) to proceed with strength and speed despite problems or difficulties

periodically (adv) fairly often and on a regular basis

the point of no return (phr) a time when it is impossible to go back to an earlier situation

tonic (n) a medicinal liquid that gives energy

rub (n) a medicinal lotion or cream that is rubbed on the skin

potion (n) a strong liquid medicine

blunt (adj) frank

a lost cause (phr) something that cannot succeed

expectant (adj) pregnant

score (n) twenty

competent (adj) having the ability to do something well

consummate (adj) perfect

wary (adj) concerned about danger; cautious

▶▶ PART 8

enhance (v) to improve; to add to

engage (v) to take part

venture (n) an undertaking involving chance, risk or danger; a speculative business enterprise

impulsive (adj) without thinking carefully

apprehension (n) fear that something bad might happen

break (n) a piece of good luck

dabble (v) to work superficially or intermittently, especially in a secondary activity or interest

downside (n) a disadvantageous aspect

budding (adj) young and promising

down the line (phr) at a point in the future

lucrative (adj) producing a lot of money; profitable

from scratch (phr) from the beginning

avid (adj) enthusiastic; eager

the ropes (phr) knowledge about a job or situation

take the plunge (phr) decide to do something difficult

PAPER 1 Reading and Use of English

▶▶ **PART 1**

ladybug (n) American English / **ladybird** (n) British English a small flying insect, usually red with black spots

habitat (n) an area where an animal normally lives

▶▶ **PART 2**

DIY (n) Do It Yourself

reclamation material (n) useful materials or items that come from old buildings

▶▶ **PART 3**

stem (v) result from

deem (v) regard or consider

▶▶ **PART 5**

nurture (n) care and encouragement given to someone while they are growing

backlash (n) a strong negative reaction by a large number of people to something that has changed in society

neuroscience (n) the study of the human nervous system

decode (v) find out how something works

buzz word (n) word that is very fashionable

run out of steam (phr) lose energy

anecdote (n) personal story

formulaic (adj) following a formula and unoriginal

angle (v) to try to get a particular response

gender (n) being male or female

array (n) range

meticulous (adj) very careful

go for the hard sell (phr) argue in very strong terms

trait (n) feature or characteristic

pendulum (n) a weight in an old clock that swings from one side to the other; used as an image to express the idea that ideas go in and out of fashion

▶▶ **PART 7**

surmise (v) to make a reasonable guess

perch (n) a resting place or vantage point

hail (v) to greet, especially with enthusiasm

swashbuckling (adj) flamboyantly adventurous

carbon dating (n) chemical analysis used to determine the age of materials

fire (v) to fill with passion or enthusiasm

tantalise (v) to offer but not satisfy; to tempt

loot (v) to rob, especially on a large scale and usually by violence

pore over (phr v) to study carefully

wry (adj) humorous, ironic or dry in manner

aqueduct (n) a waterway made of stone blocks

intricate (adj) having many complex interrelating parts or elements

toil (v) to work hard with little reward or relief

blunder (v) to move unsteadily or confusedly

annals (n pl) a written record or collection of historical events, discoveries, etc., on a certain subject

undeterred (adj) refusing to be prevented from acting

rugged (adj) hilly; (land that is) difficult to travel over

▶▶ **PART 8**

stint (n) period of time doing something

joint (n) place where two bones join like a knee or a shoulder

treadmill (n) running machine in a gym

heel (n) the back end of the foot

ball of the foot (n) part of the bottom of the foot near the toes

wind up (phr v) find yourself in a particular situation

novice (n) someone who is new to something

resentment (n) feeling of anger that something is unfair

have a head start (phr) start in front of other people

funded (n) receives financial support

PAPER 1 Reading and Use of English

▶▶ PART 1

instigate (v) to make something happen

ingrained (adj) firmly established and therefore difficult to change

quirky (adj) unusual

gimmick (n) a clever or unusual method or object used to attract attention

▶▶ PART 2

counterpart (n) a person or thing that has the same position or function as someone or something in a different place or situation

▶▶ PART 3

foundation (n) good reason

element of exaggeration (phr) a small amount of exaggeration

venom (n) a liquid poison produced by animals such as snakes, spiders or scorpions when they bite or sting

▶▶ PART 5

slump (v) sit in a position which is not upright

posture (n) the position in which you hold your body when standing or sitting

vague (adj) not clearly defined, grasped or understood

hunched (adj) formed into a hump

osteopath (n) a person who treats physical problems by pressing and moving the bones and muscles

slouch (v) to walk, stand or sit in a lazy way, with shoulders and head bent forward

with hindsight (phr) looking back

off the mark (phr) wrong; mistaken

pilates (n) a system of exercise that increases flexibility

tilt (v) to move upwards or to the side

misalignment (n) having something in the wrong position

orator (n) someone who is good at making speeches and persuading people

reluctant (adj) unwilling

sceptical (adj) having doubts about whether something is true

debilitating (adj) describing something that makes you weak and unable to function well

▶▶ PART 7

Velcro (n) a material used to fasten clothes, consisting of two pieces of material which stick to each other when you press them together

plunder (v) to steal; to take others' property by force and in large quantity

random (adj) happening at any time; unplanned

revenue (n) income

donor (n) a person or organisation that gives something, often money

hands-off (adj) separate; detached

on tap (phr) available on demand

ornithologist (n) a person who studies birds

win-win (adj) a win-win situation is one that will end well for everyone involved in it

spur (v) to encourage someone to do something

concerted (adj) strong; intense

▶▶ PART 8

put someone off (phr v) make someone lose interest or enthusiasm for something

pepper (v) include a lot of examples of something

get to grips with an idea (phr) understand an idea

glimpse (n) a brief view of something

trilogy (n) a set of three of something – books, films, etc.

atomise (v) break something up into small particles

bounce (v) jump like a ball

anecdote (n) personal story

assertiveness (n) being self-confident

diffidence (n) not wanting to talk about yourself

glut (n) a large number of something, more than is needed

gloomy (adj) sad, unhappy

sceptical (adj) full of doubt

woe (n) problem

array (n) wide range

prolific (adj) very productive

wit (n) humour

antidote (n) something that takes away an unpleasant thing; e.g. an antidote to a poison

strive (v) try very hard to achieve something

swell (v) get bigger

facile (adj) produced without effort or careful thought

PAPER 1 Reading and Use of English

▶▶ **PART 1**

foolhardy (adj) reckless; rash

stretcher (n) something used to carry an injured person

borne (past participle) from 'bear'; responsible for

limb (n) an arm or a leg

▶▶ **PART 3**

eloquence (n) the ability to use language and express opinions in a fluent effective way

call into question (phr) to cast doubt upon something

mainstream (n) accepted or including most people in society

bypass (v) to avoid

distort (v) to report an event in a way that is not true

verify (v) to confirm; to say that something is true

▶▶ **PART 5**

draw to a close (phr) to come to an end

roam (v) to go freely over a large area; to wander

glacier (n) a large mass of ice which moves slowly down a mountain valley

submerge (v) to cover something with water

deluge (n) a flood

lush (adj) having thick, healthy growth

verdant (adj) green with vegetation growth

harpoon (n) a weapon used for hunting

mammoth (n) an animal like a hairy elephant which lived thousands of years ago and is now extinct

tusk (n) a long front tooth, such as of elephants, etc.

vessel (n) a boat

deploy (n) use

ledge (n) a piece of rock on the side of a mountain

pinpoint (v) to locate exactly

shipwreck (n) a ship that has been destroyed at sea

scathing (adj) very severe (criticism)

maritime (adj) related to the sea

aggregate (n) mineral materials, used in making concrete

quarry (v) to dig stone or sand from a quarry

dredge (v) to dig up sand and debris from a river, etc.

outraged (adj) feeling great anger

perception (n) the way a person sees something

▶▶ **PART 7**

field work (n) study that is done out of the classroom

patch (n) a small area

teem (v) full of living things moving around

stilts (n) wooden posts that keep a building above the ground or water

biodiversity (n) a variety of animals or plants

crawl (v) move very slowly

to be transfixed (v) to be unable to move because something has all your attention

footage (n) part of a film

germinate (v) when a seed grows and becomes a plant

adrenaline (n) a substance produced in the body when you are excited

sprout (v) grow in large numbers

nocturnal (adj) night-time

cacophony (n) mixture of loud, unpleasant sounds

lethal (adj) something that can cause a lot of harm

anti-venom (n) a medicine used to combat poison

venom (n) the poison from a snake

▶▶ **PART 8**

rehearse (v) practice in advance of something

interpersonal (adj) between people

babble (v) to talk without making sense

get carried away (phr) to do too much of something

go off at a tangent (phr) to leave the main point; to digress

evasive (adj) not direct, clear or frank

pedantic (adj) paying too much attention to rules and details

come across (phr v) to seem to have particular qualities

insincere (adj) not showing true feelings

prospective (adj) possible in the future

blurt out (phr v) to speak suddenly

component (n) one of several parts of a machine

swollen-headed (adj) arrogant

complacent (adj) pleased with a situation

at fault (phr) responsible for something bad

PAPER 1 Reading and Use of English

▶▶ PART 1

misconception (n) a mistaken idea about something

span (n) a period (of time)

plague (n) an epidemic disease causing a high death rate

appalling (adj) shocking; deeply offensive

feudal (adj) relating to a political and social system in which a king and the people of the upper classes owned the land and people of the lower classes worked it

▶▶ PART 2

exceed (v) to be greater than something; to go beyond the limits of something

foolproof (adj) well-designed and easy to use so that it cannot go wrong

▶▶ PART 3

withdraw (v) to remove

▶▶ PART 5

hitherto (adv) up to this time

anatomical (adj) relating to the structure of a body

instrumental (adj) helpful; causing something to happen

by-product (n) something that happens as a result of something else

outperform (v) to do better than others

on a par with (phr) as good as

ligament (n) a strong, flexible band of tissue holding bones or other body parts in place

tissue (n) a mass of cells

skull (n) the bone structure of a head

spine (n) long vertical bone running down the centre of the back

pitch (v) roll

primate (n) any animal that belongs to the group of mammals that includes human beings, apes and monkeys

tendon (n) tough, fibrous tissue connecting muscles to bones or to other muscles

calf (n) the back part of the lower leg

hypothesis (n) theory

carnivore (n) meat eater

confer (v) to give

scavenger (n) an animal that feeds on dead or decaying matter

predator (n) an animal that kills other animals to eat them

carcass (n) a dead body

vulture (n) a type of bird that eats dead animals

locomotion (n) the ability to move from place to place

contentious (adj) involving a lot of disagreement and argument

dispel (n) make something, especially a belief, disappear

▶▶ PART 7

glaze (v) to cover or fit with glass

ventilation (n) a system of providing fresh air

stale (adj) not fresh

outsize (adj) very large

conservatory (n) a greenhouse for growing or displaying plants

guzzle (v) consume very quickly

emission (n) gas that is sent out into the air

trim (v) to free of excess matter by cutting

tumble (v) to decline suddenly and sharply

flashy (adj) expensive and designed to attract attention

duct (n) a tube or passage in buildings, especially for air

momentum (n) strength or force gained by motion or through the development of events

lobby (n) a group of people trying to influence politicians

break (n) a deduction that is granted in order to encourage a particular type of commercial activity

dim (v) to lower the force of, especially a light

leak (v) escape

synergy (n) the extra energy, power or capability produced by combining two or more agents, operations or processes

outlook (n) a prediction for the future

come to grips with (phr) to confront squarely and attempt to deal decisively with something

tap (v) to make use of a source of energy that already exists

at the forefront (phr) the most advanced part

▶▶ PART 8

branch out (phr v) start to do an activity you have not done before

stray (v) move away from the place where you should be

outlay (n) money spent for something

worth your salt (phr) deserving respect because you do your job well

landscape gardening (n) the art or profession of improving the ground around a building with trees, plants, etc.

cut-throat (adj) relentless or merciless in competition

PAPER 1 Reading and Use of English

▶▶ **PART 1**

pollinate (v) to transfer pollen into a flower so that it produces seeds

hummingbird (n) a very small, brightly coloured bird that lives in warm climates

pod (n) a long narrow structure that grows on various plants like peas and beans, and contains seeds

fragrance (n) a pleasant smell

cure (v) to preserve food, tobacco, etc. by drying it, hanging it in smoke or covering it with salt

harvest (v) to gather a crop from the field or plantation

treat (v) to put a substance on something or use a chemical process in order to protect, clean or preserve it

exploitation (n) the use of something for profit

▶▶ **PART 2**

flourish (v) become popular and successful

▶▶ **PART 3**

zest (n) intense interest and enjoyment

▶▶ **PART 5**

blunt (adj) not sharp

talon (n) a bird's claw, especially of predators

wingspan (n) the distance from the tip of one of a pair of wings to that of the other

soar (v) to fly high through the air with no difficulty

flap (v) move up and down

diversity (n) variety

yield (v) supply, provide

incubate (v) to sit on an egg so as to hatch it by the warmth of the body

bicker (v) to argue about little things

rear (v) to help children or young animals to grow

saunter (v) to walk without hurrying

perish (v) die

antifreeze (n) a liquid used in engine radiators to lower their freezing point

coyote (n) a kind of wolf similar to a medium-sized dog found mainly in western North and Central America

shard (n) a small piece of broken glass or metal

perforate (v) to make a hole through something

carrion (n) the flesh and bones of a dead animal that is unfit for human food

juvenile (n) a youth or child; a young animal

pen (n) a small area of land surrounded by a fence and used to keep animals in

mentor (n) a teacher and friend

glide (v) to fly through the air without power

extinction (n) when a species of animal or plant completely dies out

ingest (v) consume

▶▶ **PART 7**

amenity (n) a facility that adds to people's comfort, convenience and pleasure

boast (v) to be proud of something

following (n) a group of admirers or followers

gig (n) a performance by musicians or comedians

clutch (v) hold tightly

petrified (adj) very frightened

kid (v) to make jokes

snort (n) the act of forcing air violently through the nose with a rough harsh sound

hone (v) to improve

prodigy (n) a highly talented child

flautist (n) someone who plays the flute

abrupt (adj) sudden

audition (v) give a short performance to see whether you are suitable for an orchestra, play, film, etc

abrasive (adj) rough; making people feel bad

thin-skinned (adj) touchy; sensitive to criticism

yearn (v) to have a strong desire for something; to long for something

demanding (adj) requiring high performance

clientele (n) a group of customers

daunt (v) to make afraid; to discourage

thriving (adj) successful

bare your soul (v) show your deepest most intimate feelings

precarious (adj) dependent on chance, unknown conditions or uncertain developments

draw a parallel (phr) point out similarities

breakthrough (n) an important new development of discovery

tedious (adj) boring

misconception (n) idea based on false information or a wrong understanding

reconciliation (n) end to a disagreement

erroneous (adj) mistaken

faint-hearted (adj) lacking confidence

mute (adj) silent

bystander (n) a person who sees something happening but is not involved

deference (n) behaviour that shows you respect someone or something

overheads (n) costs involved in running a business

fiddly (adj) difficult to do because of small details

plod (n) very slow speed

side-track (v) make someone do something that is different from the main thing they are supposed to be doing

afflict (v) affect someone in a harmful way

adolescence (n) teenage years; the time in life when a person changes from being a child to being an adult

trigger (n) stimulus; something that causes a change to take place

flask (n) a bottle used to store chemicals in scientific work

fluorescence (n) special light created by radiation

spectrum (n) range of coloured lights

buzz (n) excitement

yearn (v) have a strong desire for

brainstorming session (n) when a group of people all think about something at the same time to produce ideas

ADVANCED TEST 8

PAPER 1 Reading and Use of English

▶▶ PART 1

plain (adj) ordinary, not special in any way

dietician (n) an expert on healthy eating

fibre (n) a part of food which keeps food moving through the body; an important part of a healthy diet

intake (n) what you consume by eating and drinking

stew (n) a dish of vegetables (often with meat) that is cooked slowly in water; similar to a thick soup

▶▶ PART 2

constitution (n) the set of laws and principles that govern a country or organisation

revenue (n) the money that a business or organisation receives over a period of time

valid (adj) a valid document is legally or officially acceptable

▶▶ PART 3

conduct (v) to carry out a particular activity or process

devise (v) to invent a way of doing something

merchant (n) someone who buys and sells goods for profit

intricate (adj) elaborate; having many complex elements

issue (v) to circulate or publish; to make available

▶▶ PART 5

rope someone in (phr v) persuade someone to join an activity or to help someone, even though they may not want to do this

warren (n) a collection of buildings with many narrow passages

rack (n) a piece of furniture, usually made of metal or wooden bars, where you keep things such as bottles, tools and plates

pitch (n) how high or low a sound is

sample (n) a small amount or an example of something which you try or test to see what it is like

blaring (adj) describing a loud and unpleasant noise

brass (n) musical instruments made of metal such as trumpets and horns

mingle (v) mix

thud (n) a low sound when a heavy object hits something else

predator (n) an animal that kills and eats other animals

enigmatic (adj) mysterious and difficult to understand

olfactory (adj) relating to the sense of smell

cell (n) the smallest unit of a living substance; all animals and plants are made up of cells

anesthetise (v) give a person or an animal an anaesthetic so that they do not feel any pain

clunk (v) put something down in a heavy, awkward way

physiological (adj) the way a living thing functions

odour (n) a smell

suppress (v) control or reduce

phenomenon (n) something that happens in nature

alert (v) give a warning

musky (adj) with a strong smell

toffee (n) a hard sticky sweet made by heating sugar, butter and water together

aroma (n) a smell, usually used for a pleasant smell

reservation (n) a feeling of doubt about an idea

reluctant (adj) unwilling

implication (n) possible consequence

forthcoming (adj) going to happen in the future, probably soon

▶▶ **PART 7**

temple (n) a building used for religious worship

strip (n) a long, narrow piece of something

lap (v) gently touch

peppered (v) if a place is peppered with something it has many examples of this thing on it

complex (n) a group of buildings

superlative (n) a word praising something

unearth (v) discover

Neolithic (adj) from the New Stone Age, from about 10,000BC to 2,000 BC

acre (n) a unit used to measure land – about 4050 square metres

vibrant (adj) lively

tomb (n) a large grave; some kind of building above or below the ground to house someone who has died

underpin (v) lie behind or support

dwarf (v) to be much bigger or greater than something else

precarious (adj) not safe or certain

discard (v) throw away

pottery (n) pots, dishes, cups and so on that are made by hand with clay

coalesce (v) come together to form one larger group

acknowledge (v) give recognition to

World Heritage status (n) an official recognition by UNESCO that a place has a special cultural, historical or physical importance and because of this should be protected

UNESCO (n) United Nations Educational, Scientific and Cultural Organisation

stumble upon (phr v) find by chance

settler (n) a person who goes to live in a new place

excavate (v) to dig in the ground to look for old objects

perplex (v) confuse or puzzle

settlement (n) a place where people make their homes, especially where few or no people lived before

fate (n) the things that have happened or will happen

abrupt (adj) sudden

draw (v) attract

scrutinise (v) study carefully

eclipse (v) make something else seem unimportant

further afield (phr) further away from home

confound (v) prove something wrong

carving (n) a pattern, often artistic, made by cutting away material from something

pinpoint (v) find the exact position of something

artifact (n) something made by humans

intact (adj) in one piece, not broken up

outhouse (n) a small building outside a main building

groove (v) a narrow cut in the surface of something

▶▶ **PART 8**

indifferent (adj) having no or little interest in something

universality (n) something that is true all over the world

representational (n) showing something real

stretch (n) an area of land or water; for example, a river

grid (n) a pattern of straight lines crossing each other

lavender (n) a pale purple colour; a plant with purple flowers and a sweet smell

composition (n) the way something is assembled

flap (v) move quickly up and down

cobblestone (n) small, round stones used to make the surface of a road, especially in the past

twinge (n) a sudden, short feeling of pain

haystack (n) a large pile of dried grass in a field

grim (adj) looking unattractive and depressing

ubiquitous (adj) found everywhere

pithead (n) the entrance to a mine

pylon (n) a tall metal structure used for carrying electricity wires high above the ground

supple (adj) flexible

clasp (v) hold tightly

perspective (n) a way of looking at something